A Noble Band of Worshipers

The Beginnings of Churches of Christ in Lauderdale County, Alabama

John Chisholm Church History Series

C. Wayne Kilpatrick

A Noble Band of Worshipers: The Beginnings of Churches of Christ in Lauderdale County, Alabama

Copyright © 2024 by C. Wayne Kilpatrick

Manufactured in the United States

Cataloging-in-Publication Data

Kilpatrick, C. Wayne (Charlie Wayne), 1943–

A noble band of worshipers: the beginnings of Churches of Christ in Lauderdale County, Alabama / by C. Wayne Kilpatrick.

John Chisholm Church History Series

p. cm.

Includes name index.

ISBN: 978-1-956811-79-7 (hdbk); 978-1-956811-90-2 (ebook)

1. Churches of Christ—History—Alabama—Lauderdale County. 2. Churches of Christ—History—Alabama—Tennessee Valley counties. 3. Churches of Christ—History—Alabama—19th century. I. Author. II. Title. III. Series.

286.676199 DDC20

Library of Congress Control Number: 2024947442

Cover design by Brittany Vander Maas and Brad McKinnon.

Heritage Christian University Press

PO Box HCU
3625 Helton Drive
Florence, Alabama 35630

www.hcu.edu/publications

All rights reserved.

No part of this book may be reproduced in any form or by any electronic or mechanical means, including information storage and retrieval systems, without written permission from the author, except for the use of brief quotations in a book review.

Contents

Foreword	v
Preface	xi
Introduction	xiii
1. Lauderdale County	1
2. Republican—Cypress—Liberty—Stoney Point	3
3. Waterloo	35
4. Barton's—Bluff Creek—Gravelly Springs—Macedonia	48
5. Blue Water	55
6. Hopewell—Mars Hill	58
7. Mars Hill Bible College	85
8. Bethelberry	90
9. Cypress Mills	98
10. Porter Spring—Miller's Chapel—Oliver Work	101
11. The Askew Group—Former Baptist Churches	109
12. Macedonia	121
13. Union Grove—North Carolina	128
14. The New Hope—Salem Connection	147
15. Woodland Springs	159
16. Brush Creek—Beech Grove—Killen	164
17. Sherrod Valley—Oakland Work	170
18. The Church in the City of Florence	172
19. Popular Street	176
20. Lexington The Early Work	206
21. Antioch	211
22. Burcham Valley—New Hope	216
23. Jacksonburg	220
24. Pine Hill	224
25. Threet—Hendrix Chapel	225
26. Shiloh	229

27. Rogersville	236
28. Lone Cedar	241
29. Pleasant Valley	246
30. Romine	250
Endnotes	253
Bibliography	275
Name Index	277
Also by C. Wayne Kilpatrick	281
Heritage Christian University Press	283

Foreword

Sunday lunch in the home of Kelby and Martha Smith was where the Harps were first impressed upon by Wayne and Brenda Kilpatrick. After four and a half years in the mission field of New Zealand, my young family made its way to Florence, Alabama, in the winter of 1985-86 to attend International Bible College (now Heritage Christian University). Wayne was to be one of my professors. His expertise is in the fields of history and the Bible. That spring semester, it was my privilege to sit in his World History II class. With every passing day, it was apparent that Wayne's passion was all things historical. On the first day, he said, "We must always stop and pay respects to the bridges we have crossed." And, for the next thirteen weeks, he filled the air with the stories of the past. To Wayne, it was not just information on a page that needed to be shared; it was not just the former things that needed retelling. To him, and ultimately to those of us at his feet, it was our past, our story—our history. Whether talking about John Tetzel's sales of indulgences to build Leo X's St. Peter's Cathedral in Rome, Italy, or the rise of Oliver Cromwell's Parliamentarians in the defeat of Charles I of England, we were led through a maze of factual details that resonated and gave more profound meaning to our lives.

Charlie Wayne Kilpatrick was born on Possum Creek, near Center Hill, Lauderdale County, Alabama, on December 30, 1943. He became a Christian under the preaching of Alden Hendrix, being baptized by him in 1957. After two years of undergraduate studies at the University of North Alabama, Wayne was drafted into the U.S. Air Force. Before his international assignment, he took the opportunity to continue his education by taking courses at the University of Maryland. At the height of the Vietnam War, it was not long before he was stationed in England's R.A.F. Welford in Berkshire, where he was assigned the task of ammunition inspector. During his term of service, he attained the level of sergeant. Being a history lover in an old country like England afforded him a goldmine of antiquity to examine firsthand. Whenever leave was extended, he was either playing his banjo somewhere in a show with some of his friends or striking out on his own in a planned direction to investigate Britain's ancient culture.

Returning to the U.S. after his term of service, Wayne was employed for 18 months by the Tennessee Valley Authority. He married the former Brenda Elaine Chaney of Leighton, Alabama, on December 12, 1970. At the encouragement of his brother-in-law, Milton Chaney, a gospel preacher, Wayne entered the first class of International Bible College (now Heritage Christian University) in the spring of 1972. He was part of the college's first class since transitioning from the older Southeastern Institute of the Bible. After graduating with his Bachelor's Degree in Bible in 1974, Wayne determined to return to England as a missionary. Working primarily with the Wembley church of Christ in Middlesex, just northeast of London, he and Brenda evangelized in that region. Due to a lack of sufficient support, after a year, the family returned to the Shoals area.

In the fall of 1975, upon his return to the United States, Wayne accepted an offer to teach World History, Bible Geography, and Church History at International Bible College (now Heritage

Christian University). In addition, he enrolled at Harding University Graduate School of Religion (now Harding School of Theology) to study under noted church historian Earl Irvin West. Wayne completed his studies at Harding with a Master of Arts in Religion (M.A.R.). Over subsequent years, he completed twelve post-graduate hours at the University of Alabama and six graduate hours at the University of North Alabama.

The summer following my first class in World History, it was my pleasure to travel with Wayne Kilpatrick to Newport, Wales, UK, where he directed an evangelistic campaign. For a week in the summer of 1986, we knocked on doors, conducted Bible studies in the city during the day, and worshipped with our Welsh brethren in the evenings. One afternoon, we took a break and went about five miles out of town to Caerleon, an ancient Roman city. We walked through the excavated ruins of the amphitheater and the military barracks. A few days following the campaign, we traveled to London, where we had the pleasure of having our own tour guide, C. Wayne Kilpatrick. Whether at the tower of London, Stonehenge, the cathedrals of Winchester, Canterbury, and Salisbury, and just about everywhere in between, the sheer volume of information that seemed to spill freely from this man's mind was nothing short of phenomenal.

Then, there were Kilpatrick's Church History and Restoration History courses. The names, dates, and stories of the past flowed in graceful order from his lips as if he were walking down memory lane. Wayne had a little yellow box with 4x6 index cards that he used to teach his classes. This coveted container of notes was a veritable treasure trove of knowledge he had collected and shared over the years.

Professor Kilpatrick's classes were a magnet to students. His kind-hearted and sanguine spirit filled every lecture with meaningful material that could be used in our ministry for a lifetime. Once, while teaching the history of the Restoration Movement, we arrived at class, and he told us to go to our cars and follow him a few miles from the school. He took us over to Chisholm Highway to a little shanty of a house. We followed him to the backyard, where among a few trees was the small Chisholm Cemetery. Wayne had just been lecturing about how Benjamin Lynn came to Madison County, Alabama, as early as 1809 to establish New Testament Christianity there. He had explained that Lynn's daughters had married men with that pioneer spirit, Rachel to Marshall De'Spain and Esther to John Chisholm, Jr. Lynn died in 1814 and was buried somewhere north of present-day Huntsville. After 1816, the family moved into what is now Lauderdale County, the Chisholms to Cypress Creek, north of Florence, and the DeSpains to Waterloo.

As we approached the cemetery, there before our eyes were the graves of John and Esther Chisholm. John's father, John Chisholm, Sr., was also buried there. He had been an agent for Cherokee Indian Chief Doublehead and rented land on his reserve. More importantly, these people were the first New Testament Christians in Lauderdale County, planting a New Testament church on Cypress Creek. Also buried in the cemetery was Dorinda Chisholm Hall, the young wife of Benjamin Franklin Hall, the Christian preacher who came to the region in the fall of 1826, preaching baptism for the remission of sins. Under his influence came the baptisms of Tolbert Fanning, Allen Kendrick, and others at the hands of James E. Matthews.

History is a science. With this visit to Chisholm Cemetery, pure science—the ideals, the concepts, the people, the facts on a page—became applied science—seeing, touching, experiencing. Pure history became applied history! It was a hands-on examination of the evidence of history. Later that semester, other trips were made, such as to Red River Meeting House in Logan County, Kentucky, where the Second Great Awakening in America's religious history began under the preaching of Presbyterian James McGready in 1799. We also made our way up to Cane Ridge Meeting House in Bourbon County, Kentucky, where the Kentucky Revival reached a crescendo in August 1801. From there, Wayne took us to Bethany, West Virginia, where we witnessed the artifacts, the home, the buildings of Bethany College, and the old mansion that attests to the lives and influences of Thomas and Alexander Campbell. The lectures, the trips, the discussions, and the demeanor made Wayne Kilpatrick the master of his profession.

C. Wayne Kilpatrick is known for his research and journalism. The sheer volume of hours he has spent in front of microfilm and microfiche readers, computer screens, and books in his hands is uncountable. During one Christmas break many years ago, Wayne read the 40 volumes of Alexander Campbell's *Millennial Harbinger*. He has one of the largest book collections of any historian, above 40,000 volumes. He was a staff writer for *The Alabama Restoration Journal*, and his numerous articles appear in many history-related magazines. He has lectured on church history for many churches of Christ, at numerous universities, and other education-based programs across America.

C. Wayne Kilpatrick is an evangelist and successful gospel preacher. He has conducted semi-annual evangelism campaigns through Heritage Christian University in many of the states of the United States and other countries. For 20+ years, he traveled annually to teach Bible and church history short courses in the Yucatan, Mexico.

After assisting the History Department at Heritage Christian University for 48 years, he received emeritus status in 2022. At the end of this year, he plans to retire from his position to focus on researching and writing on Alabama restoration history.

This tome is a testimony to the tenacity and pure devotion of the man. After reading it, this writer has been impressed by the voluminous sources gleaned to make this work possible. I fully commend C. Wayne Kilpatrick for this book, as it will be most appreciated by researchers of the future when they attempt to dig where he dug. It will be a much-prized resource of Restoration History in North Alabama for generations to come.

Scott Harp
TheRestorationMovement.com
May 17, 2024

Preface

For many years there has been a great need for a comprehensive history of the development of the Restoration Movement in Alabama, and the Tennessee River Valley in general. F. D. Srygley's *Larimore And His Boys* was the earliest attempt to capture any semblance of early Lauderdale County Restoration History, although it was only a partial to the whole of this study. Interest began to manifest itself in the early 1900s. In 1903 A. R. Moore presented a historical review to the Alabama State Board of Missionary Society. This was the first work of its kind, but written for the Disciples of Christ—keep in mind that the Disciples were still connected to our movement until 1906. This review was never published. In 1906 J. Waller Henry wrote "Sketches of Pioneer Times" for the *Alabama Christian*—a Disciple paper. Richard L. James and Donald A. Nunnelly wrote graduate theses on the Alabama Restoration Movement. In 1965 George and Mildred Watson published *History of the Christian Churches in the Alabama Area*. All of the above-mentioned material dealt with the Disciples of Christ part of the Restoration Movement. It was not until the 1940s that Asa M. Plyler began traveling over the state and collecting material on the early and then present-day Churches of Christ. He covered every county in the state. His manuscript was finally published upon the request of his family. The book was titled *Historical Sketches of the Churches of Christ in Alabama* and no date of publication was given. Plyler's book gave us some "personally collected information; but beyond that, it has not been of much help, as most of his sources were very limited. Today these sources are more readily available, and we have taken advantage of them.

It was needful—yes even imperative that lives of devotion to the Lord's Kingdom, such as the men and women in this study be told. Younger generations need to know what they have. They need to know that these precious servants of the Lord sacrificed so much so we could be where we are today in the Churches of Christ. A generation, now in danger of squandering away the church, needs to appreciate the fact that many of these subjects went without proper clothing, or proper medical attention many times, were constantly in need of financial means, and made many other sacrifices in order to establish the Lord's work in so many places. It would be the greatest act of ungratefulness toward the generations of these preaching brethren, who gave so much sacrificial devotion to helping save the lost and dying world if their story remains in obscurity. We truly are standing on the shoulders of giants, and these—our predecessors were the giants.

We have undertaken the task of producing a history that uses only documented sources—such as church records, journal articles, unpublished autobiographies, documented papers written for schools and universities, published and unpublished interviews, courthouse records, and even monuments and cemeteries. We have limited this study to the four Alabama counties north of the Tennessee River. That is where the Alabama Restoration Movement began.

This book is written to be used, hopefully, as a resource tool to encourage further research into local church histories. Perhaps, the lives of these forefathers in the Lord's work may inspire us to do great things for our Lord and Savior Jesus Christ.

Introduction

The four counties that lie on the north bank of the Tennessee River—Madison, Jackson, Lauderdale, and Limestone—will be the subject under consideration for this work. We will treat the counties chronologically in the order in which the Restoration Movement began.

At first, Alabama was part of the Mississippi Territory, which was ceded by Georgia and South Carolina to the United States. The Territory of Mississippi was an organized incorporated territory of the United States that existed from April 7, 1798, until December 10, 1817, when the western half of the territory was admitted to the Union as the State of Mississippi and the eastern half became the Alabama Territory until its admittance to the Union as the State of Alabama on December 14, 1819.

Prior to the War of 1812, many settlers came into what is now Madison and Jackson Counties, Alabama. Alabama was then still part of the Mississippi Territory. They could not legally, nor safely travel any further into what is presently known as Northwest Alabama because the Indians controlled the land until 1816. Some of these pioneers settled in northeastern Jackson County near modern day Bridgeport, Alabama. another group settled miles north of Huntsville, Alabama, and established Meridianville.

In the years that followed the close of the War of 1812, an influx of thousands of settlers came into the northern part of Alabama from Tennessee, North and South Carolina, Georgia, and Virginia. This was due to the promise of bounty lands to be given to men who had fought in the War of 1812. With each new settler came his own peculiar religious views, resulting in the founding of churches to propagate their views. Along with these settlers from the older states came the views of Barton Stone, James O'Kelly, and a few years later, Alexander Campbell. Just as with other religious groups, the followers of Stone, O'Kelly, and Campbell founded congregations of believers, who were dedicated to spreading the message of the Restoration Movement. Many of these congregations would prosper for a few years and then gradually disappear. Some, however, would weather the storms of time and exist down to the present.

In Northeast Alabama, the Bridgeport (Rocky Springs) and Meridianville pioneers were neither of the James O'Kelley, Barton Warren Stone nor Alexander Campbell groups. These pioneers began their New Testament churches independent of the other movements. Rocky Springs congregation was established in 1811 or 1812 by members of the Old Philadelphia church in Warren County, Tennessee, which had been established by a people who came from a mixture of religious beliefs and who wanted to follow the New Testament pattern They had established their congregation near Viola, Tennessee in 1808. The Gains and Price families moved shortly afterward to Rocky Springs (1811 or 1812). The Meridianville work was begun by Benjamin Lynn in 1808 or 1809. Both groups had studied themselves out of denominationalism without the influence of any of the three above-mentioned movements.

In Northwest Alabama, one such congregation (Stoney Point —established in 1816) has managed to endure. Several other congregations in this area that were established before the Civil

War, were not so durable. Many of them have faded into obscurity.

Much has been written about the political history of this area, but very little has been written about the religious history. Hardly anything has been written concerning the Restoration Movement in North Alabama. F. D. Srygley's biography of T. B. Larimore, *Larimore and His Boys,* sheds some light upon the history of this area and George and Mildred Watson's *History of the Christian Churches in the Alabama Area* gives some insight into this part of the state. Several histories of local congregations have appeared, but many times these works are weighted down by local traditions, rather than historical facts. Due to the lack of knowledge on the part of the average church member concerning the Restoration Movement, the purpose of this study is to give a historical account of the North Alabama movement. Our method shall be to discover who established these works and what caused them to grow or die, whichever the case may be. Since every historical work must have a beginning and an end, we have set the date of our study to begin with 1808–1809, the approximate time Benjamin Lynn came to Madison County, Alabama, and ending with the year 1914, the year World War I began. This time span covers a little over a hundred years of Alabama restoration history. It should be remembered, however, that this is in no way a complete history because there are examples of churches, such as Liberty, which appeared in *The Christian Register* of 1848 as being in Lauderdale County, Alabama, having eighty-five members, and possessing their own house of worship, then disappearing from all written records. Such incidents make it impossible to compile a complete history. History, however, does not dwell upon that which has been lost, but rather that which can be found. This historical study shall be based upon only that which can be found.

To prepare such historical undertaking many sources have been consulted. Local newspapers of the period under discussion, local courthouse records, journals of historical societies, unpublished histories, and biographical sketches have been valuable sources of material. Many books have been written by our brethren on subjects not related to the Alabama area, yet touching upon it, and literature by other religious groups have proven helpful. There are several historical collections of the brotherhood that have supplied valuable aid in this investigation, but the chief source of material has been found in brotherhood journals beginning with Campbell's first issue of *The Christian Baptist* in 1823, through most major journals until the year 2000. Where occasion has demanded and opportunity has afforded, different portions of North Alabama have been visited and much valuable information has been gained by private conversation. Such were the sources from whence this history is derived. It is hoped that this uncovering of information will give a better understanding of the Churches of Christ in North Alabama.

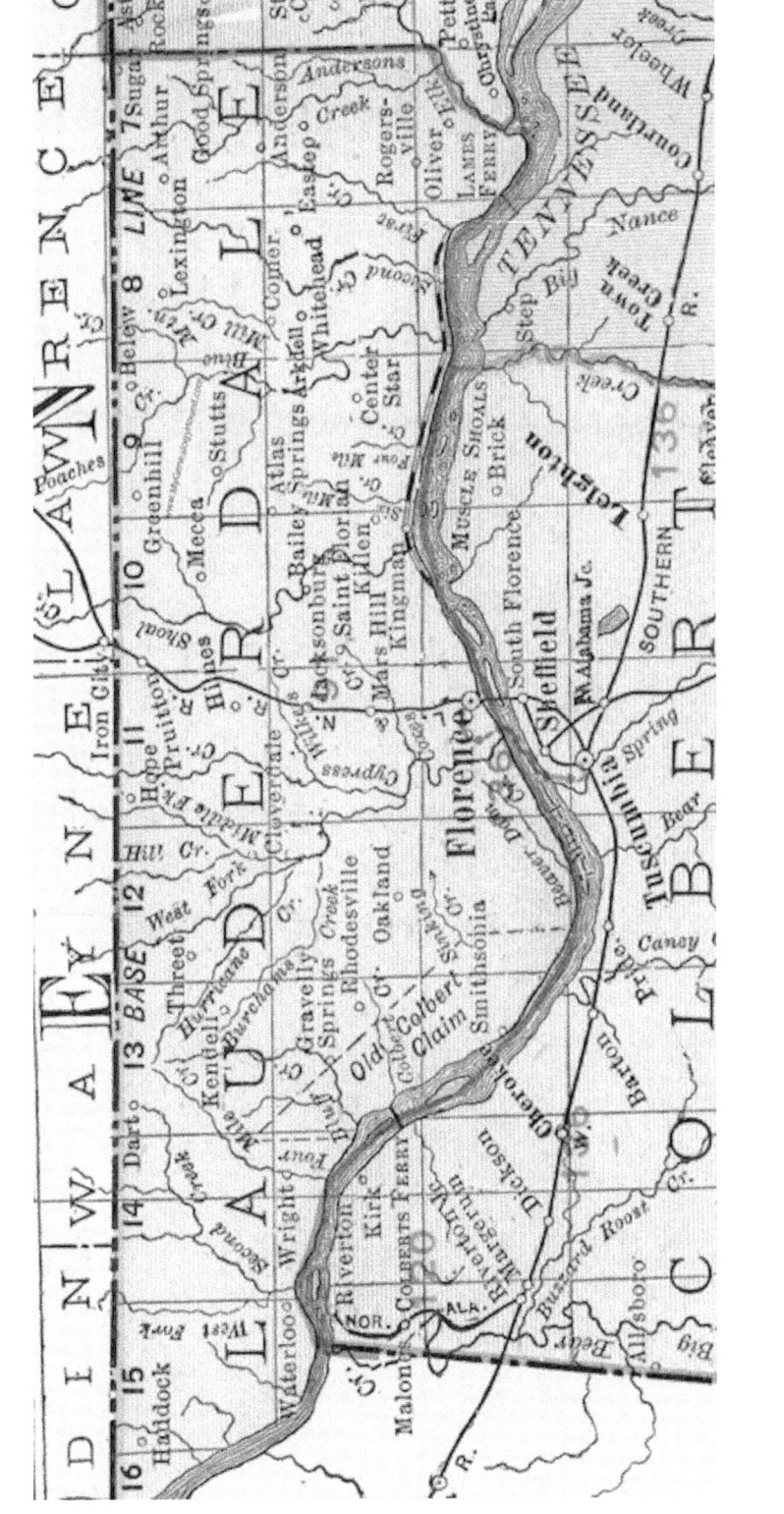

Lauderdale County

The reason we study our past is expressed very well by an old friend from the past who was native to Lauderdale County, Alabama. He had that passion for delving into the bygone years and how they related to our times:

> I think there is a desire in most all men to know something of the past when that past has some relationship to them. We study the history of our nation so that we can have some understanding of ourselves today. The same is true with God's people —we need to study the history of them in order that none of us should ever forget that we are building on the labors and sacrifices of others. Some who have sacrificed and suffered most have been forgotten.[1]

Lauderdale County lies at the extreme northwest end of the Tennessee River Valley in Alabama, lying north of the Tennessee River. It was one of eight counties created on February 6, 1818, by the legislature of the Territory of Alabama from land ceded to the United States by the Cherokees and Chickasaws in a treaty in 1816. The county was named for Tennessean Lt. Col. James Lauderdale, who died December 23, 1814, from wounds he received in the first Battle of New Orleans. In 1818 a group of investors, under the name of Cypress Land Company purchased from the government 5,515 acres of land consisting of the original town site. Other towns in Lauderdale County competing for early settlers because of their proximity to the river were Savage Spring, nine miles below Florence, and Waterloo, some twenty miles downriver. Some of the first settlements and towns included Waterloo, Florence, Rogersville, and Green Hill.

Republican—Cypress —Liberty—Stoney Point

In the years that followed the close of the War of 1812, thousands of settlers came into the northern part of Alabama from Tennessee, North and South Carolina, Georgia, and Virginia. Along with these settlers from the older states came the views of Barton Stone, James O'Kelly, and a few years later, Alexander Campbell. Just as with other religious groups, the followers of Stone, O'Kelly, and Campbell founded congregations of believers, who were dedicated to spreading the message of the Restoration Movement. Many of these congregations would prosper for a few years and then gradually disappear, as did some of the communities in which they were located. Some, however, would weather the storms of time and exist down to the present.

There was a fourth group that was not influenced by Stone, Campbell or O'Kelley. They were the first religious group to enter Lauderdale County. They had been taught by Benjamin Lynn, an independent thinker, who studied himself out of the Baptist Church and started a movement to restore New Testament Christianity. These people began to enter Lauderdale County as early as 1816, the year that the Cherokee and Chickasaw ceded this part of Alabama to the U. S. Government. The Stone wing of the movement began in Lauderdale County, Alabama, almost parallel with

Alabama statehood. Alabama had scarcely gained statehood (1819) before it felt the influence of Stone and O'Kelly. These brave pioneers came into a wide and fertile valley created by the mighty Tennessee River in northern Alabama as it made a northward turn toward Tennessee. This was the beautiful Tennessee Valley. They followed the river from Huntsville westward to the foot of the Shoals near where the Natchez Trace crossed the river. Here was the newly formed town of Florence, Alabama. Florence, situated at the foot of the Shoals and the head of the navigable waters of the Tennessee, was destined to be a trade center for northwest Alabama.

It was to this booming area that Ephraim D. Moore, the first "Stonian" preacher, came in late 1823. Moore was born in North Carolina in 1782. Later he moved to Tennessee where he became a Christian. He served under Jackson at the Battle of New Orleans as a mess cook. In 1823 he came to Alabama. B. F. Hall wrote: "He either taught school or labored on his farm for a number of years, during the week, and preached on Lord's days."[2]

Moore had settled in a small village on Cypress Creek about seven miles north of Florence known as Brandon Mills.[3] It was here in the small Cypress Creek community that Moore met young Tolbert Fanning for the first time. Several years later, upon Moore's death, Fanning wrote:

> We are more indebted to our deceased Brother, E. D. Moore, for our early religious instructions and impressions than to any other man, dead or alive. Our candid judgment is, that we never saw anyone so careful to teach, particularly young persons in the Christian religion. ... As a teacher of dignity, and elevation of style, we are not sure we ever saw superior. In affections and tenderness of heart, he more favorably impressed us than any man we ever saw; and as a lover of the truth, he had no superior. [4]

Moore's love of the truth manifested itself in many works; one of them beginning here on Cypress Creek. Moore began preaching in this little North Alabama village about three years after the Republican congregation came into existence. Even though there is no exact time in 1816 given as to when the church at Republican was founded, the evidence shows that its beginning was at the time the John and Esther Chisholm family moved to Lauderdale County. Moore began his work here in 1823 or 1824. In 1831 James E. Matthews, who came to Republican in 1826, wrote Simon Clough, editor of *The Gospel Luminary*, saying: "When I came to this county, something over five years ago, there was one small church of about 10 members..."[5] thus, indicating that at that time the work at Republican had not grown much beyond the immediate Chisholm family by 1826.

The work at Republican progressed rather slowly during 1825; possibly due to Moore's having to teach and farm during the week and only allowing himself time to preach on Lord's day. Moore, however, did not let his work keep him from teaching the young people or performing an occasional wedding in the community. Help arrived in 1826 with the coming of James E. Matthews.

Exactly at what time in 1825 or 1826 Matthews came to the Florence area is unknown. Matthews had known the Chisholms and D'Spains when they lived in Madison County. That may have been what brought him to Lauderdale County. By September he attended the meeting held on Cypress Creek[6] and by November he was listed as an agent for *The Christian Messenger* in the Florence area.[7] Matthews was born in Kentucky in 1799. Early in life he became acquainted with the views of Benjamin Lynn and was obedient to the gospel. He labored in Lauderdale County for over ten years before leaving for Mississippi. Brother Matthews was a vivacious young man when he arrived on Cypress Creek.

B. F. Hall had begun coming back to Northwest Alabama and preaching. It was during the time of the September camp meeting that B. F. Hall, who had already been working in North

Alabama from the spring of 1824 until the spring of 1826, came back to Lauderdale County.[8] He returned in the fall of 1826 and stayed until spring, 1827.[9] One must keep in mind, however, that Hall was not preaching baptism for the remission of sins during his first work in north Alabama, which was from spring 1824 until spring 1826. It was in the spring of 1826, while on his way back to Kentucky, that Hall stopped at a brother Guess' cabin on Line Creek, which ran between Tennessee and Kentucky. It was here that Hall read Alexander Campbell's debate with W.L. McCalla and for the first time in his life, he understood that baptism was for the remission of sins. Hall explained:

> I found the keystone of the arch. It has been lost a long time. I had never seen it before; strange that I had not. But I had seen the vacant space in the arch a hundred times and had some idea of the size and shape of it; and when I saw baptism as Mr. Campbell had presented it, I knew it would fit and fill the vacant space.[10]

Hall began preaching this idea on baptism to everyone who would listen. He found eager listeners when he came to Republican. Hall was set on preaching this New Testament doctrine when he came to Cypress Creek, and he did. For the first time, the congregation at Republican felt the influence of Alexander Campbell's teaching on the New Testament doctrine of baptism for the remission of sins. Hall delivered it in a plain and simple manner, yet so effective. He invited forward penitents to confess Christ preparatory to their being immersed for the remission of sins. Several presented themselves. Fanning came among them and made the good confession. B. F. Hall says Fanning was baptized the next morning by James E. Matthews for the remission of sins.[11]

Fanning told of his baptism and the impression it made upon him:

> After learning these facts, we heard B. F. Hall preach the word in a manner which was so simple and plain that anyone could understand it, At the first hearing we made the confession and submitted to baptism, at Cypress, six miles north of Florence, Alabama. As we stepped from the water, a very earnest Baptist friend exclaimed, "O bless me, when did you get religion." We, possibly, did not make a satisfactory reply; but our confidence, was that God was true, and when He promises there is perfect safety. Again, in Religious Historian of June 1873, in noticing Brother B. F. Hall's death, he says: "in 1827 we heard him preach salvation through obedience to Christ, for which we shall ever feel thankful" ... A. McGary.[12]

The preaching of Hall had been so convincing that he persuaded Matthews to embrace this doctrine. Upon Hall's insistence, Matthews wrote three articles on the subject, which were printed in the *Christian Messenger* of 1829.[13] These articles seem to be the first full-length articles ever written on baptism for the remission of sins by any of our brethren, Campbell included. Matthews, like Hall, was now convinced that the doctrine was correct and devoted the remainder of his life to spreading it.

This gave a badly needed spark to the work at Republican. This vitality, which Matthews now possessed, soon began to pay. By the end of March 1827, he reported:

> Lately, we have had a very reviving season. Last Saturday and Lord's day, eight persons were added to the church, and in a few months past, sixteen have professed faith in Christ. Last Sunday evening I baptized six, one of whom was a poor sinner, crying as they did on the day of Pentecost, "What shall I do?" I gave him Peter's direction; and being baptized, he came up out of the water rejoicing. I anticipate glorious times in this neighborhood. The people are generally in a state of serious enquiry. Prejudice is giving way. Several of the Methodists communed with us last Sunday, and the church appears to be in perfect harmony.[14]

By the middle of October that same year, Moore reports:

> We have just closed our camp meeting .... Many were there on Thursday, and continued until Tuesday 12 o'clock, and with reluctance, left the encampment ... the glorious consequence was, that forty professed faith in Christ, and 26 were baptized straitway—15 or 20 more have expressed their determination to obey the Lord in his ordinance, at our next monthly meeting .... The good work is moving on in almost every direction. We anticipate happy seasons.[15]

One can almost feel the enthusiasm that Moore felt when reporting this work. Because of Moore's renewed enthusiasm and Matthew's already existing enthusiasm, Republican could only grow. Republican was now a pulsating force in the Restoration Movement. In October 1828 Moore reported to the *Christian Messenger* that 36 souls had been baptized.[16]

An article describing the state of affairs at Republican, after Matthews had been convinced of "baptism for remission of sins" appeared in a journal called the *Christian Repository*:

> There has been a good work of grace in Lauderdale county, Alabama, in the church under the care of Elders J. E. Matthews and E. Moore. Since the work commenced fifty persons have been added to the church. The prospects of the church are highly flattering.[17]

An extract from a letter written by James E. Matthews and marked Barton's Ala. Oct. 29, 1830, was published in November issue for 1830:

> I hasten to give you some information respecting the progress of religion in this country lately. At the Camp Meeting in McNairy county Tenn. near M. W. Matthews, held on the 3d Lord's day in Sept. 22 were immersed. At Purdy in the same co. the week

following, about 10 were united with the church. At Republican, the week following 26 were immersed, and several belonging to other churches united with us in a church relationship. The Sunday following, I baptized 4 at my house. The next week a Camp Meeting was held both in Limestone county and in Morgan. In Limestone I am informed that about 25 united with the church. In Morgan 7. We have experienced great opposition at the last place, but I think that truth gained ground rapidly at the late meeting there.

At Republican, Lauderdale co. Ala. The Brethren assembled in conference. Several subjects of interest were considered, among which was the ordination of Elders in every church. It appeared to be the almost unanimous opinion of the brethren, that if our churches were on apostolic ground, they would have Elders, or men of age experience &c. set apart in every church as Bishops, or overseers, whose duty it should be to exercise discipline, administer the ordinances, and assemble the church frequently, so that in the absence of the preachers or evangelists, the churches might be kept organized. The conference recommend this subject to the careful consideration of the churches generally.[18]

In 1831 Matthews wrote Simon Clough concerning the doctrine of baptism for the remission of sins:

The doctrine of baptism for remission of sins, generally prevails, but in a more qualified sense than it is held by Alexander Campbell, Editor of the Millennial Harbinger.[19]

Matthews had been exposed to the writings of the *Millennial Harbinger* as early as 1830. Several of his friends were listed in Campbell's ledger as having subscribed to the *Millennial Harbinger* in 1830, and Matthews, himself, was listed by 1831.[20] His reading of the *Millennial Harbinger* placed him in a position to say whether his views or Campbell's were the more qualified.

Just to what extent the views of Campbell had been spread throughout northwest Alabama is reflected in a resolution adopted by the Muscle Shoals Association in 1830. The resolution read as follows:

> Through Campbellism we see the divine operation of the Holy Spirit either disavowed or so obscurely avowed, as to amount to disavowal. We see experimental religion ridiculed and reprobated. We see the apostolic mode of ordaining ministers, by the laying of hands of the presbytery, ridiculed and condemned. We therein see baptism presented as producing a change of heart and pardon of sins, when the Holy Spirit can alone produce a change, while baptism shows our faith, satisfies our conscience, adopts us into His church and makes us one with Him, by thus fulfilling all righteousness, a change of hearts being previously affected by the Holy Spirit. We therein see, as we awfully fear, an effort by man to pull down the old order of faith and practice taught by our Lord and His apostles and establish on their ruins a new order and a new name styled Campbellism.[21]

From this time forward the Muscle Shoals area, especially Republican, faced stiff opposition from the Baptists.

Our brethren were gaining strength, so much so that the Baptist lamented over not having many conversions. Hosea Holcomb expressed this best in his *History of the Alabama Baptist* written in 1840. The Shoal Creek association was:

> Constituted in 1825, of churches in Tennessee, and in Lauderdale county, Alabama, which were dismissed for that purpose from the Muscle Shoal Association. These churches were Mill Creek, Butler's Creek, Little Cypress, and Big Cypress. In 1831, there were seven churches in Lauderdale county, and the number of members was 450, and last year, (1838,) after a lapse of seven years, there were but 320 members in these seven churches, and from the year 1831, to 1838, there were only 46

added by baptism. May we not inquire, "will the Lord cast off forever! and will he be favorable no more! Is his mercy clean gone forever! Doth his promise fail for evermore! - Hath God forgotten to be gracious! Hath he in anger shut up his tenderness!"[22]

From this statement and lament by Holcomb, one can see that our brethren had affected the growth of the Baptists in Lauderdale County. The opposition was going to become much more fierce. Despite this opposition, Matthews and Moore made increasing gains, not only at Republican but throughout all of Lauderdale County. Matthews, by 1831, had moved westward from Cypress Creek into the community of Bartons (modern day Gravelly Springs, Lauderdale County). He wrote that there were upwards of 200 at Republican and that he had planted a church of about 60 members in his own immediate vicinity.[23] The strength and influence of Republican caused it to be the site of a Christian Conference in 1830. A detailed description is given by Matthews:

> At Republican, Lauderdale co. (sic) Ala. (sic) The Brethren assembled in conference. Several subjects of interest were considered, among which was the ordination of Elders in every church. It appeared to be almost unanimous opinion of the brethren, that if our churches were on apostolic ground, they would have Elders, or men of age experience. . .set apart in every church as Bishops, or overseers, whose duty it should be to exercise discipline, administer the ordinances, and assemble the churches frequently, so that in the absence of the preacher or evangelist, the churches might be kept organized.[24]

With this decision, not only Republican but all the churches across north Alabama were taking a giant step toward the restoration of New Testament Christianity. The steps were slow, but each step was deliberate and was placed upon solid ground, the

Word of God. Another step was taken in the next conference which began the last day of September in 1831 at Republican. This time the brethren decided to dismiss all of the usual formalities and call no one to the chair, nor choose a president for the meeting. Matthews says:

> In Conference, we dispensed with the etiquette usually observed. No bishop was called to the chair, nor was any clergyman or lay-member chosen President. We entered no resolutions upon our minute book, nor did we take the name of an "Advisory Council." But "with one accord, in one place" we mutually engaged in arranging the appointments for our next annual meetings, so as to best promote the cause of the Redeemer; and agreed to request you to publish said appointments in the Christian Messenger. Jas. E. Matthews.[25]

With the proceedings in this conference, the brethren in North Alabama had taken a monumental step toward completely abandoning any human organizations. They had now become autonomous congregations. No doubt this very act in 1831 helped shape the thinking of the brethren in this area concerning societies.

The next conference, which was held at Republican in October of 1832, reflected the changing attitudes of the brotherhood toward conferences. Only ten persons were baptized, and Matthews' report read:

> Barton's, Lauderdale Co., Alabama, Oct 24, 1832. Dear Brethren Stone & Johnson: —Our Camp Meeting and Conference terminated about a week since. About 10 were immersed, but prospects were not so flattering as formerly. Some unfortunate excitement was occasioned by immersion being made a test of communion in the preaching of some of the brethren. I am fearful if brethren are not careful, much evil will be the result.
>
> I have long been the advocate of reformation, but I view

with extreme regret the spirit which to me seems to prevail among many of those who profess to be reformers. We should certainly proclaim the truth fearlessly. but we should avoid that precipitancy which I fear too much prevails in adopting a new idea. Teachers of the religion of Jesus, should feel so solemnly the responsibility resting upon them, as not lightly to proclaim as truth that which is questionable. But this is probably not the greatest evil that is obtaining among us, especially our young brethren. It appears to me that there is too much rashness and self-confidence with a censorious spirit manifested in their discourses, for them to be profitable. They seem to justify themselves by the plea that they are teaching the truth, not remembering, I fear, that they should "Speak the truth in love." I have seen so much of this, as I think, that the cry of reformation from such, has almost become disgusting to me. Many of us have reformed in theory, but there is a greater and more thorough reformation needed. Where is that humility, kindness, forbearance and love—that contempt of show and parade—of popularity and worldly advantage which shone so conspicuously in the primitive saints? Where is love, holy joy, peace, long suffering, gentleness meekness, goodness, temperance, patience and fidelity, which are the characteristics of genuine piety? The fruits of the spirit? Alas! they appear almost to have fled, And to the disgrace of reformers—yes of those who call themselves Christians, these things are rarely to be found! Do we complain of the pomp, the pride, and persecuting spirit of the popular sectaries? And shall we not blush that we who profess to be Christians are found tracing their steps? A reformation in spirit and practice is what we mostly need; and until professors, by their Godly walk, and conversation, become the salt of the earth, and the lights of the world, we may vainly flatter ourselves with the belief that the day of millennial glory is opening on the world.[26]

It seems, also, that a question had arisen over baptism being made a test of communion. Up until this time, the practice at

Republican had been to let all denominations partake of the communion. Men such as Moore and Matthews had believed such an act was scriptural. They felt that by allowing the denominations to commune with the Christians, they could win them to the truth by speaking the truth in love.

Things seem to have improved somewhat during 1833. Matthews reports in a letter to the *Christian Messenger* dated August 8, 1833, that eight persons had been added, and again on September 3, 1833, he reported 30 had been added. He stated that "The churches in Alabama are gradually increasing, and the prospects brightening. The preaching brethren are becoming alive to the work."[27]

The next Christian Conference was to be held in Lauderdale County beginning on the second Lord's day in August of 1834. [28] The mainstream of the restoration in north Alabama had, by this time, focused on Lauderdale County, and Republican in particular. But all of this was soon to change. E. D. Moore had already moved to Texas sometime during 1832, and James Matthews was having to attend all the churches in Lauderdale and Limestone counties. Matthews had already complained of having a broken constitution and fasting declining health.[29]

He had also, by now, begun to center his Lauderdale County work around the western end of the county toward Waterloo. This is evidenced by the fact that Barton Stone had sent several songbooks to Matthews through the Waterloo Post Office in January of 1833.[30] The facts are not exactly clear concerning the work at Waterloo. We will discuss the Waterloo congregation later. The work had been established there in 1816 —the same year Republican was established.

Even though by now Matthews had centered his work around Bartons and Waterloo, the Republican work continued to thrive. James Young was emerging as a prominent figure at the Cypress Creek work. He had been ordained as an evangelist sometime after the 1830 Christian Conference in which it was decided to ordain elders and evangelists in every congregation. By August of

1834, Young was the agent for the *Christian Messenger* in the Florence area.[31] Several members in the area were currently taking the *Christian Messenger* at the time. Several members, including Young, were subscribing to the *Millennial Harbinger*, also. This list also included John Chisholm, George Cockburn, and A. Amonet.[32] Subscriptions to the brotherhood journals indicate an interest in one's spiritual condition, as well as an interest in what was going on in the brotherhood. Such was the attitude of the membership at Republican during the mid-1830s. Young also gave his testimonial to the Lauderdale County, Orphans Court, on September 17, 1835, by which he was given authorization him to perform weddings.[33]

In March of 1836, James Matthews describes the condition of the church throughout north Alabama as being rotten to the core and needing radical reform. He authored a dismal article to Barton Stone as follows:

> Bartons, Alabama, March 10, 1836. Elder Barton W. Stone, Beloved Brother. Alas! I fear, brother Stone, that the opinions of brother McCorkle are going to prove true. I am almost out of all hopes of seeing the world, or even the church radically reformed until it is done by the fire of the Almighty's indignation! The church, so called, is rotten to the very core. Truth, justice, mercy, and all the lovely attributes of Christian character, are becoming strangers on the earth!! I am led to exclaim in the language of Jeremiah. "O that my head were waters, and mine eyes a fountain of tears, that I might weep day and night for the slain of the daughter of my people!" I cannot but believe that impending vengeance is hanging over our guilty land. The retributive justice of the Almighty will not sleep, nor be withheld forever. Yet I trust that as it was at the destruction of Jerusalem and the Temple, so there are some now who love the statutes of the Lord, and who will escape the fiery indignation that awaits an ungodly world. But my sheet is full, and I must desist. The Lord willing, you shall

shortly hear from me again. Your brother, James E. Matthews.[34]

Perhaps Matthews' constitution having been broken and his ill health helped shape this dismal picture of the Alabama work. He remained in Lauderdale County until after May 1837, because he recorded a wedding in the marriage book on May 22, 1837. We lose track of Matthews until he reappears in Mississippi in 1842.

Brother James Young gives a different picture entirely in his letter of October 23, 1836.[35] He states that the church at Florence (Cypress Creek) had five additions and that the prospects for the Florence work was good. He goes on to report nine baptisms elsewhere. According to Young, the church was still growing at Republican.

Between 1836 and 1844 the only journal that covered the North Alabama work, was the *Bible Advocate* which was published in Paris, Tennessee. It only sporadically printed anything about North Alabama and two times was the Cypress Creek work mentioned. J. H. Dunn sent one of the Lauderdale County reports. The following is one report on Republican:

> At Cypress, Bro. Henderson and I preached three days, and gained one by confession and baptism. At this point, the audience was very large and quite attentive. And although there was the emotion and interest clearly, manifest, the people could not, it seemed, be induced to obey the Lord, by submitting to the institutions of the Gospel. J. H. Dunn.[36]

Another example was James Young of Florence, Alabama, listed in the *Bible Advocate* as paying for volume one.[37] That was only one of very few references to Florence, Alabama, and Lauderdale County. One thing that hurt the work in this area was that by 1835, Stone had moved his *Christian Messenger* to Jacksonville, Illinois, and was giving more attention to the work in

Missouri and Illinois. Alabama no longer had a prominent place in the *Christian Messenger*. Stone's publication seemed to have been the cord that bound the North Alabama brethren together. Once the *Christian Messenger* was removed, the work in north Alabama seemed to be retarded, especially in Lauderdale County. Another thing that helped retard the growth at Republican, as well as elsewhere in north Alabama, was the fact that Christian Conferences were no longer held, or if so, no mention of them can be found after 1834. Camp meetings were still held, but they did not draw the crowds in the capacity that the conferences had drawn them. This was a visible sign that the work was slowing down.

The brethren needed a new motivating force in the form of a journal. The *Millennial Harbinger* was being read by many Lauderdale Countians but was looked upon by many as being too harsh toward the denominations. Matthews expressed the sentiment of most North Alabama brethren when he compared the *Christian Messenger* to the works of Alexander Campbell. He wrote, "I think the latter have too much severity attached to them."[38] The brethren believed the truth was to be spoken in love. Apparently, they felt Campbell did not always speak in this manner. The search for something to replace the *Christian Messenger* and its influence is evidenced by the names of many north Alabama brethren which appeared in other brotherhood journals, such as Walter Scott's *Evangelist*; D.S. Burnet's *Christian Preacher*; John R. Howard's *Bible Advocate*; and *The Christian Repository*. It was not until Tolbert Fanning's *Christian Review* appeared in January of 1844 that the problem was solved. By Fanning having grown to manhood in this area, it was felt that once more the work in north Alabama would receive the proper attention. It now had been over nine years since the *Christian Messenger* had dominated this area. The first report on the work was an indirect report on Cypress Creek and was reported by Tolbert Fanning published the report:

> Friday, November 1, 1844, we journeyed to the neighborhood, of Florence, in Lawrence (Lauderdale) county, Ala., and spent the night with our faithful friends in the family of John Chisholm, Esq., Saturday, Nov. 2d, we reached Florence, where we met our brethren, Ligon. McDonald, Dunn, Hackworth, Young, Houston, and many others of our brothers and old acquaintances. The Methodists were kind enough to open their house of worship, and we addressed the citizens for three days, on the first principles of Christianity.[39]

Even though this was more about downtown Florence, most of the attendees would no doubt have come from the Republican—Cypress work. That was the only congregation in Lauderdale County within sixteen miles of Florence. A point of interest: Fanning had preached in the same Methodist meeting house two years earlier with no visible results. He only gave a one-sentence reference to it.[40] The work in Florence would not develop for another fifty years.

Many changes had taken place in Lauderdale County during these nine years. By 1844 Matthews had moved to Mississippi and had become involved in politics.[41] The work at Bartons was in decline and was doomed to eventually disappear completely. Waterloo had already ceased as a congregation in Lauderdale County, because of its removal to Texas, thus there was no church in the western-most part of the county. Dr. W. H. Wharton, from Tuscumbia, made an unsuccessful attempt to establish a work in the Middle Cypress community (Bethel Berry) in 1838.[42] During this meeting, five persons were baptized, one being John Ijams, the grandfather of our beloved E. H. Ijams.[43] Several years later (1869), a young gospel preacher fresh out of Franklin College, by the name of T. B. Larimore helped organize a permanent work in this same community.[44]

Republican was slowly undergoing a name change during the late 1830's. Locals began to refer to it as "Old Cypress." This name remained until the early 1850s when the brethren either bought or built a building on the west bank of Little Cypress Creek near the mouth of Ijams Branch. For a brief time, it was called "Liberty."[45] But it relocated and began to be called Stoney Point by early Fall of 1856.[46] Two of the preachers mentioned in Fanning's report, as attending the meeting that Fanning held in Florence in 1844, were James M. Hackworth and James Young. For some time, the burden of spreading the message of the Gospel in this country had been solely upon Young and Hackworth. Hackworth admired Fanning greatly but would not hesitate to disagree with Fanning when the occasion arose. One such instance is illustrated by Hackworth after Fanning had alluded to the establishment of the church in Russellville, Alabama, as being providential. Hackworth wrote: "I am of the opinion that your pen rather slipped when you said the gathering of the church at Russellville was a providential thing."[47] It seems that he never agreed with Fanning on this point, but it never ended their friendship. Later, Hackworth developed some rather strange views concerning the Holy Spirit and again he and Fanning disagreed.[48]

During the time Hackworth was at the church on Cypress Creek, he wrote concerning the state of the congregation there:

> We are in a tolerable state of spiritual health. We meet weakly (sic) and break the loaf, sing praises, teach and exhort poor sinners to obey our blessed Lord and we are often much refreshed.[49]

Despite the continuance of weekly meetings to break the loaf, sing, teach, and exhort, the past glory of the Cypress Creek work was fading. In 1848 its membership was only 67; however, they had by now secured a meetinghouse near Cypress Creek that faced the south, standing in front of a post oak tree, and was entered from the south end.[50] Here Alexander Hall's *Christian*

Register gets Bluff Creek confused with the Cypress Creek congregation. There was only one other meetinghouse in the county owned by our brethren at that time. The congregation at Liberty boasted of having their own meeting house and a membership of 85 souls. The congregation, at that time, was meeting in a shared house or union meeting house. They finally purchased the property in 1853.[51] James Young was minister to the Liberty and Blue Water congregations; Blue Water had only 13 members.[52] Both congregations have long since passed from the pages of recorded history. Other churches, no doubt, came and went during this period, but only the Cypress Creek work endured.

There was, however, a disturbing event that occurred at Cypress in 1849. The matter of the church at Cypress Creek having withdrawn from James Young, yet Young had baptized a woman and had requested the congregation to receive her into the fellowship. They refused because he had been disfellowshipped. J. H. Dunn wrote a letter to Philemon Gresham (Gresham was the future father-in-law of T. B. Larimore.) In Dunn's letter, he explained that he would not come and preach at Cypress unless the matter with Young was settled. He wrote his explanation:

> Although I would be glad to see my good brothers and sisters at Cypress, I am determined not to preach there until that matter is settled. There is no use in it. I cannot do any good for saint or sinner under such circumstances. I have this day written to bros. McDonald and Liggon (sic) to go forthwith and try to save the cause at Cypress and I want you, my good brother, to go after or write for them, encouraging them to come and settle the matter immediately.[53]

The matter was resolved, obviously, because Dunn made several trips afterward and preached at Cypress.

Republican was now being addressed as Cypress. Things

begin to revive at Cypress. In the summer of 1851, one such period of revival came when J. H. Dunn and J. J. Trott came to Old Cypress in early July and collaborated with the brethren for seven days. This resulted in seventeen confessions and one restoration. The brethren had "all things in common," sharing both their joy and their food. Trott referred to their eating together as a "basket meeting." He describes the feeling during this time by writing:

> They manifested zeal and Christian hospitality of the primitive disciples in 'having all things in common' and being of 'one heart and soul.'[54]

The feelings experienced during this meeting, no doubt, reminded the older brethren of days gone by when "Old Republican" was the pride of the North Alabama brotherhood.

J. M. Hackworth was now gone from Old Cypress leaving it without a regular minister. With the arrival of the 1850's, the work here was on good footing. The burden of keeping the flock together fell on the eldership, which was composed of Philemon Gresham, C. W. Wesson, Andrew J. Grisham (Gresham), and probably others. An occasional visit from Brother J.H. Dunn of Limestone County helped to keep the congregation revived.

By this time brethren in the Tennessee Valley were relaxing their feelings somewhat towards some sort of cooperation among the churches, especially in evangelization, but not without some opposition. By 1850 they were planning to have a cooperation meeting at Green Hill in Limestone County. Tolbert Fanning was to attend.[55] Either the meeting never materialized, or it was a complete failure because Fanning never printed anymore in his *Christian Magazine* concerning the meeting. Some of the churches joined in with the Tennessee Evangelizing Association the next year. J. H. Dunn was the State Evangelist of North Alabama in 1851 and only received $208.25 for that year's labor.

The blame for such a small amount of pay was that the Evangelizing Committee never received any funds for Alabama, and at our late state meeting there was no representation for that state. Their connection with us seemed more formal than real.[56]

By June of 1852, James Young of Florence and David G. Ligon of Moulton were placed on the Board of Directors for the Tennessee Evangelizing Committee.[57] This shows that some of the brethren, at least, were now interested in seeing the preaching conditions in their area remedied. By September, the north Alabama area had in mind to try another cooperation meeting at Green Hill in Limestone County.[58] Again, nothing much was ever reported on the outcome of this organized effort. It seems that many brethren were still skeptical of this type of cooperation. James Young's involvement in the Tennessee Evangelizing Committee may indicate, however, that the Cypress Creek brethren were in favor of some sort of cooperation, because by October 27, 1860, the Stoney Point—Old Cypress congregation, had sent two of its elders to the cooperation meeting in Lafayette County, Alabama.[59]

During the organization attempts of the 1850s, several preachers visited Lauderdale County; some to preach and some for other reasons. In April of 1852, J. B. Ferguson came to the resort community of Bailey Springs, about eight miles east of Florence, apparently to recuperate from some illness. He wrote concerning himself: "We have been communing with the deep spirit of affliction ...."[60]

Sometime between May 1849 and June 1853 the church on Cypress Creek had relocated to a building across the Creek. It was on the west side and near where Ijams Branch empties into Little Cypress Creek. The congregation referred to itself as "Liberty."[61] The deed was signed by Andrew I. Gresham, William H. Gresham, George Herndon, Joseph Ijams, C. W. Wesson, I. H. Thrasher, and William B. L. Thrasher. These men were the trustees of the church property. The deed mentioned the church building as "the late brick church," as though something had destroyed it. Just what happened to it was never mentioned by anyone in the journals, which is highly unusual.[62] The church had given the trustees permission to sell the property. The transaction occurred on June 6, 1853. This would be near the time when the congregation moved south on the road to a rocky point and built another building—thus the name "Stoney Point."

J. H. Dunn and John Taylor visited the county many times during this period and helped keep the churches alive. Brother Dunn drafted a report concerning one such visit in 1856:

> I visited Old Cypress —now called Stony [sic] Point — Lauderdale County, Alabama, and held a meeting of three days continuance, including the Lord's day in last month (November), at which time we had three additions by confession and baptism. The dropping spirits of the brethren and sisters were much revived during the very pleasant interview.[63]

By 1858, Dunn was writing:

> The cause of primitive Christianity progresses slowly in North Alabama, owing the scarcity of proclaimers of the pure testimony of God.[64]

In the same letter, he reported only one addition at Stoney Point during that preaching engagement. The next month he reported three more additions.

John Taylor's work was about the same as J. H. Dunn's work. Taylor writes:

> I attend the congregation at Stoney (sic) Point, in Lauderdale once a month, and have thus far made fourteen additions. This congregation now numbers over one hundred, meets every Lord's day, and in a prosperous condition-and they expect

brother Fanning to spend a week with them during the present fall.[65]

In that letter, Brother Taylor gives an insight into the congregation's condition at that time. In this same letter, he says the brethren at Stoney Point were expecting Tolbert Fanning to spend a week with them. Fanning was already, at that time, preaching across north Alabama.

The same year (1860), Fanning was on his north Alabama visit, and the cooperation meeting was held in Lafayette County. George L. Brown was selected to be the state evangelist for Lauderdale, Limestone, and Franklin counties, for the year 1861.[66] At this time, Stoney Point had contributed one hundred dollars to the evangelizing association. Thomas B. Trotter reported 58 members at Stoney Point at this time.[67] John Taylor had earlier reported that the congregation numbered over one hundred, but this figure, no doubt, reflected the number of young children and non-members in attendance there.[68]

It seems that the brethren in Lauderdale County were coming into the Civil War period on a relatively weak footing and one would wonder if they would survive the coming crisis. Sadly, very little has been said concerning our Lauderdale County brethren during the war. The Civil War ended a glorious period of the Restoration Movement in Lauderdale County. From its beginning in 1816, and especially from 1824 down to 1861, the work here had been blessed by many great workers for the Master. Preachers like E. D. Moore, James E. Matthews, James Hackworth, and James Young, who worked on a permanent basis, and men like B. F. Hall, Tolbert Fanning, J. J. Trott, J. H. Dunn, John Taylor, and other itinerant workers, all made a lasting impression on this county. They helped mold its basic beliefs, which have been handed down to the present.

The work at Cypress Creek had come to a crossroads in its prominence in Lauderdale. The war hastened and a huge change was about to occur. Families would be affected, and some would be isolated at times from the meetings of the brethren at Stoney Point (formerly Old Cypress). John Taylor came to Stoney Point and preached once a month.[69] J. H. Dunn came twice a month, traveling from Fort Hampton, Limestone County, Alabama. These two brave old soldiers helped keep Stoney Point alive during these trying times.

The Philemon Gresham family, and possibly others, were troubled by occupying Union Armies that sporadically controlled Chisholm Road. This road was a major road from Tennessee into Northwest Alabama. It was the lifeline between Clifton, Tennessee, where boats offloaded supplies for the Union Army during Confederate control of the river from Savannah, Tennessee up the river, and to Florence, Alabama, the destination for these supplies. The Union Army controlled those who needed to cross Chisholm Road, sometimes turning the people back. This happened to the Gresham family many times. They eventually decided to meet in their own house or a neighbor's house for Lord's Day worship. This would eventually result in a new congregation being established, which will be discussed later.

The country along the Tennessee River was hotly contested ground during the Civil War. The river, in connection with the Mississippi, opened direct steam-boat transportation to the base of supplies for whichever army had possession of it. By holding the Tennessee, the Confederate Army could reach the rich agricultural regions of west Tennessee, Arkansas, Mississippi, and Louisiana, and communicate with such important supply-centers as Paducah, Memphis, and New Orleans. With this same facility the Federal Army, if in possession of the river, could reach Paducah, St. Louis, and all ports along the Ohio River. For this reason, the Tennessee Valley was one of the great battlegrounds of the Civil War, second only to the Shenandoah Valley of Virginia. Each army managed to possess the transporting supplies and munitions of war over it. The armies moved back and forth across the river so that the country was almost constantly a battleground. Lauderdale County was a part of this perpetual battleground. The war set the Lauderdale County brethren back a few years, as compared to many years in other Alabama counties.

No pen can properly describe the chaotic conditions which prevailed in Lauderdale County, Alabama just after the close of the Civil War. Alabama had only been admitted into the Union in 1819 and was hardly out of the pioneer stage when war came in 1861. The demoralization brought on by invading armies, the derangement of the labor system by the sudden emancipation of the slaves, the depression sustained in their loss as property, and the shock of disappointment at the failure of the Southern arms —all these conspired to produce deep and universal gloom. For once, society was launched upon a wild and stormy sea of disorder. Men and women wept in the midst of crushed hopes. Soon the weather-beaten Confederate soldiers began to return to their homes to find prevailing the wildest disorder. But the Confederate brought with him the same spirit, which had carried him through hundreds of battles. He exchanged the battlefield for a field of cotton or corn. This was a period of distress and gloom, which was not relieved by the events of the immediate future, as we shall later see. Stoney Point suffered like fate.

Gravelly Springs and Stoney Point had just gone through the most traumatic period of their history. The task of attempting to tell how our brethren functioned as the Lord's body during these dark and bloody years, now, seems almost impossible. These were the silent years of the Restoration Movement, concerning our history. The religious historian is left to pick his way and gather up the fragments of history as best he may. Since this fragmentary information will not justify a discussion concerning the war, we begin post-war 1866, when the *Gospel Advocate* with Tolbert Fanning and a new helper—David Lipscomb.

One saving grace to the situation with the churches of Christ was they, unlike most all other American religious groups, never divided over slavery. The division would eventually come, but not over slavery. This was because men in leadership positions, like editors of brotherhood journals, took the position that slavery was a political issue, rather than a religious issue. Alexander Campbell wrote in the *Millennial Harbinger* in 1845:

> To preserve unity of spirit among Christians of the South and of the North is my grand object, and for that purpose I am endeavoring to show that the New Testament does not authorize any interference or legislation upon the relation of master and slave, nor does it either in letter or spirit authorize Christians to make it a term of communion.[70]

Positions such as Campbell's helped to keep the unity over slavery. The war would bring a change in attitude and eventually tension arose after the war and the brotherhood moved toward multiple disagreements—such as instrumental music in worship and the missionary society. Finally, the brotherhood began to divide into northern liberal churches and southern conservative churches. That was a result of the Civil War.

The war set the Lauderdale County brethren back a few years, as compared to many years in other Alabama counties. During the four years of war, some of the churches were either completely disbanded or suffered heavy membership loss. Before the war, three organized churches were in existence. Stoney Point, Gravelly Springs (formerly known as Bartons), and Bluewater. (Gravelly Springs and Bluewater will be discussed separately). By the end of the war, Gravelly Springs was not to be found. It was gone from the pages of history. Bluewater was almost gone. It was to be revived for a brief period of time and then vanished. One can see the setback the Restoration Movement suffered by the loss of two congregations in Lauderdale County—imagine what this was like all over Alabama and the South.

The congregation at Stoney Point had been nurtured enough by J. H. Dunn and John Taylor, and along with strong leaders such as Gresham and Wesson the congregation survived. In 1860 it numbered over 100, but afterward, it would be a few years before we find a definite number of members.

Lauderdale County had been without a resident minister from the time James Young relocated to another county in 1850, until the coming of Larimore in the summer of 1868. There was an absence of ministers in the church of Christ in the marriage records in the courthouse at Florence, for this period, except for occasional weddings performed by Dunn or Taylor. This is most evidently shown by the absence of any minister for the churches of Christ in the census of 1860. There were five Baptist, four Presbyterian, and thirteen Methodist ministers in Lauderdale County, but no minister for the churches of Christ.[71] J. H. Dunn and John Taylor had held Stoney Point together during the war and continued to be the life-giving force in the struggling congregation until Larimore arrived in 1868. From 1868 until 1874 nothing could be found relating to the Stoney Point work. Even the membership had nothing specifically relating to this period.

Our next written record was from the membership book given to the church by T. B. Larimore. In 1874 Larimore gave the congregation a church book in which the church kept their membership roll until 1920.[72] From this book, it is revealed that the church lost many members to new congregations as they were being established.

A funny story about one of Larimore's boys is related by F. D. Srygley. He told of George P. Young's attempt to preach at Stoney Point sometime in the early part of 1876. He gave the following account:

> One Sunday evening the usual quartette returned from Stony Point, four miles distant, much earlier than usual. G. P. Young was the main preacher on that trip, and we all considered him the "big preacher" of the school. Supposing he would preach one of his very biggest sermons that Sunday, we were not expecting them back till late, and Professor Larimore said, in some astonishment, "Why, young gentlemen, you are back unusually early." With an air of general disgust, one of the "non-professionals," his coat on his arm and his handkerchief in his

hand, strode wearily by, mopping the perspiration from his forehead, and remarking in answer to the Professor's expression of surprise: "Yes; Mr. Young preached for us today, and he just put the thing right through." Further inquiry revealed the fact that Mr. Young's big semon would not materialize that day, and after a few unsuccessful efforts to make it visible to the naked eye, he gave up in despair and dismissed the congregation. That "non-professional" had been induced to walk to Stony Point to hear the big preacher's sermon, hence his disgust. [73]

During this period Stoney Point had several of Larimore's boys come and preach for them. Stoney Point, in a way, became a training ground for the Mars Hill students. This is the reason there are so many churches of Christ in Lauderdale County, Alabama in 2024. C. E. Holt, who grew to manhood in this area, wrote in 1906 of the boys from Mars Hill:

> This is the beginning point for many of the Mars' Hill preachers. Here it was that I preached my first sermon, which resulted in one confession and baptism.[74]

After Young's episode, the next report came from C. F. Russell. While at Mars Hill students were expected to use their school breaks and weekends in some sort of teaching or preaching. C. F. gladly performed that expectation. On one occasion Larimore asked Russell to fill an appointment at Stoney Point near Florence He described the appointment as follows:

> On 2nd Lord's day in May at Stony Point, four miles from Mars Hill College, after trying to talk to a little band on the necessity of being faithful, growing Christians, we gave the invitation and were agreeably surprised to see seven arise from their seats and come forward, five from the world, one from the Methodists and l one took membership. What made it such a glorious time was five noble young men and one young lady all just starting

out upon the sea of life Prudent enough to take a chart and compass by which to be guided over the breakers and through rough seas and thoughtful enough to take Jesus us a friend who will never forsake them.[75].

C. F. Russell's home was Apple Grove, Morgan County, Alabama. He was a student at Mars Hill at that time. F. D. Srygley wrote of Russell in *Larimore And His Boys*. He described Russell as:

> C. F. Russell, of Apple Grove, Ala., was one of Mars' Hill's brilliant young preachers; but unfortunately, his labors were cut short by failing health soon after he left school. While yet a student, he held several very successful protracted meetings, and but for the failure in health would unquestionably have taken high rank in our Southern pulpit. He was modest, quiet and unassuming; original, earnest and untiring. Professor Larimore once had an appointment he could not meet, and asked brother Russell if he could fill it for him. With characteristic modesty and willingness to do his best, he said: "I don't think I could fill it for you, professor; but if it will accommodate you and do any good, I am willing to go and wriggle about in it."[76]

The records show that he never married and was of ill health most of his life. His preaching was very limited because of his prolonged illness. He died in Arkansas. It was not clear why he was in Arkansas at the time of his death. Following C. F. Russell's report written May 2, 1883, Larimore made one about two other Mars Hill students. They were O. P. Speegle and John T. Underwood. He wrote:

> Fourteen accessions. Oscar P. Speegle and John T. Underwood, "workmen" – "workmen that need not to be ashamed." As the "Mars' Hill Boys" almost always do, Oscar and John closed the meeting, when interest was highest. Four confessions after first

discourse. This is according to their training, but it is not best. T. B. L. Stony Point.[77]

The next report was made by T. E. Tatum, another Mars Hill boy. In the report, he gave a list of his preaching points during the Summer of 1883 and Stoney Point was a regular point for him.[78]

By 1885 Brown Godwin was preaching at intervals for Stoney Point. He was working with the church at that place when they bought the property at a new location with the intentions of building a new house of worship. He, however, was not a regular member at Stoney Point. His name is never found in the church's roll book. He sent a report to the *Gospel Advocate* on this project; but communications were mixed up and the report made it sound as though he was reporting on a house already finished, instead of one still to be built.[79] The truth of the matter is that the land purchase had not been made when Godwin made his first report. The land transaction was made September 10, 1886.[80]

A brother Alexander McArthur wrote on July 7, 1885, concerning the Godwin report:

> Since Bro. Godwin's report of my work, ten have been added at Young's Factory, and seven at Pine Grove. Expect to commence protracted meetings ere (sic) long. Stony Point brethren are moving on earnestly. Aim to build their house of worship soon. The brethren in this country think Bro. Godwin did Bro. Rutherford wrong in his report of our work together. Bro, Rutherford did the principal part of work at Stony Point, which is reported in the Advocate as done by me. Bro. Godwin says he regrets that the mistake was made but that it was made at the Advocate office and says he is satisfied it was done unintentionally.[81]

The Stoney Point deed of 1886 and the church's roll for 1885 reveal some interesting information about this period. In the original list for 1885 William Bryant Stevenson's name is missing from the roll, however, September 10, 1886, it is on the deed for the new location for Stoney Point. Stevenson was a country preacher. Another preacher's name was enrolled in 1876—George Smallwood. He had been preaching for ten or fifteen years or more. He became a member there between 1874 and 1876 because his name was not on the 1874 list. This shows that Stoney Point was not without a preacher on any given Sunday, yet they allowed the boys from Mars Hill to come and practice at their congregation.

It would be five more years before there would be a written record of activities at Stoney Point. Larimore reported on a meeting by W. H. Gresham:

> Bro. T. B. Larimore writes: "Bro. W. H. Gresham, whom all our "Mars Hill boys and girls" remember, of course, as one of our faithful Mars Hill elders, has just closed a three-day meeting at Stony Point, resulting in fourteen accessions to that patient congregation that, in the bitter-sweet long-ago, suffered so many of 'the boys' to 'make a beginning' there. Patient, long-suffering, 'Old Stony' is still solid.[82]

Gresham was a brother-in-law to T. B. Larimore and had served as a trustee for the old Liberty congregation.[83] He also was a member at Stoney Point before the Civil War.

As material from this period is very scanty, the next report is twelve years later. It was a report by W. W. Barber relating to a meeting he had just closed at Stoney Point. It read:

> Lobelville, September 1: On the first Lord's day in August, I began a meeting at Stony Point, Ala, The meeting continued only six days. The audiences were large, and the attention was good. The interest was growing when we had to close. Four persons were baptized ... W. W. Barber.[84]

One can see from this report that interest in religion was

fading away. It perhaps was because the attitude of society had become so disconnected from God that they felt they did not need God anymore—they could do everything for themselves. Bad mistake.

The next meeting to occur was reported in 1906. C. E. Holt was to do the preaching.[85] Then two years later another report gave the condition of the congregation. It was reported by William Behel (Uncle Will). He wrote:

> It may be of interest to the readers to give a brief statement of the cause in Lauderdale County. There are but few congregations in this county where I have not preached. My work is almost entirely where no other gospel preaching is done. Stony Point is seemingly improving, judging from the appearance of the congregation lately. Wm. Behel.[86]

In October C. E. Holt sent another report to the *Gospel Advocate* about another meeting at Stoney Point:

> Our meeting at Stony Point, six miles north of this place. and one of the oldest congregations in the country, is progressing nicely. Thirteen persons have been baptized, and the interest is good.[87]

He sent another report nearly a year later on Stoney Point which reads:

> Florence, August 23.—I am now engaged in a good meeting with the church of Christ at New Hope. Six have entered the fold and the interest is very good. Recently I have assisted in meetings at Belmont, Miss.; Stony Point, Ala.; and Good Springs, Tenn. There were twenty-five additions in those meetings....[88]

October 1910 came from Holt as he was reporting on his coworker—J. T. Harris. His first report said: "Brother J. T. Harris is in a good meeting at Stony Point seven miles north of Florence." [89] The second report stated that Harris had twenty-seven baptisms at Stoney Point.[90] This was the last report in the *Gospel Advocate* concerning Stoney Point, within our time frame of 1816–1914. We now shall look at the next three congregations to be established before the Civil War.

WATERLOO

A group of French Huguenots and Scotch-Irish settled in northern Alabama, just after the American Revolution. Through the influence of a Huguenot preacher—Benjamin Lynn, the little community had dropped all human names and creeds, prior to leaving Madison County Alabama, and agreed to take the New Testament as their rule of faith and practice. Among the families that composed this community at Waterloo were the D'Spains, the maternal ancestors of Addison and Randolph Clark leaders in the Restoration Movement, and pioneers in Christian education in Texas.

Very little is known concerning the church at Waterloo. Perhaps more is known about the little band after they were no longer at Waterloo. The birth of the Waterloo church was about the same time the Republican—Cypress Creek work began. Marshall D. Despain [D'Spain—later Spain] had moved his family from Meridianville, Madison County to Waterloo at the same time the John Chisholm family moved to the Cypress Creek area. These men were brothers-in-law and the sons-in-law of Benjamin Lynn. When land opened to settlers these two families were among the very first families to move into Lauderdale, which would have been 1816. The D'Spain family brought the teachings of Benjamin Lynn with them.

The family, like the Chisholms, worshipped in their houses until other families joined them later. It was not until a young school teacher by the name of Mansell W. Matthews moved into their community, that the Waterloo congregation began to be placed on a firm foundation. He was the first cousin to James E. Matthews. He arrived at Waterloo as a schoolteacher. He was baptized by John Mulkey in Spring Creek near Tuscumbia in 1823. He wrote of his baptism in the *Gospel Advocate*:

> I confessed my Savior and was buried with him in baptism by Bro. Jno. Mulkey in spring Creek, Franklin county, Ala., in 1823. Commenced publicly proclaiming his cause in 1825, having Brother B. F. Hall for my co-laborer, often associated with B. W. Stone, Scott, Johnston, Smith, Palmer, the Mulkeys, Moore, Hill, Griffin and a host of other pioneer preachers of the restoration ....[91]

B. F. Hall wrote of Matthews:

> I had also taken a young man of the name of Mansel W. Matthews to travel with me. His venerable father gave him to me saying: "Take Mansel and make a preacher of him, if you can; and if you cannot, send him back home to me." He became a useful, popular and influential preacher; but has removed about so much that he has "wasted his fragrance on the desert air."[92]

Obviously, Matthews came as a schoolteacher to Waterloo first and then began preaching. He was at Waterloo in 1823, before he was converted. He began preaching by 1825. He and Lynn D'Spain shared the role of preaching at Waterloo. D'Spain was baptized in the fall of 1826, and Tolbert Fanning and Allen Kendrick were baptized at the same time. During the time Matthews was just teaching and before he was preaching,

Ephraim D. Moore preached at intervals at Waterloo. In December 1824, when Marshall D'Spain made out his will, one of the executors of the will was Ephraim D. Moore.[93] This trust had been developed through Moore's preaching at Waterloo.

Before we move on to the 1830s one sad note should be noticed here. The death of Marshall D'Spain occurred on January 4, 1825. He was the patriarch of the D'Spain family and son-in-law of Benjamin Lynn.

Our next mention of Waterloo was a notice on December 1832. Barton Warren Stone had sent 300 songbooks to Mansell W. Matthews and his cousin James E. Matthews. The books were divided between Waterloo and Barton's congregation.[94] The church seemed to be growing well at this time.

By 1834 Allen Kendrick, who grew to manhood ten miles eastward on Bluff Creek (Barton's) was one of the preachers for the church at Waterloo.

The next item shows Allen Kendrick as being in Waterloo in 1834. Another report was sent to the *Christian Messenger* about the work at Waterloo. It read as follows:

> Bro. Allen Kendrick, of Waterloo, Ala. has lately baptized 12 or 14, in that place or vicinity. Bro. L. D. Collins of that place wishes us to give our views with regard to the faith of the subjects, and of the administrator, of baptism. We still plead that the subjects of baptism should have an operative faith, such as will lead them to repentance and obedience; and that the administrator perform the act of immersing with an unwavering faith that it as a divine appointment. Editors.[95]

Kendrick had been baptized at the same time as Tolbert Fanning and Benjamin Lynn D'Spain. These three men grew up knowing one another. They all began to preach at the same time and many times all preached in the same meetings. Kendrick was sharing the pulpit with Mansell Matthews at Waterloo.

The Collins family seemed to be one of the prominent families at Waterloo. P. M. Collins' name was published as serving as an agent for the *Christian Messenger*. There were other names of subscribers as is seen in the list:

> Waterloo. P. M. Collins for A. Parker and Jackson Webb 8; Bartons Jas. E. Matthews for Simeon Eckols 8 and $9.00 for H. Books.[96]

The L. D. Collins was a strong Christian at Waterloo. He seemed to be very active in the congregation. His name appears along with Allen Kendrick at Waterloo in a report on those who had paid Stone for his journal and other items that appeared in the *Christian Messenger*:

> Waterloo, L. D. Collins for self-1.25; A. Parker, 1.25; R. Johnson 1.25; W. Welch 1.25; Eld. A. Kendrick paid 1.00. to agent, all for vol. 9.[97]

The year 1835 would eventually prove disastrous to the church at Waterloo. That was the year the church moved to Texas, leaving a very struggling little church behind. Eventually, this first planting of the church was completely gone by 1848. In the *Christian Register* only three congregations in Lauderdale County were listed—the old Barton's church, a new congregation called Bluewater in the Elgin Community, and of course the Cypress congregation.[98] The Matthews Papers spoke of this relocation of the Waterloo church to Texas:

> During the last half of the year 1835, practically the whole Alabama community (Waterloo) where Mansil Matthews had taught school and a number of families from Tennessee and Mississippi formed a company and started for Texas There were two Christian ministers in the company, Lynn D'Spain and Mansil W. Matthews. The caravan, on its long and tiresome

journey, did not travel on the Lord's Day. The members spent the day in worship and rest. They sang, prayed, partook of the Lord's Supper, and listened to the Word, which was proclaimed by either one or both of the preachers. Religion was to them a vital thing, and inconvenient circumstances were not powerful enough to deter them from doing their duty as they interpreted it. Almost the whole company was made up of Disciples. It was a Church on foot, on wheels and on horseback.[99]

In 1860 Carroll Kendrick, who grew up at Bluff Creek—Gravelly Springs, wrote of the impact in Texas by these Christians from Waterloo. He wrote:

> Brother Fanning: We have just concluded another happy meeting some-thirty miles west of this place on N. Gabriel. There were thirty-one additions, one a Baptist preacher. It was a truly refreshing time. A number of our old Alabama friends were there, and still pressing on in the service. How they delighted to talk of old battles fought and victories won. We concluded, as the best guests we could make, that from. Lauderdale County, Ala., twenty-five. Years ago, we might now count some 50 preachers and, perhaps 50,000 disciples and you know we did not. wait then, to be especially sent nor had we any pledges, or promises of support, except God's promises.[100]

Kendrick gave a beautiful picture of what a small, determined group can accomplish with a strong faith in God. This will always be the legacy of the Waterloo congregation.

After the 1836 report, there was no other report until the 1880s. A John Nelson Vandiver was living at Waterloo in 1884 and was a converted Baptist preacher who was now preaching the New Testament plan of salvation. He was appealing through the pages of the *Gospel Advocate* for aid in preaching to the people in his area. His story is as follows:

> Dear Brethren: I have been a Baptist minister for nearly thirty years and have been tantalized as being a Campbellite. Not knowing the ground, they occupied, I would deny. But after becoming acquainted with some gospel ministers, I was astonished to learn that a people had been so misrepresented. I have just returned from a three years' tour in the West, and have mingled with many orders, have made many new and happy acquaintances. I find many here inquiring for the old landmarks, and now I ask, through your dearly beloved columns, for ministerial aid to visit those ends of the earth. We want men who can defend the gospel plan of salvation, and I will warn them in time to not come expecting an easy time. Any minister who can come, and will address me at Waterloo, Ala., I will take great pride in publishing the appointment, and will serve him as a pilot, and defend him to the best of my ability. They call me a Campbellite, a turncoat, and I know not what all. I assure you that I have made no changes in gospel sentiments, but feel that I have gained strength, like Apollos, from acquaintance with Aquilla, and I expect to prove my faith by my works. John R. (N.) Vandiver.[101]

Vandiver mentions that there were people "inquiring for the old landmarks" in Waterloo and the surrounding area. Could it be possible that Vandiver was responsible for planting the seed that grew into the re-established church of Christ at Waterloo? He mentioned that he would help anyone who wanted to come and preach at Waterloo.

He sent a second report to the Advocate which gave more information on his conversion and baptism; but included information in relation to the Waterloo area. It was as published below:

> I am now writing to inform my brethren about my whereabouts. I am in receipt of two letters desiring to know where Waterloo is, and how to get there. Waterloo is on the Tennessee

River, twenty-five miles below Florence, Ala., and thirty miles above Savannah, Tennessee, and has about 200 Inhabitants. I am a great deal better off in the way of ministerial aid than I thought when I first wrote. Notwithstanding, we still invite and urge the brethren in the ministry to come; there is work for all. I met with a cousin of mine, P. J. Vandiver, at the Poplar Spring Church, the State Line Ferry, on the Tennessee River, in this county. He preached three discourses. Four were baptized, and three from the Baptists, me being one. He could not give me a correct statement of all his labors; but said he had met with great success and considerable ingathering. Prejudice is dying away. I handed out all the Advocate I had and have several promises to subscribe my next visit. I have promised to visit Bro. Vandiver, (he lives 20 miles from me,) and put in one month in the Master's cause, after which I hope to have something to report worth hearing. John N. Vandiver.[102]

He mentioned the church at Poplar Springs. That church had been mostly converted from the Methodist church at Poplar Springs in October 1880 by Murrell Askew.[103] Vandiver mentioned that his cousin P. J. Vandiver preached three discourses and that three came out of the Baptist church and were baptized, including himself. We know that Vandiver, as a preacher, must have preached several times at Waterloo.[104] So, it seems likely that he was the one who re-planted the church at Waterloo.

We know there were some strong Christians in Waterloo because an invitation from West Tennessee Christian College (now Freed-Hardeman University) was published in the *Gospel Advocate*, and it contained the name of a local boy from Waterloo. He was James L. Haddock, and he received a Bachelor of Literature (BA) degree.[105] He was trained as a teacher so he could support himself in his preaching. He did report a preaching appointment at Poplar Springs while a student at West Tennessee Christian College.[106] Years later he was preaching in other states.

It was not until 1898 that a report spoke of Waterloo church as being established. The report was very short, and it was announced that E. W. Sewell intended to hold a meeting at Waterloo. It was to begin on the second Sunday of August 1898.[107] Brother Sewell never gave a report on the meeting. We do not know if the meeting did or did not transpire, or if it did and was so unsuccessful that he never thought it worth mentioning.

The following year W. S. Long came and conducted a meeting in July. He wrote of the meeting:

> Waterloo, June 28.—I reached this place on June 15. Almost all of the people being busy, I preached only at night. After preaching about a week to a people who are interested in the word of God, I visited Florence, Ala., and preached at Rhodesville on my way. The brotherhood at Waterloo and surrounding country are weak indeed. I think it should be the duty and work of strong congregations to send good gospel preachers there and preach the truth, especially to the promising young ladies and gentlemen. God bless the Young! May they be an honor to Christianity and humanity. I found a faithful band at Iuka, Miss. W. S. Long, Jr.[108]

Long made an appeal to the stronger churches in the area to help the weaker congregations such as Waterloo.

There were, however, some members who wanted to go the extra mile in studying the Bible. One such member was R. Higgins. He wrote an inquiry to F. D. Srygley concerning fellowshipping nonmembers. It was as follows:

> Brother Srygley: Is it right for members of the church of Christ to commune with other churches? Is there anything wrong in our holding school when we meet on the first day of the week to break bread? R. Higgins.[109]

In 1901 W. S. Long returned for another meeting. This meeting was somewhat successful. The report is given:

> Ramer, August 31.—Brother W. S. Long, of Henderson, ... On the third Lord's day in August, he commenced a meeting at Waterloo, Ala.., and continued for eight days. On the fourth Lord's day in August Brother A. G. Freed joined him and preached some strong sermons. Six persons, five of whom were from the Methodists, were added to the church. Brother Long is now with us at this place (Ramar). He is appreciated by the brethren wherever he goes; for he preaches the truth boldly, yet with love. Jephthah Fowlkes.[110]

Arvey Glen Freed joined Long seven days later and preached some "strong sermons." Long and Freed had six responses for the two-week meeting.

The congregation was growing slowly and by 1903 they were looking for a preacher to work with them on a regular basis. A. V. Bevis had the *Gospel Advocate* publish an advertisement for a preacher at Waterloo. The advertisement read as follows:

> Preachers Wanted—Brother A. V. Bevis, of Waterloo, Ala., under date of September 21, writes: "If you know of a good young preacher whose services we could secure, please give us his name and address. We want one who will locate here or have his headquarters at this place." Waterloo is in Lauderdale County, North Alabama. Any young preacher who realizes that he can accomplish good in that field, or more good there than elsewhere, should reply at once to this inquiry. The desire to accomplish the greatest good to the greatest numbers should govern us in regard to fields of labor. There can scarcely be a doubt that many preachers could accomplish more good in such towns as Waterloo and fields of labor surrounding them than to settle in cities where they have no special field of work.[111]

In September P. H. Hooten came and conducted a meeting that lasted ten days resulting in two baptisms.[112] The next recorded meeting was in 1907. Sometime in January, William Milton Behel came and held a meeting at Waterloo.[113] He wrote of that meeting: "My first meeting at Waterloo, which resulted in twelve additions, has already been reported."[114] Again, in July he returned and held another meeting. The second meeting continued for thirteen days, and nine persons were baptized. Behel said of this success: "Brethren Owen, Fuqua, Sewell, Long, and others sowed, and I have done the reaping."[115]

C. E. Holt came and preached at Waterloo in October of that same year. This is probably not an extended meeting, as the congregation had already had two extended meetings that year. Holt just said: "I am now preaching at Waterloo, Ala."[116]

In June 1908 Behel wrote a comprehensive report on the Lauderdale County work. He wrote of Waterloo:

> There are several places in this county that would be good mission points, and my intention is to see that some of these have the gospel preached this summer. Some congregations, North Carolina especially, will see that I am assisted in this work.
>
> One was restored at Waterloo on last Lord's day. I have been preaching at Waterloo for over a year and am glad to say that the church there is doing fine now. The attendance continues to increase, and the preaching of the gospel is surely triumphing over error. The brethren there are zealous. And their zeal is "according to knowledge," which will prove to making the work permanent. Brother Harris will conduct a meeting for them, beginning on the second Lord's Day in July. We look for (sic) a good meeting. "Be thou faithful unto death, and I will give thee a crown of life." Wm. Behel.[117] [118]

In July, the *Gospel Advocate* reported that J. T. Harris was in a "good meeting" at Waterloo.[119] The meeting closed with three baptisms.[120]

C. E. Holt had a debate with a Baptist minister by the name of Lewis at Waterloo. He wrote on February 26, 1909, concerning the debate:

> I spent a part of last week at Waterloo, Ala., in a discussion with a Mr. Lewis (Baptist) from Memphis, Tenn. I am quite sure that much good was accomplished. Waterloo is a place where much prejudice exists against the church of Christ. The debate gave much encouragement to the "faithful few."[121]

Sometime following Holt's debate problems arose from the lack of knowledge and understanding of the scriptures. A sister had an illegitimate child; she confessed her sin to her sister and her sister told a brother in the church who told it to the congregation. The penitent sinner wanted to be accepted by the church but then comes the problem. Some wanted to accept her, and some did not. One of the members wrote to E. G. Sewell of the *Gospel Advocate* and inquired what should be done in this situation. The inquiry and answer were published in the *Gospel Advocate*.

The inquiry:

> Brother Sewell: Miss — had an illegitimate child; and she acknowledged to her sister of doing wrong, and her sister told it to Mr. B —. and Mr. B —. told it in the church. Some of the members want her in the church and some do not. I want to know what you have to say about it Waterloo, Ala. F. E. H.
>
> Sewell's answer:
> It is certainly very plain that if the sister has made an honest confession and desires to remain in the church and do right in the future, it is the duty of the brethren to forgive her and encourage her to be faithful to the Lord from this time forward. All that manifest a disposition to do right should not only be

allowed the privilege but should be assisted as the word of God directs, that they may be saved.[122]

Things such as this demonstrated the church at Waterloo was weak, yet willing to grow in knowledge and understanding. They needed more Bible study. At the same time the inquiry was printed in the *Gospel Advocate,* J. T. Harris was engaged in a meeting at Waterloo.[123] This was good timing because any further questions on the matter could be addressed by Harris. Nothing else was ever heard of the matter through the pages of the *Gospel Advocate.*

We usually do not give obituaries in their entirety, but the following one needs to be given just as it was published. It gives an insight not only into the life of the deceased but also, the church life at Waterloo. It reads:

> Brother Zack Higgins, of Waterloo, Ala., was born on March 19, 1877; was married to Miss Ollie Spain on January 15, 1904; and departed this life on September 18, 1910. Brother Higgins was good in every sense that the word implies; he was a good citizen, a good neighbor, a good husband, and a good Christian. He leaves a young, heartbroken wife, an aged father and mother, and several brothers to mourn their loss. As I remarked the day of his burial, I do not think the church at Waterloo could have lost a member who would be missed more than Brother Higgins; but we all rejoice in the faith that our loss is his gain. Florence, Ala. J. T. Harris.[124]

Brother Behel returned for another gospel meeting in 1912. The result of the meeting was two souls rescued from the devil's clutches.[125] During the period from around 1900 until 1914—our ending for our study of the North Alabama Restoration Movement you may have noticed three names kept showing as holding meetings at Waterloo. They were William Behel, C. E. Holt, and J. T. Harris. This faithful trio kept the church at

Waterloo faithful and growing spiritually. From all of the above reports, one can see that the church was never numerically strong but was spiritually strong. That is why the congregation still lives in the westernmost part of Lauderdale County, Alabama. One last report for this set period was that the church at Waterloo gave $8.50 to the Emmerson Bible School and Orphans' Home.[126] This demonstrated their willingness to reach outside their immediate community and do good. With this kind act, we close the history of Waterloo.

Barton's—Bluff Creek—Gravelly Springs—Macedonia

As was stated earlier in this book the years that followed the War of 1812, thousands of settlers came into the northern part of Alabama from Tennessee, North and South Carolina, Georgia, and Virginia. Many families came to the fertile and well-watered Tennessee Valley to live. Among those families were the Fannings, the Kendricks, and the Youngs, the Houstons, and Hightowers. These had all moved into the Bluff Creek Valley between 1816 and 1820. The community went through different name changes. First: Barton's, after James Barton's store. Second: Bluff Creek after the stream that ran through the community. Third: Gravelly Springs after the springs near where the creek bends westward toward the river. Many of the settlers who moved there became members of Bluff Creek Church of Christ.

Tolbert Fanning and his brother James Madison Fanning grew to manhood along with Allen and Carroll Kendrick. The Kendrick brothers' father Jesse Kendrick purchased seventy-nine acres plus in September of 1827 on Bluff Creek and built a grist mill.[127] Tolbert Fanning's father signed this deed as a witness. Carroll Kendrick wrote of this in Tolbert Fanning's obituary the following:

When I was a mill boy, in Bluff Creek, Lauderdale county, Ala., I knew Bro. Fanning, his father and mother, brothers, and sisters well and intimately. Father Fanning used to send to our mill, and I went to school with most of his children. The aged father and mother left us some years since. So did James Madison Fanning, one of our purest preachers. Perhaps several other members of the old family have gone; and now Bro. Talbot is gone [May 3, 1874, aged nearly 64].[128]

These four men, along with Benjamin Lynn D'Spain, Samuel Giles, and James Young all rode and preached together many times in their early days at Bluff Creek. Julian Carroll Kendrick (Carroll's son) wrote of his father:

Carroll Kendrick—Was born Dec. 29, 1815, on Bigby Creek, eighteen miles from Columbia, Tenn. When about four years old, his parents moved across the Tennessee line into Lauderdale county, Ala., where he grew up. His Sunday schooling was largely rolling huge stones in to Bluff creek valley, fishing, etc., with an occasional visit to the Baptist monthly meetings. There were no Christian Lord's day schools, and but a poor showing of any kind of schools there...Carroll Kendrick was early and deeply impressed with the necessity of being a Christian—mostly by the prayers and teachings of his mother; but it took him four years careful reading of the Old Testament, and twelve reading of the whole of the New, to rid himself of popular doctrines, and learn what to do to become a Christian. When he understood this (1832), he wrote to his brother, then an active evangelist, met him forty miles on the way, and was immersed "for the remission of his sins." He was then nearly eighteen and has never for one moment regretted this start. Two things only he regrets —that he did not start sooner, and that he has not been more devoted and useful.[129]

My friend, Frank Richey has a PowerPoint lesson about this

community at Bluff Creek and what an impact it had on the Restoration Movement in general. He calls it "The Community of Influence."

The approximate date for the establishment of the Bluff Creek church is given by James Evans Matthews. He wrote: "I have planted another church in my immediate vicinity, of about 60 members.[130] Matthews had moved to the Bluff Creek Community by April 25, 1831, because his name appears along with Ephraim D. Moore and William Fanning as purchasers of a parcel of land at Bluff Creek and the date was April 25, 1831. When James Evans Matthews moved to Bluff Creek-Gravelly Springs, the community was known as Barton's, after James Barton's store and post office at Bluff Creek. His removal to Barton's in 1831 and his article saying that he had planted a congregation in his "immediate vicinity" all happened the same year. We can safely say the church was established in 1831. February 27, 1832, Matthews negotiated a land deal that included a sawmill, a cotton gin, and a grist mill.[131] In 1831 he and William Fanning (Tolbert's father) were subscribing to Alexander Campbell's *Millennial Harbinger*.[132] This sounds as though Matthews was planning to stay on Bluff Creek for a long while.

Apparently, the congregation had not grown enough to acquire a building of their own until 1833. By this time, the congregation was called Bluff Creek; any reference to "Barton's" now related to the community only. In 1833 property was secured and a building was constructed, according to a deed made in 1848. The deed was written as follows:

> This indenture made and entered into this 22nd day of August 1848, between Robert M. Patton of the first part and Hardy Hightower, Ross Houston, and Pugh Houston, trustees of the Church of Christ, meeting at Bluff Creek, in the county of Lauderdale and state of Alabama, witnesseth that when as Ephraim B. Reed by his writing obligatory dated 10th day of September 1833, commonly called a little band undertook with

Hardy Hightower, David Houston, and Samuel Young, then trustees, and their successors in office, that in consideration that they would build, or cause to be built, a meetinghouse for the public worship of God (for all religious denominations which worship God as Christians and more especially the denomination known as Christians, and also the United Baptists) on two acres of land known and described as follows:[133]

The precise location of the property was given. We learn that the property was first purchased in 1833 and that something must not have been clarified at that time; thus, another deed had to be secured from Robert Patton.

The second title was granted in 1848. Also, another interesting item was included as a kind of "creed in the deed":

Record Book of the Church of Christ meeting in a Brickhouse on Bluff Creek in the County of Lauderdale and State of Alabama. The members of this church take scriptures of the Old and New Testament as their only creed and believe most firmly that no other rules but those of the Bible should be adopted within the faith and practice of Christians. Hardy Hightower, Ross Houston, and Pugh Houston—Trustees.[134]

These Christians had learned to protect their property by placing in the deed things that distinguish them from other groups that might try to take their property. Even though our brethren built the building they did specify, in the beginning, that other groups could use the building for worship—thus the "creed in the deed." This made the building a "union house."

By 1844 James Matthew Hackworth and James Young were working in the community and preaching regularly. Hackworth wrote the following:

At Bluff Creek, (a place with which you are well acquainted,) there are about 18 or 20 excellent and intelligent Brethren, (not organized.) We have added to the good cause since last fall, at different points, about 25. We direct all our efforts, not at the animal, but at the intellectual powers of man. We are not fond of Brethren created in a storm. If we could compensate your labors, we would be pleased to have them for a time at Florence and Bluff Creek, this summer. The Review is a good work, may it prosper. Yours in hope. James M. Hackworth.[135]

By this letter, we now know that the church on Bluff Creek did not have elders and deacons. The church for eleven years had not appointed these officers in the congregation.

However, the matter was soon laying heavily up the mind of one of the leading men of the congregation. Ross Houston, one of the church's trustees wrote on this subject to Tolbert Fanning's *Christian Review*:

The Christians move in harmony, on Bluff Creek. We number 27. We have no deacons or Bishops yet, owing to the fact, that we have none qualified for the Bishop's office. You know, to attempt to make Bishops of unqualified members, would be placing ourselves in a condition never to be able to come to a perfect and full organization. All the ordinances and laying on hands, would never make a Christian Bishop, of one not possessing the qualifications found in the Holy records. The Apostles have put it in our power to know when we are right, and why then conjecture or speculate. I would as soon see a good old sister set apart, to the Bishop's office, as to see a Brother set apart to it, who did not possess every qualification found in our book of discipline.[136]

Houston was correct about qualifications for elders. We do not know if the congregation ever elected elders and deacons.

By 1848, as we have already seen, the Bluff Creek congregation had a brick meetinghouse, according to the 1848 deed. That same year the *Christian Register* was published by Alexander Hall as a one-time project. It was published to give statistics on congregations in the United States and around the world. It listed only three congregations in Lauderdale County. It had the church at Bluff Creek listed as Cypress. That was a misunderstanding, perhaps because at the time Hackworth gave his address as Cypress Springs, Alabama, March 24, 1845.[137] As Hall was not familiar with Lauderdale County, he easily made mistakes with the facts. For example, he placed the second grouping of Lauderdale County, Alabama churches in the Tennessee section.[138] It appears that Hall may have used part of Hackworth's report to Fanning, in the *Christian Review* in 1844, for his list of Lauderdale County churches.[139]

The 1848 *Christian Register* material was the last time Bluff Creek was mentioned as an existing congregation. Silence until after the Civil War ended.

Lauderdale County was a part of a perpetual battleground in North Alabama and suffered heavily. The war set the Lauderdale County brethren back a few years, as compared to many years in other Alabama counties. During the four years of war, some of the churches were either completely disbanded or suffered heavy membership loss. Before the war, three churches with their own buildings and two house churches were in existence. Bluff Creek at Gravelly Springs (formerly known as Barton's), had built a building before 1848 and James Young served as their minister.

During the winter of 1865, the Union Army under the command of General James H. Wilson, located his headquarters at Gravelly Springs. His camp extended from Gravelly Springs to Waterloo. He was waiting for the rain-swollen Tennessee River to recede. He was preparing for his drive to South Alabama to destroy all the industry on his way. Wilson wrote in the Official Records:

> The troops were all cantoned on the north bank of the Tennessee River, Long's, Upton's, and Hatch's divisions and Hammond's brigade, of Knipe's division, at Gravelly Springs,

and McCook's division at Waterloo. The aggregate force was about 22,000 men, 13,000 of whom were armed with Spencer carbines and rifles, 16,000 were well mounted on horses, simply requiring a few weeks' rest, feed, and attention to become fit for active service. The balance was poorly armed and dismounted.[140]

When he left on March 22, 1865, for Selma, Alabama, he left the valley on the north side of the river in a desolate condition. Upon leaving, they burned any public buildings that could be used to house troops. The Bluff Creek church building must have been destroyed in this burning spree. One can only conclude that the Civil War destroyed both the Bluff Creek congregation and their building.

The next mentioning of Gravelly Springs was a note in the *Gospel Advocate* about J. M. Bevis purchasing a copy of H. T. Anderson's New Testament through the office of the *Gospel Advocate*.[141] Nothing was mentioned, however, of a church at Gravelly Springs. The Bevis families were strong members of the Macedonia congregation. He later would become an elder there.

The next report to mention Gravelly Springs was in 1880, when Brother Murrell Askew traveled through Gravelly Springs, on his way from Savannah, Tennessee, and never mentions a church there.[142] If there ever was a time to mention a church at Gravelly Springs, that would have been the time to do it.

This closes our Bluff Creek phase of this history and transitions to the Macedonia phase, which was near Gravelly Springs. That connection will be more obvious later in our discussion of the Macedonia work, which will be discussed in the post-Civil War period.

BLUE WATER

Shoal Creek Association was constituted in 1825, of churches in Tennessee, and in Lauderdale County, Alabama, which were dismissed, for that purpose, from the Muscle Shoal Association. The Blue Water Baptist church was constituted of eleven members, from Mill Creek: in 1823. David Lancaster, their preacher, ministered to them for about 16 years. It was the largest church in the Association in 1840. Aaron Askew, Murrell Askew's father, (who was the preacher at Little Cypress), held his membership there.[143] Typically, Murrell Askew followed his father in some of the older Baptist churches in his preaching. Blue Water Baptist church was a likely place for Murrell as it was not but a few miles from where he was living during the 1870s when he left the Baptists. It was to this church community that James Young came in the Fall of 1843 and began to preach the gospel of the Lord. He soon established a small congregation. It seems they met in the Baptists' house for a few years and finally built their own house of worship.

Bluewater has been a mystery to the study of the Lauderdale County Restoration Movement. It was only found in our brotherhood's printed material three times and only one person whom we knew, who even knew anything about it. It was mentioned in Hosea Holcomb's book on the history of the Alabama Baptist.

In 1844 a short statement was published in the *Christian Review*—a journal published by Tolbert Fanning. The statement read:

> We have a little band of Brethren on Blue Water in this county, numbering 13 or 14 members, gathered since last fall, principally by the labors of Brother James Young, (not organized). (James M. Hackworth).[144]

At that time there was no mention of a house of their own house of worship.

In the *Christian Register* in 1848, only three congregations in Lauderdale County were listed—one of them was a new congregation called Bluewater in the Elgin-Mitchell Town Community.[145] It was noted in the *Christian Register* that Cypress Creek (then called Liberty and later Stoney Point) and Gravelly Springs had their own houses of worship; but Bluewater did not have a house of their own.

The war set the Lauderdale County brethren back a few years, as compared to many years in other Alabama counties. During the four years of war, some of the churches were either completely disbanded or suffered heavy membership loss. Before the war, two organized churches were in existence. Stoney Point, Bartons at Gravelly Springs, and Bluewater, an unorganized congregation. By the end of the war, Barton's was gone from the pages of history, leaving Stoney Point, Bluewater, and Hopewell—which was a newly formed congregation that was established during the war. One can see the setback the Restoration Movement suffered by the loss of Macedonia. Imagine what this was like all over Alabama and the South. Bluewater, though a struggling church, managed somehow to survive. We believed this was due to Murrell Askew's efforts among the Baptist churches in his community—as the Bluewater church was only four- and one-half miles from the Salem church.

The last note on the Bluewater congregation was printed in the *Gospel Advocate* in 1894. It was short and read as follows:

> Florence, Dec. 25: I have spent the last five and a half months preaching at the following places: North Carolina; Lauderdale county, Ala., one week, with five additions; four days at Bluewater, with good attention; one week on Middle Cypress... A. P. Holtsford.[146]

This congregation was always a small band of Christians from its beginning until it ceased to meet. It was located northwest of Mitchell Town a couple of miles. As late as World War II the Bluewater church was still meeting, though it was a very small group of Christians from that community. Charles Beavers said that his parents took him there several times, as a small boy. He remembered that the membership was small at the time.[147]

Why was there such a scarcity of information on the Bluewater church? One explanation is that it was a poor backwoods congregation with many uneducated or little educated people. They would not be sending reports to any publication, The only likely reports came occasionally from preachers who sporadically came through the Blue Water community. James Young, the founder of the congregation, is the only documented preacher of the New Testament church to have worked with Blue Water on a regular basis; but Askew's influence heavily overshadowed this work after the Civil War. Thus, the history of this small congregation in Lauderdale County, Alabama that nearly slipped through the cracks of Restoration History has been partially rescued.

Hopewell—Mars Hill

The history of the Mars Hill church began with Stoney Point. During Union occupation travelling to Stoney Point and back to the Mars Hill community was many times very difficult. Chisholm Road was a main artery to Clifton, Tennessee where most of the Union military supplies were offloaded from boats and hauled down to Florence. The Chisholm Road was heavily guarded and many times the Christians, and especially the Gresham family, from Mars Hill had to cross that road to attend worship at Stoney Point. Brethren from communities east of Chisholm Road were turned back. This caused this family and their Christian neighbors, who were members at Stoney Point, to start worshipping in their homes. Their numbers grew to the point that after the war they decided not to return to Stoney Point but rather establish a congregation in their community.

The brethren secured the use of an abandoned church building from the Methodists. It was known as "Hopewell." Brother J. H. Dunn preached occasionally at Hopewell, as well as at Stoney Point and in the Middle Cypress community. Upon his first visit to Hopewell, he wrote:

A New Family Gathered For The Lord. Lone Mulberry, Ala., Oct. 5, 1867. Bros. Fanning and Lipscomb: On last Saturday I commenced a meeting at Hopewell meeting house, near Florence, Ala., which continued up to Thursday. We had quite an interesting time, this being a new field, where our brethren hitherto have preached but little. I immersed six during the interview three of each sex, two of them heads of families-one from the Methodists, one from the Baptists, and one or perhaps two from the mourners' bench. They have enrolled their names and pledged themselves to watch over each other for good, and to keep the ordinances of God's house faithfully. They number twenty-six, and the prospects for additions are flattering.

Hopewell is situated on the Military or Nashville Road four and a half miles north of Florence. It is a neat, well-finished frame house, of good size. It is a neat well-finished house of good size. It was built by and belonged to the Methodists, and for some cause, they offered it for sale, and two of our liberal brethren and a good sister became the purchasers, paid for it, and have a deed to it.

Preachers are affectionately solicited of man-to call and preach for them. Inquire for Bro. John A. Thompson or Bro. Andrew J. Gresham, who reside near the meeting house either of whom will gladly receive a preacher and entertain him and will not send him away empty. Your old and devoted brother in the one hope, J. H. Dunn.[148]

By May 31, 1868, the brethren had bought the building from the Methodists.[149]

It was to this congregation that T.B. Larimore came to hold a meeting in June of 1868. Srygley described Hopewell as being four miles from Florence, and "scarcely more than a stone's throw from Mars Hill."[150] The brethren did not think Larimore preached well enough, so they took him across the county to Brother Young's (Thomas W. Young) house to preach. Larimore wrote of this event at Hopewell:

I came to Hopewell to hold a protracted meeting (June 1868). They let me try to preach once, and they were so pleased with that 'sarmint' that they let me off—suddenly! The meeting closed with a jerk and a bang. It was not wound up much, hence required but little time to run down; or perhaps it ran down so very fast is why it struck bottom so quick. It was wound up for eight days and it ran down in an hour. An Irishman once said: "They thuck me into the charch for six months on trial; but I did so well they let me off in three months." Hopewell did better by me than that—they took me for eight days and let me off in sixty minutes. Well, they did exactly right. They reasoned thus: "We have had none but good preachers here; we are few and weak; our enemies hold the fort and camp on the field. Now, if we let *him* try to preach here, it is goodbye to our prospects. Better have no preaching than his sort." Then they said: "What shall we do with him? This will we do—Brother and sister Young live a way back—good preachers rarely go there; they will appreciate any kind of preaching; to them will we send him." They said to me: "We will take you to Bro. Young's; he and sister Young and Frank and another one or two are the church there; they are good people and will treat you well." They sent me—I believe Bro. Andrew Gresham took in a buggy.[151]

Brother Andrew Gresham (one of Larimore's future brothers-in-law) drove Larimore, in a buggy, to Thomas Young's house. The result of Larimore's trip to the Youngs was the establishment of the Middle Cypress congregation, from what had been, up until this time, a house church. Middle Cypress will be discussed with the Bethelberry congregation.

Larimore, perhaps unknowingly, pointed out a weakness at Hopewell. He wrote:

This congregation is small but devoted to their Master's cause. They never learned to wait for the preacher to come around to serve the Lord for them; but, like valiant soldiers of the cross, they are ever at their post. They meet every first day of the week, preacher, or no preacher, and spend usually, three hours or more in teaching the children, reading the Holy Scriptures, exhorting each other in psalms, hymns, and spiritual songs, in breaking of bread, and in prayers.[152]

The weakness was their numerical strength. They never seemed to grow in number. The congregation had already begun to make plans to relocate to another site. The brethren continued to meet at the Hopewell site until 1870 when they relocated to the old foundry building near Mars Hill College [the site of the present-day congregation].

Larimore and the brethren had heard that someone intended to buy the old foundry property and start a brewery. So, Larimore and the brethren approached the owner of the property and purchased it. They began remodeling the old foundry building and fashioned it into a reasonably good meeting house. It was upon this change in location that the congregation took on the name "Mars Hill church of Christ." They occupied the newly renovated building sometime late in 1870. Srygley gives the date —1870 as when the brethren began using the foundry building. [153] Brother Granville Lipscomb mentioned a meeting that he held at Hopewell on the 2nd and 3rd Lord's Days in August 1871, which contradicts Srygley's statement. Apparently, Srygley got several dates incorrect in his book *Larimore and His Boys*

> Brother David. We had the pleasure of attending a series of meetings held by the brothers and sisters meeting at Hopewell five miles North East of Florence Ala., commencing the 2nd. and 3rd. Lord's days in August. The meeting closed with 18 accessions, 10 by baptism, 4 from the Baptists, 3 by commendation, and one from the Presbyterians, yet unbaptized. The cause seems to be advancing rapidly in this section. The brethren and

sisters meet every Lord's day to attend the ordinances; they have much to encourage them; we trust they will continue zealous in the good cause...G. Lipscomb.[154]

The history of the congregation is closely tied to the history of Mars Hill College. Therefore, to retrieve the congregation's history, we must also look at the school's history.

The first report to appear in the *Gospel Advocate*, after the congregation relocated from the Hopewell site to Mars Hill was sent by F. D. Srygley, a student at the school, but also a member of the Mars Hill church of Christ:

> Bro. Larimore reached home Saturday night about midnight. He has added about 130 to the church since July 15. I met him at church Lord's day morning; the first time I had seen him since July 1. After a warm greeting, he opened his Bible, and, pointing to a passage in the sixth chapter of John, said, "Did you ever notice this," He then gave me a new and brilliant idea, after which he continued in a voice that trembled with emotion, "Oh, this blessed book? I wish I could tear my mind from every other subject and make it my constant and only study for life." I relate this to show his manner of teaching the Bible. Whether in school or out he modestly communicated every idea he thinks a student will appreciate and utilize. Brethren, this Institution, especially the Bible College, is doing much for the church. We have many good schools —-probably more than we can support. If any must perish let us have those that do most for Christianity. If the preservation of our best schools will not save Mars Hill, I shall try to be reconciled to the death of my Alma Mater... [155]

This report gave two interesting facts.

1. Larimore's style of teaching and preaching.

2. Confirms Larimore's working with the Mars Hill congregation while at home.

Larimore seemingly refers to the work at the Mars Hill church:

> T. B Larimore writes from Mars Hill College near Florence, Alabama, Oct. 13, 1879: Our Mars' Hill work has begun. Two confessions, yesterday Bro. Clayton (J. C.) McQuiddy has just returned from Mountain Mill-three accessions, one over three score and ten.[156]

When school began each session, Larimore was working, mostly, for the school and the Mars Hill congregation. So, "Our Mars Hill work has begun" is to be understood as both school and church at Mars Hill.

In the late Spring of 1880 Robert Wallace (R. W.) Officer was raising money for his mission work amongst the Indians. He traveled throughout North Alabama and South Middle Tennessee preparing for his mission work amongst the Indians. In the fall of 1880, he moved to Texas where he began full-time work with the Gainesville Church of Christ. This was the beginning of his work among the Indians north of the Red River in Indian Territory (Oklahoma) where he distributed books, papers, and tracts with the aid of an interpreter. Officer came to the Florence area and to Mars Hill in June and preached a few sermons. He also brought T. C. Biles, a disenchanted Methodist preacher, with him. While at Mars Hill Officer baptized Biles and gave the following report:

> Bro. Biles made the good confession, and I baptized him at Mars' Hill. He went to Florence and began preaching in the City Hall. His congregation grew through the week at night. I spent the rest of my time with Bro. M. Askew, preaching at night at his house: Returned to Mars' Hill, Lord's day and preached for the brethren

> in the morning; one young man came forward and made the good confession, and went with me to Bro. Askew's 10 miles below on Tennessee River where I preached at 7 o'clock Lord's day evening, where 7 others confessed the lord Jesus. All were buried with the Lord, filled the grave that Jesus left empty, and arose by faith in the promise. We found Bro. T. B. Larimore, all the faculty, and all the young men working together for good. One of the essentials there, is the untiring labors of sister Larimore... Yours in hope, R.W. O. Lewisburg, Tenn., June 7, 1880.[157]

Officer was a diligent missionary and won the hearts of many people in Alabama and Tennessee. He was especially loved by the Mars Hill congregation.

Our next insight into the work at Mars Hill came from H. H. Turner, one of "Larimore's boys." He gave another view of the mission-minded congregation. Under the heading of "A Commendable Example," he wrote:

> The church at Mars Hill Ala., collects through its regular contributions, such sum as it can, and sends a couple of young preachers to the nearest destitute section to labor so long as they can on the support given. In July or August, it started two out a foot. The last report gives sixty-seven baptisms as the result. Why will not other churches do likewise? Scarcely a church in the land but can do as much if it will.[158]

One of the editors at the *Gospel Advocate* wrote the following:

> "I had good news to tell, and was determined to tell it," Bro. Turner says, was the inspiration to him to labor under difficulties. Earnestness is worth a thousand-fold more in reaching men with the gospel, than eloquence or learning. The Mars Hill church last year, helping Bro. Turner, added one hundred and nine persons to the Lord, planted five young congregations, kept three Sunday-schools at work in a destitute and needy field.

Mars Hill is a weak congregation, financially and numerically. Who can show a better record? Mars Hill congregation could not have brought a preacher from a distance and sustained him, but an earnest man living close by, with the help he could get in the field of labor, was supported. The way to clean the street is for everyone to sweep before his own door. The way to convert the world, ill for every church and every Christian to convert his neighbors. The Mars Hill church "is a good example to other churches in Alabama and everywhere.[159]

These two articles demonstrate the concern for lost souls and the determination to do something about it at Mars Hill. It would be two more years before another report came forth in the *Gospel Advocate*. T. B. Larimore writes:

My homework for the present closes with the writing of Bro. Wade's obituary: He was a devoted personal friend of mine. One of the best friends of the needy I have ever known. He read the Bible and the Advocate, seemed to care for no other paper, no other book. I enter the evangelistic field tomorrow, to evangelize till Jan. 1, 1887, 'the Lord willing.' Our month's work at Mars Hill and Florence resulted in great good.[160]

The Wade mentioned by Larimore was John D. Wade of the Antioch congregation near present-day Iron City, Tennessee. Wade had a terrible accident and one of his arms was torn off at his gristmill on Wolf Creek and died a few days later. He was one of the strongest supporters of Mars Hill College and a very close friend to Larimore. Larimore's report concerning his work at the Mars Hill church was supported in another segment of the *Gospel Advocate* by Brown Godwin:

Bro. Larimore closed his school with a series of meetings at Mars Hill and at Florence. Last report said 10 accessions. Meeting still going on. Bro. Larimore aims to teach 10- or 12-weeks next year.

Brethren remember this school is striving to teach pure religion, will you help, or will you send your children to sectarian schools or to others that only try to get them through their books. This school will begin in January; therefore, you can go to school and then cultivate a crop. Those preparing for preaching will find this to be the place for them. Brown Godwin, Linden, Tenn.[161]

For some unknown reason, nothing was printed in the *Gospel Advocate*, relating to the work of the church at Mars Hill, for five years. A report about Larimore's work as an evangelist finally broke the silence. The *Gospel Advocate* printed part of a letter that Larimore had written:

> Bro. Larimore is now at home, Mars' Hill, near Florence, Ala. In a private letter he says, "I am preaching for the home folks every night and Sunday too. There is no rest for the weary—in this world." He will begin a meeting with Campbell street church, Louisville, Ky., the first Sunday in April—possibly a few days earlier.[162]

Later, in October the *Gospel Advocate* printed an excerpt from another private letter of Larimore's, and it gave another bit of information on the Mars Hill church work. It was a letter from Eddie Blalock of which Larimore pointed out facts about the Blalock families' involvement with the church at Mars Hill. We take the liberty to give a few facts from this letter:

> Bro. Larimore encloses for me a letter from Eddie Blaylock, whom I (F. B. Srygley) knew as a little boy studying "second reader" and trying to learn the "multiplication table" a few years ago at Mars' Hill. On the margin of this letter. in Bro. Larimore's well-known writing I find these words: "Eddie is not only one of the Mars' Hill boys, but one of our neighbor boys. His father is a deacon in our home congregation, and one of the best of men. I prophesy good concerning Eddie." I understand that

"Eddie" graduated from the Florence State Normal College after Mars' Hill College was suspended. He was one of the small boys then. He is now teaching at Mountain Mills and making himself useful in the vineyard of the Lord as well. May the Lord bless him.[163]

This lets us peek into the private lives of a family very much involved in the work at Mars Hill (and members of that family still are involved with the Mars Hill work, presently [2024]).

In December of that year, Larimore reported on another member at the Mars Hill congregation. This time it was an elder at Mars Hill that he gave a report. It was Larimore's brother-in-law W. H. Gresham. Larimore wrote:

> Bro. W. H. Gresham, whom all our Mars Hill boys and girls remember, of course, as one of our faithful Mars Hill elders, has just closed a three days meeting at Stony Point, resulting in fourteen accessions to that patient congregation that, in the bittersweet long-ago, suffered so many of "the boys" to "make a beginning" there. Patient, long-suffering, "Old Stony" is still solid.[164]

This report shows the close ties between Mars Hill and Stoney Point. Remember that Mars Hill was formed out of Stoney Point during the Civil War. Families in both congregations were related. This bond still exists in 2024.

The next report we give in full. It contains so much information about the church and community it deserves full attention:

> Private Letter from Bro. Larimore. [The following letter was not intended for publication, but we take the liberty of publishing it, thinking it will be of interest to many of our readers. Ed.]
>
> Our all-day meeting at Mars' Hill yesterday was delightfully pleasant. A joyous reunion of families and friends. Two discourses and one dinner, of course. The L. & N. R. R. contributed much to the success of the meeting by furnishing

comfortable conveyance to and from Mars' Hill. Iron City, West Point and St. Joe sent a special train to Mars' Hill, "literally packed with people— men, women and children— from engine to rear platform." The youngest visitor from afar was "the charming little Miss" Anonymous Myers, of Iron City, whose age, according to the "official report" and record thereof, was (is) six weeks and seven days. The oldest was — old. "The tariff question, of which you have heard or seen some mention in political papers or elsewhere, has been so learnedly, logically, lengthily, thoroughly and frequently expounded and discussed in these favored parts of our great country recently, that I think the railroad authorities wisely and generously allowed the seven-week-old customer to be "put on the free list." This is not "official," however— simply my opinion. For various reasons, one of the most seriously important of which was that I had just been compelled to close a meeting at Mooresville when the interest demanded its continuance, I was in no condition to perform my part of the programme; but I did the best I could, and the people possessed too much magnanimity of soul to tell me what they thought. This is one of the many marvelous blessings vouchsafed to preachers here below. Few things can crush me more completely than to be compelled to close a meeting when the most joyous and glorious results are at hand, and few have been more frequently thus crushed than I. I have long been promising myself, among other things, these three: 1. To rest a few weeks, in the warmest part of every year. Faithful friends who love me earnestly entreat me to do so, and I believe duty to myself demands it; but how can I? All this year, I have been preaching twice or thrice a day, and, yet how little I have done! How much needs to be done, and that without delay! "Some sweet day," we shall "pass over the river and rest under the shade of the trees." "Meet me there." 2. To never make or agree to any engagement or arrangement that promises to compel me to close a meeting before it ought to be closed—to have but one engagement at a time and fight every fight to a finish; but it is so hard for me to say no! In all these years of tearful toil, I have never finished but one meeting. I work at one place as long as other engagements and positive promises will permit and then go elsewhere, instead of remaining at each place as long as the interest demands. The latter is evidently the correct way. The former is the way I do. 3. To build at Mars' Hill, just such a church house as ought to be here, for all time, viz: A commodious, solid-stone structure; not fine, fashionable and showy, but neat, plain, substantial, comfortable and durable. A house that will stand for ages and always be appreciated by the humble workers and worshipers "in the vineyard of the Lord." Few know how we have struggled, how we have economized, or what we need here; yet the name and place are near and dear—almost sacred—-to thousands who love the Lord, his people and his cause. When the railroad that has done so much to elevate and almost make this country was completed and Mars' Hill was made a station— not a post-office, however, Florence still being our post-office— the authorities, as a compliment to me, changed the name from Mars' Hill to Larimore; but, though I appreciated their kindness and the compliment, I immediately appealed to them to reverse their decision and rescue from "oblivion" the name by which the place has so long been known; and, though Larimore, instead of Mars' Hill was on their time tables, etc., they graciously and generously granted my request, and thus has been preserved, perhaps perpetuated the name Mars' Hill. T. B. Larimore. Mars' Hill, Ala., Sept. 5,' 92.[165]

Larimore's refusal to accept the new name "Larimore" for the train station near Mars Hill, shows his modesty and no desire to be honored in that way. But the battle shifted to brethren thinking Mars Hill had a post office. That was not Larimore's desire either. He wrote a short request to the brethren and pleaded with them that there was not a post office at Mars Hill. It read as follows:

> Will you please tell them again that Mars Hill is not, never has been, and probably never is to be, a post office? Some letters addressed to me at Mars' Hill reach me, after long delay—how, I do not know. Ten times as many may never reach me. Of course, the writers feel about them just as if they knew I received them on time. Mars' Hill is simply a suburb of Florence, and Florence is our post office—Box E — T. B. Larimore.[166]

Larimore was in such high demand to hold meetings he had to mark off August for the annual meeting at his own home, Mars Hill. The following report reveals this:

> ... He is now at Winchester, Tenn., and he has set apart August for the annual meeting at his own home, Mars' Hill, near Florence, Ala. The Mars Hill meeting is attended every year by more or less visitors from different parts of the country, and those who propose to attend this year may make their arrangements to go sometime in August. While at home he will probably do some preaching at other points in that part of Alabama, as he does every year, and then, by the blessing of God he will begin another series of evangelistic labors in the early fall, which will probably continue without cessation from point to point till the end of the year ... He should always be addressed at Florence, Ala. His mail is forwarded regularly from Florence, no matter where he may be.[167]

His popularity as an evangelist is one reason for his closing of Mars Hill College. Another was that he was getting burned out from constantly having to raise funds for the school. He believed he could be more effective as an evangelist than he could as a schoolteacher. This writer believes he made a bad mistake. Looking at the end results of his school shows that he multiplied himself hundreds of times and the proof is the churches that were established by his "boys." Basil Overton had a saying: "I love what I'm doing because I don't know what I'm doing"—meaning we never know the end results of the work we do. "Blessed are the dead which die in the Lord from henceforth: Yea, saith the Spirit, that they may rest from their labors; and their works do follow them." (Revelation 14:13). Larimore did, however, live long enough to see much good results from his school and his "boy." The congregation at Mars Hill owes him much gratitude, because of his influence almost at the beginning back at much gratitude. Larimore may have saved the Mars Hill congregation through his quick thinking to purchase the old foundry property and prevent a brewery from being built on the doorsteps of his school, which was about to be launched. Through this purchase, the church could have a large building in which to worship and grow. They used this old foundry shop until 1904 when their new house was completed.

For their annual meeting in 1894 Larimore's brother-in-law—R. P. Meeks came and helped him in the meeting. A. B. Simpson of Waverly, Tennessee wrote concerning this meeting:

> Brother Meeks will go to Mars Hill, Ala., to join Brother Larimore in a meeting. Where could be found a stronger team? May the Lord bless them, together? with the brotherhood. A. B. Simpson.[168]

It seems that Larimore was not well at that time, which is perhaps the reason Meeks came to help Larimore in this meeting. Larimore wrote of this situation:

> It grieves me not to be able to preach as these perfect days are going by. I baptized three gentlemen in Florence last night but was not able to preach. I am going to Lawrenceburg tomorrow, but my judgment and friends here tell me to quit trying to preach and try to get well. We had eleven confessions at Mars' Hill, but I had to close the meeting in the midst of the best interest we have ever had here. Aug. 14, 1897. T. B. Larimore.
> [169]

Three weeks later the *Gospel Advocate* published a final report on the Mars Hill meeting:

> Mars Hill, August 17. Brother Meeks' meeting at Mars Hill added eleven to the fold-just eleven more than we expected, material being so scarce that additions were scarcely to be expected. Material never accumulates about Mars Hill.[170]

Larimore continued to hold meetings at Mars Hill each August. He held one in 1898 while still very exhausted and sick. F. D. Srygley wrote of his condition:

> Brother Larimore spent the night of May 23 at my home on his way from Springfield, Mo., where he had just closed a meeting, to his home at Mars Hill, near Florence, Ala. He was in feeble health, and in his body bore the marks of serious exhaustion from overwork when he ought to have been resting and recuperating his nervous system and general health... F. D. Srygley.[171]

Srygley wrote again in September of that year concerning Larimore's health and his work at Mar's Hill:

> The latest news from Brother Larimore is encouraging. His health is steadily improving, and he hopes to be able to resume regular work as an evangelist by the first of September. For several years he has held an annual protracted meeting at his home, Mars' Hill, Ala., in August of each year. These meetings have always been well attended by people from a distance as well as by the neighbor around Mars' Hill. The interest from a distance has for some years attracted the attention of railroad authorities, and special excursion rates have been given to Mars' Hill during Brother Larimore's annual protracted meetings. The congregation this year was probably the largest that ever assembled there. The house though large for a country congregation, would not hold the women; and if it had been four times as

large, it would have been packed. Brother Larimore preached twice on Sunday and expressed the opinion next day that he would be all right and ready for regular work again by the first of September. If a prophet is always without honor in his own country, then Brother Larimore is certainly no prophet. He has more honor, and he draws larger congregations at his own home, where he has been heard most and known longest and best, than anywhere else F. D. Srygley. [172]

In October Strother M. Cook, a missionary to Africa, came and solicited funds for his work abroad. Since Mar's Hill was so mission-minded, we believe that they contributed to his work. He wrote:

At the present time I am among some of the churches in North Alabama. The churches at Florence, Mars' Hill, Sheffield, Russellville, Bear Creek, Haleyville, Buttahatchie, Lynn, and Jasper have been visited and most of them have given cheerfully to our mission... [173]

Mars Hill demonstrated time and time again their concern for mission work, both at home and foreign. Perhaps this was no exception.

Little information between 1898 and 1903 can be found in the journal. 1903 was a mixed year for Larimore and Mars Hill. Larimore's son Theophilus Brown Larimore, Jr., better known around Mars Hill as "Toppie" died on August 4, 1903. G. C. Brewer gave an account of this sad story:

On August 4, 1903, death invaded for the first time the home of Brother Larimore. His son, Theophilus (tenderly called "Toppie") passed away. He was an osteopathic physician, thirty-one years old, and had his office at Winchester, Tenn. From childhood he had been a cripple. He suffered with what used to be called "white swelling," but which is tuberculosis of the bone.

When the final fatal attack seized him, his mother went to Winchester and brought him home to Mars Hill. The family physician, Dr. Bramlette, said an operation was necessary. Arrangements were made to take him to Nashville to Dr. Eve. The Louisville and Nashville Railroad runs by Mars Hill, about one mile from the Larimore home. This railroad company had arranged a stop and built a small station booth there for Brother Larimore and called it "Mars Hill." Automobiles were unknown, and such a thing as an ambulance did not exist in that section then. But good neighbors were in abundance, and kindness and love were the law of the community. Neighbor men, with "Toppie's" brothers, carried him on a cot to the train; and when they came to the Creek, spanned by a one-person foot log, they waded it without hesitation. "Toppie" and Brother Larimore reached Nashville safely, and the operation was performed successfully. Brother Larimore had already written a telegram of hope for the loved ones at home, when a sudden change came, and death was almost immediate. "Toppie" was brought home and buried at Mars Hill on Thursday. The following Sunday, August 9, the annual meeting began. Brother Larimore was so overwhelmed with sorrow that he feared he could not preach. The brethren talked of getting someone else, but no one seemed to be available on so short a notice, and Brother Larimore, looking to the Lord for strength, agreed to go on with the usual plans. He preached with a deeper pathos and a more compelling tenderness because of the bleeding heart that throbbed in his bosom. G. C. Brewer.[174]

During the death of "Toppie" there was much sadness at Mars Hill. Emma Page wrote a tribute to Toppie in the *Gospel Advocate*:

The time of the annual meeting at Mars' Hill (usually in August) is reunion time for Brother Larimore's family. The children who have left the home nest always come back then if

possible. Toppie had never failed to be at one of these meetings. Thirty Augusts he had seen come and go; thirty of these memorable meetings he had attended. Even when he was just recovering from his long spell of suffering and sickness, — unable to walk, he was carried to the meetings, where propped up in a chair, he enjoyed the services as much as anyone else and contributed his share to the general happiness. The meeting this year began on August 9 — five days after Toppie passed away, and three days after his burial. It was a sad meeting for Mars Hill family, especially for the father and the mother, who missed the bright face of their son who had never failed to be with them at their reunion time, always happy and cheerful, always doing everything in his power to add to the happiness of others — many little things which no one else seemed to think of doing.
[175]

For some time talk around the Mars Hill church had been concerning the condition of the old shop in which the church had been meeting, since they left the old Hopewell building. In 1903 Mrs. Horace P. Lucas, who was a member at Mars Hill, took it upon herself to send an appeal to the brotherhood concerning helping build a new meeting house at Mar's Hill. Since the appeal was the catalyst for getting things in motion for the new building, we give the appeal in full:

> Mars' Hill, Ala., four miles from Florence, Ala., is the home of our beloved brother, T. B. Larimore. While nearly all of the people of that community are members of the congregation of Christians worshiping there, there is no wealth in the congregation, because there is none in the community.
>
> Florence is my home now; but my membership is still at Mars' Hill, where I was born and brought up and where Brother Larimore baptized me when I was a little child.
>
> While Brother Larimore and the members of the congregation at Mars' Hill have helped many others in many places and in

many ways, always trying to respond to every call for help, we have necessarily denied ourselves, that we might help others, which, of course, it was our duty to do. One result of this is that we worship in what was once a blacksmith shop, now nearly fifty years old.

Now we are not ashamed of the dear old shop, the sacred memories and sweet influences of which are felt in ten thousand homes that have been made better, brighter, and happier thereby; but we have resolved that, the Lord willing, Brother Larimore shall have a better house in which to preach, and his friends a better house in which to hear him, when he is at home. We know that there ought to be, and we believe that there are, thousands of grateful, faithful friends who will be glad to contribute liberally to this important work (who, indeed, would sincerely regret not having an opportunity to do so); and to all such the privilege is now, once for all, extended.

Brethren, to all who really appreciate the privilege of giving not grudgingly, but gladly and literally little or much to this important work we appeal for help, and to no one else. We will build the best house that we can build; we will build it this year; we will pay as we go, owing nothing when the work is completed; and we will be careful to put into it not even so much as one penny, farthing, or mite that is not a freewill offering —a love offering, gladly given. Therefore, if you really wish to help us, please do so now. You shall not be worried by a repetition of this appeal. If you help us, we shall be grateful, and may the Lord bless you; but if you refuse to respond to this appeal, you reject the only opportunity that you will ever have to help us. It is now or never. We want no pledge or promise; we want cash. and nothing but cash, as we shall plan and build according to the cash on hand, contracting no debt. So, then, "what thou doest. do quickly;" and may the Lord abundantly bless you.

Please send all offerings to Mrs. Horace P. Lucas, Miss Ettie

Larimore. or Mr. L. C. Moore, Florence, Ala., or T. B. Larimore, 900 South College Street, Nashville, Tenn.

(Mrs.) Horace P. Lucas. Florence, Ala.

Brethren D C. M. Southall, W. H. Gresham. J. B. White, H.C. Blalock, and L. C. Moore indorse the foregoing statement and appeal, as follows: "We, the elders of the churches of Christ at Florence and Mars' Hill, commend Sister Lucas as worthy of all confidence, love, and esteem; we approve and appreciate her unselfish labor of love; and we direct and request that the foregoing important, worthy, and righteous appeal be published by order of the churches that we represent."[176]

The new building was no longer just a dream. By November it was under construction, according to a report in the *Gospel Advocate*:

> Work has begun on the new house of worship at Mars' Hill. Ala. A few days ago Brother Larimore preached the last sermon in the old shop which has done such useful service. Brother Larimore is now in a meeting with the Tenth Street church of Christ, this city [Nashville].[177]

In 1904 Sister Lucas requested Larimore to make a statement through the pages of the *Gospel Advocate*, concerning the former appeal, which he reluctantly wrote. We also give his statement in full:

> Sister Lucas, who recently resolved to build a memorial meetinghouse at Mars' Hill, (my home), insists upon my submitting to my friends, for her a statement, that the situation and the status of the work may be better understood by all interested or concerned.
>
> As Chicago, Nashville, and St. Louis all postponed their great expositions one year because of not being ready on time, so, while our memorial meetinghouse, of much more impor-

tance to us than all of those combined, was to have been built this year, it is to be built next year — is to be completed, seated, and made perfectly ready for service in time for our annual protracted meeting in 1904. So many friends expressed regret that it was to be built before they could contribute to it as they desired that duty seemed to demand this delay, that none might be thus disappointed. Now all who will, can help.

Sister Lucas wishes me to state that all contributions, great or small, will be gladly and gratefully received till the work is done; that every penny received will be appreciated and shall be properly applied; that she is anxious for every one of my friends to contribute something to the work that nothing but freewill, love offerings is desired, that no tricks, traps, or schemes or shows shall be resorted to in order to raise a dollar; that the house shall be for service, not for show; that it shall contain nothing that any conscientious Christian cannot recognize as right; and that absolutely no debt shall shadow it when work and worship begin therein. She wishes me to also state that, while she hopes all our friends may manifest an interest in our work, she herein and hereby request some true friend in every community reached by this call to make a careful canvass of the community and write to friends in the interest of the work.

Contributions may be sent to Mrs. Horace P. Lucas, Miss Ettie Larimore, or Mr. L. C. Moore, Florence, Ala., or T. B. Larimore, 900 South College Street, Nashville, Tenn. Now having submitted the statement that Sister Lucas requested me to submit, I wish to say of my own volition and on my own responsibility, that she, whom I have known all my (her) life, who was my pupil in school, whom I baptized when she was a little child, is worthy of all confidence, love. and esteem. No sinister motive prompts her to do anything that she does. She seeks no notoriety, praise, or position, and would not under any circumstances, accept a penny for the labor of love she is performing. She longs to see the work accomplished because of the good it will do; and it is the dream and desire of her heart that every friend I have on earth shall contribute something to it. When she first mentioned the matter to me, I protested earnestly against it; but she insisted. and said: "Your friends all love you; you love them and want to please and bless them; it will be a sweet pleasure; and a great blessing to them to build the house, and they will gladly build it."

T. B. Larimore.[178]

The building was finished in late summer of 1904, just in time for the annual meeting at Mars Hill. The new building was the talk of the town as can be seen in the Florence Times report:

Big Meeting At Mars Hill. First Services held In New Christian Church.

The new Christian church at Mars Hill was opened for service for the first time Sunday, when Elder T. B. Larimore preached to two large audiences morning and afternoon.

Much interest was manifested in the meeting, people coming from far and near and listening with the closest attention to the eloquent sermons of the distinguished preacher.

A basket dinner was spread on the grounds and many hundreds of people enjoyed a royal feast.

The meeting will continue until August 28, services being held at 10 a.m. and 8 p.m. on weekdays and at 11 a.m. and 8 p. m. on Sunday.

The music will be in the charge of Dr. I. K. Harding of Bowling Green, Ky., who assisted at the recent meeting at the Christian church in Florence, assisted by John T. Glenn of Nashville.

There were two additions at the Sunday services. The church building is a modern structure and entirely out of debt, the last cent of indebtedness having paid off.[179]

Sister Lucas' dream of having the building paid in full by the time of the meeting was realized, as can be seen in the *Florence Times* report.

Larimore's brother-in-law, J. C. Ott kept a diary religiously and wrote of the first meeting in the new building. He wrote:

> Sun. 14 —I went to church at Mars Hill. Bro. Larimore preached for the first meeting in new church.
>
> Mon. 15 —I went to town and returned and hauled a load of hay.
>
> Tues. 16 — I went to church at 10 a.m. Hauled two loads of hay in afternoon.[180]

Nothing more can be found on Mars Hill until 1907. That year was a sad one at the Mars Hill congregation—it seemed to be the year of death. In March Larimore's wife Esther died from an extended illness. J. C. McQuiddy, a Larimore Boy, wrote of Esther's death:

> Sister Larimore died early Monday morning, the 4th inst., and was buried at the family burying ground at Mars' Hill at three o'clock Tuesday afternoon. Thus, a noble mother in Israel has fallen. She was a woman of firm convictions, sunshiny nature, and one who wielded a great influence for the cause of truth. She ably assisted her husband in the great work which he did at Mars' Hill for seventeen years. When it was thought best to discontinue the school, she stayed at home and thus made it possible for her husband to do the great work he had done in the field. The influence of her life will be far-reaching. A large crowd attended the funeral, which was conducted by Brethren Meeks and Elam and me.[181]

Then in July, Emma Page authored a memorial essay about Esther Larimore:

Sister Larimore-Julia Esther Gresham-was born, on July 11, 1845; "born again"-born into God's family-October 21, 1859; married, to T. B. Larimore, August 30, 1868; went home, March 4, 1907. This is a brief record of a life filled to overflowing with the fruits of the Spirit — a life that shall live in the memory of those it blessed as long as they shall live and live in the fruits of its influence forever. She grew to womanhood in the house in which she was born, Florence, Ala; spent most of the years of her married life in sight of her girlhood home; and her body sleeps in the family burying ground near that same peaceful, country home. Her life, however, near Mars' Hill, was not circumscribed by narrow bounds. Her sphere of usefulness was broad, her influence, far-reaching.[182]

F. D. Srygley, one of the Mars Hill students, wrote of her, in his first book, *Larimore and His Boys*, the following tribute to the mistress and "mother" of Mars Hill:

She is dignified in bearing, kind in manner, calm under trying circumstances, firm in her convictions, constant in her affections and patient in hope. She has the fortitude of a martyr, but she is neither fanatical nor excitable by nature. She is forever at work, and an incessant singer. She sings over the cook stove, sings while arranging the dining room, sings in the nursery, sings at the sowing machine, sings in the garden-wherever she goes she sings and works with an earnestness that defies penury: and mocks despondency. "As a mother, wife, Christian, she is the equal of the best-an honor to Christ and a blessing to his cause"-is the estimate a distinguished man who knows her well has expressed of her. In formulating and carrying out practical business plans, she is an invaluable assistant of her distinguished husband, In this line she is peculiarly well adapted, both by natural gifts and early training, to be a true helpmate for him.[183]

F. B. Srygley dearly loved the Larimore family. T. B. Larimore was his idol and mentor. He loved his memories of Mars Hill. He had observed the Christians at Mars Hill and was always remembering their influence upon his life.

In October Larimore reported the death of another faithful Mars Hill woman. She was Mattie Price Moore, an enthusiastic worker for Christ. She was constantly concerned with the cause of Christ and the church of God at Mars Hill. She worked for Christ for a third of a century. She was one of the loyal, faithful, and true who went home from that historic Christian home of Christian workers in 1907. Larimore wrote:

> Sister Moore (nee Miss Mattie Price) was born in Lauderdale County, Ala., where she lived all her life, May 8, 1844. She was married to L. C. Moore, February 28, 1867. She was not a charter member of the Mars' Hill congregation, but became a member thereof shortly after its establishment, and was a willing, worthy worker therein from the day on which she was "born again" till Heaven called her home.[184]

Like Esther Larimore, she was one of the very earliest members of the church at Mars Hill.

We know very little about the church at Mars Hill from 1907 until 1911. Our only reference to the church was a report on support sent by members of Mars Hill sent to the Tennessee Orphans Home:

> L. C. Moore, Mars' Hill, Ala., $2; Miss Maggie Gresham, Mars' Hill, Ala., 50 cents; W. H. Gresham, Mars' Hill, Ala., 50 cents; G. N. Daugherty, Mars' Hill, Ala., $1; Herschell Larimore and wife, Mars' Hill, Ala., $1.50.[185]

Two years later Isaac C. Hoskins wrote about his association with Mars Hill. He gave an insight into Larimore's work there. The following article reads as follows:

Florence, Ala., July 7.-Brother T. B. Larimore has been telling "the wondrous story" at Mars' Hill with characteristic pathos, sweetness, and power. The meeting began on the second Lord's day in July and closed on the third Lord's day, with three sermons both Sundays and two each day between. Six were immersed and one restored. The meetings were well attended-immense crowds on Sundays-and the interest fine. It has been five years since I heard Brother Larimore, and it was exceedingly gratifying to note how well he looks (though suffering from an ailment that will quickly pass, I think) and how forcefully he preaches the word. As I preach once a month at Mars' Hill, there was, in addition to the pleasure of hearing Brother Larimore, the added pleasure of meeting these dear friends; and it will be a great pleasure, if the Lord permit, to have this godly man back again next year to "preach the word" at Mars' Hill. Isaac C. Hoskins.[186]

Next to the final report on the Mars Hill church came in October of 1914. It was a short and to-the-point report as follows:

David Lipscomb Cooper, Fisherville, Ky., August 30 to September 13, fourteen baptisms, two from the Baptists, two restorations, six by letter; Mars' Hill, Ala., September 20-30, five additions, two restorations.[187]

J. Paul Kimbrell gives a report on his work in Lauderdale County in which he mentions going to Mars Hill during a meeting and hearing Brother Cooper preach a sermon:

While in Florence, I went out to Jacksonburg, where Brother Hoskins was holding a meeting, and heard him deliver a sermon. Before returning on Monday, I drove out to Mars' Hill, in company with Brother W. G. Wallace, of Rogersville, and listened to a sermon by Brother Cooper, of Kentucky. Yesterday (the first Lord's day in October) I began a series of meetings at the Bradley School house, in the southern part of Wayne County. Large crowds were present at both services. I am expecting some results, as there is plenty of material to work on. After the meeting closes, I will go back to my home at West Point and will probably enter school after Christmas. J. Paul Kimbrell. Iron City, Tenn.[188]

This being the last entry in 1914, closes the study on the church of Christ at Mars Hill. Mars Hill is still a vibrant church in 2024. It is still active in mission work and evangelism in general. May it continue to be a shining light for many years.

Mars Hill Bible College

Even though Larimore had come to Lauderdale County, he left temporarily to teach at Mountain Home Academy near Moulton, Alabama, which was under the leadership of J. M. Pickens. Larimore taught there for the fall session and then taught for six months in West Tennessee at Mansell Kendrick's school. He left there and taught at Stantonville, Tennessee, for ten months, and returned to Florence, Alabama. On January 1, 1871, he opened Mars Hill Academy.[189] Larimore had gotten the idea for Mars Hill while teaching at Mountain Home Academy.[190] The founding of Mars Hill was the founding of a new era in Lauderdale County church history and was proof that this area was well on the road to recovering from the war.

I like F. D. Srygley's idea of allowing Larimore to tell his own version of Mars Hill Bible College. Srygley wrote the following account:

> The story of the school at Mars' Hill can best be told by him who established it and did so much to make it what it was. A few years ago, one of Mr. Larimore's friends, C. M. Southall, of Florence, Alabama, wrote him a letter in which he said: "I can never forget your work at Mars' Hill what you did there for

North Alabama, in particular, and the whole world, in general; for, doubtless, the influence for good of the work done there has been felt in every land beneath the skies."

Upon receipt of this letter, Mr. Larimore wrote of Mars' Hill and the work there as follows:

"I appreciate this pleasant reminder of my work at Mars' Hill, of course, notwithstanding my work was only a part of the wonderful work to which our brother alludes.

"Brother Southall has long been a prominent and a model citizen of Florence; and I believe there is not a worthier elder, a truer Christian or a better business man in Alabama. He is, and has been through the sorrows, struggles and vicissitudes of many eventful years, my personal and appreciated friend; and he has never failed or faltered when he knew I needed sympathy or succor. May the Lord always abundantly bless him and his.

Mars' Hill is about four miles from Florence. Florence is on the right bank, the north bank, of the Tennessee River. Mars' Hill is about four miles from the river, on the same side. Although I soldiered and scouted, in the sanguinary sixties, along the left bank of the broad, beautiful Tennessee, all the way from Decatur to Shiloh and from Shiloh back to Chattanooga and heard the mournful music of Minie balls within less than a dozen miles of both Florence and Mars' Hill, I never saw either of them till after the war till the spring or summer of 1868, three years after the war closed.

In 1868, I married Miss Julia Esther Gresham, at her home near the spot subsequently named 'Mars' Hill', so named by me, about four miles from Florence. She inherited twenty-eight acres of land from her father's estate. Ten dollars an acre was the price of land there then, but that tract of twenty-eight acres of woodland was worth, probably, three hundred dollars, because of its location and beauty.

About the beginning of 1870, free from debt, but without a dollar, a man in size, but scarcely more than a youth in judgment, experience and appearance, I conceived the idea of establishing on the tract of land constituting Esther's inheritance a school for boys and girls, such a school as I believed to be needed then and there. I think I never thought of the possibility of failure, believing success to be a necessary certainty.

All available financial assets for the work, in sight or out of sight, so far as I knew, consisted of that tract of land. But Esther and I went hopefully to work, or probably I should say we continued to work. She was bright and beautiful and as good as she could be. Withal she was an incessant worker not a club woman, not a meddler in other people's matters, and as far from a gadabout as possible. She had neither time nor taste for such pestiferous things. I could preach, some people who had not heard much preaching thought, and I was willing to preach and teach to the limit of my ability and do all I could to advance our work.

Somehow or other success crowned our efforts. I have never been able, in the realm of reason, logic and mathematics, to explain how; but have always attributed it to Providence. Within twelve months from the time, I first thought of the school, Mars' Hill opened for pupils in the house we had built on the hill, with all the pupils, boys and girls, that we were prepared to take care of.

The school succeeded from the very start. The people in the territory in which it was known and patronized seemed to prove by common consent that it was worthy of all the patronage it received. Additional buildings had to be erected soon and were promptly filled.

A clear, cold spring bunt from the bosom of the forest covered level at the foot of the hill on which the house was built, a beautiful brook babbled by just beyond, and covering the bottom were a grove of green and growing trees and a foundry, established long before the war between the North and the South, where munitions of war were manufactured during that sad, fratricidal struggle.

A few miles from Mars' Hill was a colony of industrious,

thrifty Germans who attended to their own business and bothered nobody. But after we established the school, some of those Germans resolved to build a brewery in the bottom where munitions of war had been manufactured, or somebody started that report to scare me and practically force me to buy the approximately seven hundred acres of land pertaining to the foundry. Esther and I strolled among the tall trees in the bottom one bright night and talked about the gloomy prospect till we decided it was not gloomy at all; for we believed, trusting the Lord and doing our duty, we could meet the situation successfully and surmount all the difficulties in the way, and that thought made the prospect bright.

We lived hard and worked hard, practicing the principles of self-denial and strictest economy till the estate of seven hundred acres was free. Once when I went to make a payment on the place, our creditor said he had no use for the money then, and we could continue to use it, without interest, as long as we needed it. But my opinion then was exactly what it is now: the best time to pay a debt is when you have the money; and we paid it, but no interest on the indebtedness was accepted.

Contrary to Esther's judgment and over her earnest protest, I deeded or had deeded the entire estate to her, believing she would be left a widow and desiring to protect her against trouble to the limit of my ability. Her health seemed to be perfect then, while mine was apparently very poor.

Our school lasted seventeen years. Our seven children, four sons and three daughters were born there: Dedie, Granville, Topple, Herschel, Ettie, Virgil and little Minnie Belie, whose span of life was so short that she can scarcely be said to have lived in this world at all. In due process of time, I baptized the six children as they one by one reached the proper age and voluntarily made the good confession. Topple and Granville have since gone home, as has also their mother, and only four remain, two sons and two daughters. Allowance must usually be made for the opinion of parents relative to the merits of their children.

Conservatively speaking, however, and correctly, our children were as good as the average, and there was not a bad one in the bunch. Being absolutely sure of that, I am happy in the thought of meeting all of them in that sweet home where there is rest for the weary, with bliss unspeakable and eternal, for all the faithful in Christ Jesus our Lord."[191]

The far-reaching influence of those seventeen years of labor cannot be measured in human terms. The immeasurable good that was done brings to mind a quote from Basil Overton:[192] "I love what I am doing because I don't know what I am doing."—Meaning he did not know what the ultimate results of his work might be. The old Mars Hill Bible College work is still impacting the southeastern part of the United States of America and may for years to come.

BETHELBERRY

Baptist churches in Tennessee and in Lauderdale County, Alabama, were dismissed from the Muscle Shoal Association to form the Shoal Creek Association in 1825. These churches were Mill Creek, Butler's Creek, Little Cypress, and Big Cypress. The Little Cypress was later renamed as Middle Cypress. The Middle Cypress Baptist church was originally the Little Cypress Baptist church.

Little (Middle) Cypress Baptist church was organized in July 1818, by the Muscle Shoals Creek Association, and it was left with no minister. There were no Baptist ministers at that period on the north side of the Tennessee River, in that region; but in the next year, Elder Jeremiah Burnes moved from Tennessee, and became the minister at Little Cypress. Mr. Burnes was well known as an evangelical minister of the New Testament. Elder A. Askew took charge of Little Cypress.[193] Middle Cypress was in a weak stage by the Civil War, which may be why Larimore so easily held his meeting in the "house of Hard-Shells" or more commonly called "Old Iron Jackets."

In his history of the Churches of Christ in Lauderdale County, Alabama, Eris Bonner Benson wrote:

No record has been kept of the name of the preacher who established the church at Bethelberry; nor is the year of its beginning known. One lady of seventy-four years of age has said that it was established before her birth. T. B. Larimore, W. B. Young, Castleberry, and William Behel conducted meetings for the church. Before 1910, during a meeting held by Larimore, several persons were baptized, but the condition of the building and lack of leadership caused the members to quit meeting for some time. However, a few years ago, they erected a new meetinghouse and began meeting each Sunday to worship. During 1948 Earl Prater preached once a month for them. With only about eighteen members the church was almost a mission point itself; hence, it did not contribute to foreign missionaries or to orphan homes. Located about sixteen miles from Florence, the church property was valued, in 1949, at $2,500.[194]

W. H. Wharton from Tuscumbia came into this community as early as 1838. He is listed in the Bethelberry church book and shows members who had been baptized by him that year. Mary H, Freeman was baptized by Wharton on January 21, 1838.[195] Thomas W. Young was baptized by James Young, who disappeared from Lauderdale County records by 1850. These examples prove that there were Christians in that community long before Larimore came and helped organize the congregation.

Larimore's account of his rejection at Hopewell after preaching one sermon reveals that Christians were already in the Middle Cypress community in 1868. He tells of the discussion among leaders at Hopewell over what to do with him:

> Well, they did exactly right. They reasoned thus: "We have had none but good preachers here; we are few and weak; our enemies hold the fort and camp on the field. Now, if we let him try to preach here, it is good bye to our prospects. Better have no preaching than his sort." Then they said: "What shall we do with him? This will we do—Brother and sister Young live a way

back—good preachers rarely go there; they will appreciate any kind of preaching; to them will we send him." They said to me: "We will take you to Bro. Young's; he and sister Young and Frank and another one or two are the church there; they are good people and will treat you well." They sent me—I believe Bro. Andrew Gresham took in a buggy.[196]

Larimore spoke of the (Thomas W.) Young's family as being the church there. So, there was a church there; but not yet organized. That would be done very soon.

Larimore came down from Franklin College to preach at Rock Creek in Colbert County, in the summer of 1868. After the meeting there, he went back to Hopewell for a protracted meeting. Larimore's reception has been described above.[197] The brethren at Hopewell felt that Larimore did not have enough experience, so they sent him across the country to the Middle Cypress community, which resulted in the establishment of permanent work which is still strong today (2024). A twist of fate occurred at Hopewell. Upon leaving Hopewell in June 1868, Larimore was taken to Thomas W. Young's house to preach in the Middle Cypress community. The Baptist's building was secured for a meeting. Larimore reflected upon the meeting:

> What teachers and preachers came out of that meeting. That was a wet nest, and the house was a Hard-Shell house; but some wonderful birds were hatched then and there... I am drifting, before the Providence Mattie, George, Bennett-these are some of the converts made at that meeting.[198]

The Mattie of that last sentence became Mattie Y. Murdock, who taught school at Ennis, Texas, and who authored several articles in brotherhood journals. George was George P. Young, who became president of Orange College, Stark, Florida, and Bennett was W. B. Young who attended Bethany College in West Virginia and became a prominent preacher also. No wonder Larimore said: Hopewell sent me to the right place.[199]

The Bethelberry church book's first entry recorded the following:

> June 21st, 1868— In the year of our Lord one thousand eight hundred and sixty-eight on the 21st of June we the undersigned by permission of the Baptist (commonly known as the "Old Iron Jackets") met at their house of worship known as Little Cypress Church and had preaching by Brother T. B. Larimore and organized a Christian Church and to be known by the name of.[200]

Seven men signed the above statement:

> Thomas W. Young, Jasper W. Wilson, John J. Jones, Thomas J. A. Young, George P. Young, Ben F. Young, and William B. Young.[201]

Jasper Wilson, a member of this newly formed congregation wrote concerning this meeting:

> Florence, Ala., August 31, 1868. Bro. Lipscomb: We wish to bring to the notice of the readers of the Gospel Advocate, the condition of our Church, (or in other words, the Church of Christ) in this place. We were as sheep scattered, without a shepherd. Bro. T. B. Larimore preached for us on the third Lord's day in June. We organized it with about 22 members. We now number 38, and there are a great many others that seem to be very anxious to learn the way of salvation and we have no one to preach for us, only as we can prevail on some kind brother to give us a call occasionally. Bro. H. J. Spivey preached for us yesterday. Two came forward and made the good and were baptized today; and as he is obliged to start home tomorrow, we wish to call the attention of those who may read this — that

preach Christ and him crucified, should they pass this way, we request them to give us a call and preach for us; for if we had preaching regularly,

I verily believe that in twelve months we will number over a hundred. Our place of worship is thirteen miles a little west of north of Florence, Ala., on the waters of the Middle Cypress Creek. Fraternally yours, J. W. Wilson.[202]

According to Wilson's report, H. J. Spivey (of Lawrence County, Tennessee) preached for them on August 30, 1868. He baptized two. He was on Middle Cypress for part of three days before he had to return home. He was probably the first preacher to visit after Larimore's meeting in June of that year.

In two months, the congregation grew to thirty-eight members. Wilson expected the number to reach a hundred in twelve months. The congregation did not grow that fast but within two years it was over that number.

On June 21, 1869, it was entered upon the record, that the congregation was to be called the Middle Cypress Creek church.

In the year 1869 and June 21st, we whose names are recorded here, having put on Christ by compliance with his laws do hereby congregate ourselves as a Church or congregation of the Lord (to be known as the Middle Cypress Creek Church or Congregation) and giving ourselves to the Lord and to one another, obligating ourselves to live as followers of Christ and as Brethren in the Lord by being governed by his laws, as laid down in the Scriptures which is the truth in all things.[203]

By the end of 1869, the congregation was still meeting in the old log church building owned by the Baptists. In December 1869 they decided to build their own meeting house. The entry for December 2, 1869, records:

> We the undersigned agree to pay the amount, attached our names for the purpose of building a Christian Church house. This December 2nd, 1869.[204]

At that same meeting, Thomas pledged the land upon which the meeting house could be built. The pledge was as follows:

> I will give the land and timber to build it and the amount attached to my name, besides. Thomas W. Young.[205]

The land was donated by Thomas W. and Francis Young.[206] He was the father of Mattie, George, and Bennett Young.

On August 13, 1870, John Taylor came and held a meeting at Bethabara.

The congregation decided to raise money to build a building. The following entry was recorded that day entry:

> August 13, 1870. In the year of our Lord 1870 and on the 13th of August, having for our preacher John Taylor (Evangelist).[207]

Upon completion of the new building, the congregation was to be called Bethabara.[208] This name has been handed down to the present in the corrupted form of Bethel Berry. The record book is filled with names of persons baptized, who did the baptizing, and persons from whom fellowships had been withdrawn. Some financial statements are contained therein, and sometimes a re-numbering of the charter membership. Also, there will be found a clue to its contribution to the kingdom.

Thomas W. Young wrote:

> Brethren L. & S.: It will be gratifying to you and many others to learn that Bethabara congregation, in Lauderdale county, is advancing in our Master's cause. Bro. David Mills, of Florence, Ala., recently held a meeting with us, resulting in five additions —all from the world. A mother, two daughters and two sons

and to one young man that joined at Hopewell a few days before under Bro. Granville Lipscomb's preaching. Oh, what a beautiful scene it was to see five of one family marching into the water, putting on Christ in baptism and to arise to walk in newness of life. There is prospect of much good being done here. We have preaching twice a month, but we need a more experienced teacher to teach us the work of the Lord's house. May God bless our efforts in his cause, that we may enter into the gates of the city to enjoy his presence forever. Thomas W. Young, Middle Cypress, Ala.[209]

It would be twelve more years before a report relating to Bethabara would appear in the *Gospel Advocate*. Brown Godwin, a Mars Hill student, reported on some of the preaching points of other Mars Hill students. He listed T. E. Tatum as preaching monthly at Bethabara.[210] Tatum wrote of having preached there:

> By request of one who is dear to me, I will give a report of my labors since Christmas ... I have preached some since school closed, June 6, and occasionally before, at Bethabara, Stony Point, Bethel, Barton Station, on M. & C. R. R., Mountain Mills, and Rock Creek, which has resulted in twelve additions ... T. E. Tatum, Mars' Hill, Ala, July 11, 1883.[211]

This congregation contributed much to the Lord's work in Lauderdale County and its influence was felt in several states. Mattie Young taught in Mississippi and Texas, George P. Young started Orange College in Stark, Florida, and W. B. Young preached in Alabama, Tennessee, and Missouri.[212] The Jasper Wilson family moved to Arkansas and started a work.[213] The George Smallwood family, along with the John D. Wade family, returned to his plantation; near present-day Iron City, Tennessee, and established Wade's Chapel (Antioch which was on Wade's farm).[214] Only God knows how many more states have felt the influence of this little band formed on a stormy night in the summer of 1868.

John T. Underwood, a former Mars Hill student, came in 1890 to Bethabara and preached. A report followed:

> Preached at Bethabara, commencing the second Lord's day, live discourses, one confession and baptism, one reclaimed. Preached at the Lime Kiln the second Lord's day; three made the good confession and were baptized the same hour of the day. John T. Underwood. Barton, Oct. 21, '90.[215]

The next report came from the pen of A. P. Holtsford:

> Florence, Dec. 25: I have spent the last five and a half months preaching at the following places: North Carolina; Lauderdale county, Ala., one week, with five additions; four days at Bluewater, with good attention- one week on Middle Cypress...A. P. Holtsford.[216]

Unfortunately, this would be the last information from brotherhood journals within our parameter of time. There were unsure notes in the church book, but nothing important, just membership rolls, which might be of some value to genealogists. The next report would come thirty-two years afterward, in 1926.[217] This brings us to the end of our discussion on Bethabara.

Cypress Mills

One of these congregations was established in the company community house, which became a union house for religious purposes. Sometime in 1878 some of Larimore's students came to Martin's Factory and began a congregation in the union house. H. H. Turner gave an excellent account of the beginning of the congregation, to be known as the Cypress Mills congregation:

> Brethren L. & S.: The Cypress congregation is situated within two and a half miles of Florence, Ala., at the factory known as the Martin Factory—turned by the flowing waters of Cypress Creek. This little band of disciples has been planted and nourished by the young preachers of Mars' Hill College. We commenced here two years ago with five or six scattered members. We went to work in good earnest, though strongly opposed by the sects; we held our position, using no other weapon but the one spoken of by the apostle, (Eph. vi: 17), persuading sinners to become Christians, as Paul of old. This little band of disciples has increased under the teaching of the brethren, who handle the word of God aright, until it now numbers about twenty-two members. We set it in working order last year, and they met twice a month all year to keep house for

the Lord. They would have met every Lord's day, but the house of worship is a union house, and we are not allowed but two days, Some of the members having moved away, our deacon being one, we met on the fifth Lord's day in April and reorganized according to the directions given by the apostle Paul (Tim, iii: 1-8, Acts vi.) warning the selected ones of their duty; that they must take charge of the flock. The congregation selected Bro. William Stephenson bishop, and Bro. Thomas Rackard deacon, both men of zeal and courage. I will venture to say that this little hand is getting along better than many of the old congregations. We have endeavored this year to follow the teaching of the Bible, meeting upon every first day of the week to commemorate the death and sufferings of our blessed Redeemer. When the weather is so bad, we cannot go to the church, old sister Stephenson, who loves the Lord and entertains the preachers, who is almost on the brink of the tomb with age, care and trouble, gives us free access to her dwelling in which to worship. There is, too, Sister Holt, who when we were opposed by the sects, opened her house and bid us welcome and Godspeed. Her good husband is not a member of Christ's church, but we hope and pray will be soon, before the brittle thread of life is snapped. May God bless this and all congregations, is my prayer. H. H. Turner, Mars' Hill College, April 18, 1880.[218]

Nearly a year later another report came from the pen of Turner:

H. H. Turner, Florence, Ala., writes as follows: I preached for the little congregation at Cypress Mills near Florence Ala. the second Sunday in March for the first time in twelve months, had a good audience two were added one reclaimed. This is a noble little band of worshipers, composed mostly of sisters of the noblest character. May God prosper them. They are poor in this world's goods, but rich in faith, hope and charity: One good old sister told me she was not long for this world, but that her Father whom she served was rich, possessor of all things and that would give her plenty in the sweet bye-and-bye. Oh, may we all have faith like this.[219]

After the mills closed the membership dispersed to several places including different states, but according to Sister Irma Matthews Plott some of this little band of Christians remained near North Florence and became part of the charter members at Sherrod Avenue Church of Christ.[220]

Porter Spring—
Miller's Chapel—
Oliver Work

In his thesis, Eris Bonner Benson states: "No record seems to have been kept of the name of the person who established the church at Oliver in about 1878, the first church of Christ in that section of the county." I believe Benson was correct in all but one point in this statement about the establishment of the Oliver Church of Christ.[221] He was wrong on the date of establishment—it was much earlier.

A note of caution here: The name "Porter Spring" has been mistakenly called "Potter Spring" by preachers who reported their meeting at this congregation; but the two earliest deeds for the church plainly read—"Porter" not "Potter."

Robert Wallace Officer, an unusual Baptist preacher lived just north of the vicinity of Porter's Spring. Officer had been preaching "baptism for the remission of sins" for some time. He, like Murrell Askew, would eventually leave the Baptist Church, join the Restoration Movement, and preach the New Testament gospel. He seems the likely preacher to have first preached at Porter's Spring. This would have been in 1869 or earlier, because the first deed to the church and school was made on February 25, 1870.[222] The deed reads— "for a church and school" which infers that a church was already in existence at the time of the writing of the deed. So, it can safely be said that the church had been established before 1870.

The first trustees were William J. Chandler, Charles, and John C. Houie.

The building sat on a half-acre lot near the Spring on Porter's property and thus named the Porter's Spring Christian Church. It was to this newly formed congregation that Granville Lipscomb came and held a meeting in August 1871. Lipscomb wrote:

> Dear brother David. I spent some days between the 3d and 4th. Lord's days in August with the brethren and friends at Jonesboro Ala. There were two additions at this point. I also labored six days including the 4th Lord's Day in August at Potter's (Porter's) Spring near Rogersville, Lauderdale co. Ala., where there were ten additions. At both these points we have only a few brothers and sisters who are struggling in the midst of much opposition to maintain the good cause. Much good could be affected (sic) at these points by a faithful preacher and the brethren would extend to such a one a hearty welcome. Affectionately G. Lipscomb, Hunts Sta. Tenn. Sept. 4th. 1871.[223]

Lipscomb stated that the two congregations were struggling to survive. Ten souls were added at Potter (Porter) Spring. That gave excitement to the new congregation. The church grew to the point that a new building was needed.

One of "Larimore's Boys" C. F. Russell came and preached in 1877. He wrote:

> C. F. Russell writes, Aug. 9, 1877: I have just closed a meeting at Potter (Porter) Springs, near Rogersville, Lauderdale County, Ala., resulting in five additions by confession and baptism. The brethren are going right to work to build them a new house of worship. Not five years from now, if the band here will be faithful, there will no doubt be a large, thriving congregation here. [224]

This creates questions. Which building was Russell mentioning? Was there a building between the Porter's Spring schoolhouse and the Oliver building? From what Benson said in his history of the Church of Christ in Lauderdale, County, Alabama there was a building called Miller's Chapel. Tom and Chunk Miller led in getting the new building, so for a short time the congregation was called Miller's Chapel.[225] If this is so, where else is it mentioned? Was this the Miller's Chapel building? You see more questions than answers.

In 1880 Robert Wallace (R. W.) Officer spoke of a church at Rogersville:

> Dear Bros. L. &: S.: I left Lewisburg on Monday after the 3rd Lord's day in May. Met with the brethren at Bunker Hill, Shoal Bluff, Temperance Oak, Big Creek, and Rogersville, at night in connection with Bro. T. C. Biles-of Florida, who joined me at Shoal Bluff.[226]

A rather unusual event occurred at Porter Springs in September 1888. Bro Thomas G. Nance reported the event to the *Gospel Advocate*. We give the entire report due to the nature of the event:

> Thos. G. Nance writes from Athens, Ala., Sept. 15, '88: "In connection with Bro. T. L. Weatherford, of Limestone county Ala., I held a meeting at Brook's schoolhouse, in said county; thirteen added, Thence to Zions Rest, in Giles county. Tenn., in connection with Bro Wm. Smith of Giles county, Tenn.; no additions. The next was at Shoal creek, same county, with Bro. Smith; six added. Next, to Beech Grove, in Limestone county, Ala.; two added. Thence to Big Creek, Bro. Weatherford's home congregation, in connection with Bro. Weatherford; twenty-seven added. Thence to Riverside, five miles east; five added. From there we made a passing visit by Mt. Carmel, in said county; one added by confession and baptism and one from the

Baptists. On to Martindale's schoolhouse, in Lauderdale county, with two baptisms which we reported to Potters Spring church a few miles away. Made Potters Springs a passing visit; baptized two and received one from the Baptists and one from the Methodists. Thence to Hurricane Springs, baptized four and returned back to Potters Springs and held them a two day and three nights' meeting; counting those added at Martindale's schoolhouse and some others, making twenty-three in all there. Next to the last night of our meeting, I am sad to say, the devil sent one of his agents while the house was packed to its utmost capacity, to take his stand at a window and direct his death dealing instrument right into the house amid all that throng of men, women, and children and shot one man through the thigh while standing between young ladies, and in as dense a crowd as could be, lodging the ball in a bench by him. All things had gone off pleasantly till after being dismissed, when without a word, while moving towards the door, the pistol fired, and dozens of voices were heard screaming. He made his escape into the dark and is at large. Numbers of people are seeking his arrest. Hope they will find him, and the Lord rewards him. This leaves me at Athens on my way to another meeting at Limestone fifteen miles away."[227]

That was one event folks remembered for a few generations. The next report was five years in coming; but nothing as shocking as the 1888 meeting. John T. Underwood visited during a meeting conducted by W. H. Sanday and a brother Curtiss. Underwood reported what he observed. He seemed impressed at the way this meeting ended:

Atlas, Oct. 4.: I preached five days at Salem, Lauderdale County, Ala., commencing the fourth Lord's day in July, with eight added to the one body. I preached one discourse at Hurricane Springs the fifth Lord's Day, with two added. We went from there to Porter Springs and joined Brother Sandy and Brother

Curtis in a meeting on Monday, which closed the first Lord's Day in August with thirty-nine added...John T. Underwood.[228]

W. H. Sanday sent a report concerning a new preacher—J. P. Jones of Lexington, who had preached his second ever sermon and it was at Porter's Springs. It was a very complementary note about the young preacher. The note read:

> Rogersville, Oct. 30. Brother J. P. Jones, of Lexington, Ala., preached his second discourse in life for us last Lord's day, at Porter's Springs, and I must say that he did well for a new beginner. He seems to be the right man for the work he has chosen, for he shuns not to declare the whole counsel of God. Dr. Jones is sound to the core, and I think the core is sound too. Brethren, give him a helping hand, and enable him to devote more of his time to the ministry ... W. H. Sanday.[229]

Two years later W. H. Sanday held a very successful meeting in September 1895. Sanday was a local preacher from the Rogersville-Oliver area. He sent the following report:

> Anderson's Creek, Sept. 18. Our meeting at Mount Carmel, Ala., conducted by Brother Weatherford and me, lasted five days, with eleven added. I then preached at Porter's (Potters) Springs, near Rogersville, Ala., on Lord's Day following, which was last Lord's Day, and had twelve additions. The twelve added last Lord's Day made sixty-one that have been added to the congregation at Oak Ridge (?) in two weeks. W. H. Sandy.[230]

This may well have been the last gospel meeting ever held in the Miller's Chapel building because the following year the congregation re-located.

On March 27, 1894, a U.S. Post Office was established near Porter Spring to be known as the Oliver Post Office.[231] In 1896 the congregation relocated on the road between Athens and Florence (later known as US Highway 72). Their building was finished in 1896.[232] The congregation was then named the Oliver Church of Christ.

In the obituary of Earl M. Hodson, of Moulton, Ala., J. T. Harris wrote:

> When on November 21, 1934, Earl M. Hodson, of Moulton, Ala., passed this life; I lost one of the best friends I ever had. I first met him in Oliver, Ala., thirty years ago. J. T. Harris.[233]

That would have been about 1905 when the two men first met. Brother Hodson was probably teaching at the schoolhouse at Oliver, as his profession was school teaching. He also preached some, when needed. Oliver, at this time, needed someone who could step up when needed. J. T. Harris held a meeting, at the time he met Hodson, at Oliver.

Harris held several more meetings at Oliver over the next several years. In 1906 he reported one such meeting:

> Weakley, August 14.-on the fourth Lord's Day in July I began a meeting at Oliver, Ala., which continued seven days, with five baptized and four restored. J. T. Harris.[234]

He reported on this meeting again in his final report for the summer's work. His report read:

> As I have reported only two or three meetings this year, I will let the readers of the Gospel Advocate know that we have not been idle in this part of the Lord's vineyard. My first meeting was with the Oliver congregation, in Lauderdale County, Ala. The meeting began on the. fourth Lord's Day in July and continued for seven days, with five baptized and four restored. I found a faithful little band at this place, who seem perfectly contented

with God's way of doing things. I have agreed to preach for them monthly next year.[235]

He described the congregation as being "perfectly contented with God's way of doing things." He reported another meeting in July 1907:

> Brother J.T. Harris, of Minor Hill, Tenn., began a meeting at Oliver, Ala., on last Lord's day. He recently preached at Minor Hill and baptized one person.[236]

He made another report on the meeting in another communication:

> Brother J. T. Harris, of Minor Hill, Tenn., recently closed a very interesting meeting at Oliver, Ala., with fourteen additions-twelve baptized, one restored, and one from the Baptists.[237]

By the third week in September 1908, he was engaged in a meeting at Oliver.[238] Harris sent the final report on his meeting at Oliver:

> Brother J. T. Harris recently closed a meeting at Oliver, Ala., with forty-four additions-thirty were baptized, twelve restored, one from the Methodists, and one from the Baptists. He is now in a meeting at Bunker Hill, Giles County, Tenn.[239]

That meeting, no doubt, was the most successful meeting ever held at Oliver. The next reported meeting was five years later. Harris also conducted that meeting. He reported that meeting as well:

> Florence, Ala., December 3.-On the second Sunday in November I began a meeting at Oliver, Ala., and preached there one week, then moved two miles to Rogersville and continued

another week. Both meetings resulted in three baptized and two restored. I was at Rogersville in October; preached three times and baptized seven persons. The brethren at this place are making ready to build a nice church home, which is badly needed. They have been using the Presbyterian Church for a number of years. The Lord willing. I shall preach for the above-named congregations occasionally next year. J. T. Harris.[240]

The next report is the final report in the *Gospel Advocate*. J. T. Harris came and held the final meeting at Oliver as reported in the brotherhood journals within our set time frame (1914). It is given in full below:

Florence, Ala., January 11. The work in this (Lauderdale) county continues to grow. I preached at Oliver on Saturday night and Sunday morning, at Rogersville, Sunday afternoon and at night. After the afternoon service a noble young man was buried with Christ in baptism. J. T. Harris.[241]

These two reports also mentioned the newly established church in Rogersville, Lauderdale County, Alabama, as well as Oliver. With these reports, we leave the Oliver Church of Christ history, as completed with what available information we have.

The Askew Group— Former Baptist Churches

While Larimore was busy trying to get Mars Hill College on a firm footing. Another struggle was going on between the Missionary Baptist Church and their most popular preacher, Murrell Askew. This struggle developed into a Restoration Movement led by Murrell Askew.

To fully understand how the following four churches became churches of Christ, we must study the life of the man who brought this movement about. Murrell Askew is virtually unknown outside of Lauderdale County, Alabama. To add to the confusion of some folks, he was sometimes addressed by the Indian Creek Missionary Baptists Association as E. M. Askew.[242] He is not well known, even within the families who descended from him. One might even question how much these families really know about Askew. Much misinformation still circulated about his life. Despite all this anonymity and being misunderstood, Askew was a major catalyst in causing the Baptists of North Alabama to restudy the Bible, and to question the creeds of the day.

The purpose of this writing is to give documented information on this forgotten "soldier of the cross." Murrell was born in Williamson County, Tennessee, not far from Franklin. He was born to Aaron and Elizabeth "Lovey" Askew on March 4, 1811. His father Aaron was born in North Carolina in 1789.

At the age of 22, he moved with his wife to Tennessee. Hosea Holcomb says that Aaron was a "wicked, profane man, but felt a keen conviction for sin ...." He continues: "In 1816, he removed to Lauderdale [County, Alabama], a profligate deist." In 1818 he was converted and "forsook some of his evil practices, such as profane swearing, Sabbath breaking, etc." and he was baptized in the beginning of 1819.[243]

He was ordained to preach in 1826. Just how serious he was as a preacher has been questioned. Percy D. Wright kept a journal and wrote several things about the Askews. His aunt Elizabeth had married Murrell Askew on March 2, 1845.[244] Young Percy heard many tales about Aaron and Murrell Askew. He wrote: "Askew would preach and say, 'Do as Askew says, not as Askew does." He further stated that Askew was a "drunken preacher." [This was said of Aaron before he became a preacher; not Murrell].[245] Young Murrell grew up under these circumstances. Whether all these charges about his father were true or not true, we know not.

We do know that young Murrell became religiously inclined early in life. He managed to get a fair education and used the Bible as a main source of reading. In 1844, we find him subscribing to Tolbert Fanning's *Christian Review*.[246] Murrell had grown up in a very volatile time when the Baptists in Northwest Alabama were rethinking their theology, and many were becoming members of the Church of Christ. In 1830 the Muscle Shoals Baptist Association passed a "Resolution" against "Campbellites."[247] This must have influenced his later thinking of the Bible.

Murrell tried his hand at farming but was not very successful. In 1850, Murrell owned a hundred and sixty acres of land, but only had 20 acres as improved or tenable land.[248] He was listed as a schoolteacher and had a wife and three young daughters.[249] Sometime between 1850 and 1854, he began to preach. Mid-year, 1854, he established the Mt. Pleasant Baptist Church in Lexington, Alabama. The church officially organized on November 30, 1854, in "newly built house near Lexington, Lauderdale Co., Ala."[250] Askew preached on an irregular basis until 1857 when he became their regular minister. He was listed as a Missionary Baptist minister in the US Census for 1860 and was living near Center Star, Lauderdale County, Alabama.[251] He was their minister until 1861.

This was the year the Civil War began. The war took its toll on churches. Churches struggled for survival, and many did not survive. During the war, most rural churches completely disbanded. This may explain why Askew was not listed as their minister. G.W. Garrett served as minister for a few months and left. Askew did, however, continue to preach during the Civil War on an irregular basis. The year of 1862 was an especially bad year for Murrell. His father, Aaron died that year. After the war, to vote, Southerners had to take an oath of loyalty to the United States government. On September 16, 1867, Murrell Askew took the oath of loyalty and was enrolled.[252] Mt. Pleasant was nearly dormant until 1868 when they re-hired Askew as their regular minister.[253] During the war, his brethren had begun to rumble about his theology, which they called, "Campbellism." Askew was preaching: "that the sinner must obey all of the requirements of the gospel." He stated, "that the sinner could not claim the promise of the pardon of sins save through obedience to the condition."[254] He tried to get his accusers to discuss the subject with him, and they refused.

Murrell continued to preach as he understood the Bible, but many Baptists searched the Scriptures to disagree with him. Many honest hearts saw the truth and aligned themselves with him. One such man was William Comer, who was already a member of the Church of Christ, and R. T. Lanier, who was one of those honest hearts in the Baptist church and was diligently searching and would soon abandon the Baptists. Both men would subscribe to the *Gospel Advocate* and share their learning with their neighbors.[255]

Comer explained his actions to the *Gospel Advocate*:

> When I find a person that I think will lay down their prejudice, enough to read and investigate, I get them to read them.[256]

The *Gospel Advocate* and T.W. Brents' *Gospel Plan Of Salvation* were the two sources to which Comer referred. He further speaks of Askew's reading these publications. Also, he mentions that other leading Missionary Baptists were now changing their views on salvation.

In 1874 trouble arose from some of his brethren, after some eleven years of peace. He was brought before the Indian Creek Association and charged with preaching "Campbellism" again (the same year he was rehired as a regular minister for the Mt. Pleasant Baptist church near Lexington.) He asked the Association to define the doctrine of "Campbellism." They told him that he was teaching that all sinners had to do was believe and obey the gospel in all its requirements, and they would be saved. They told him to stop preaching this kind of doctrine. He told them he would stop for twelve months (which would have been until the next Association meeting) if the Association would agree to discuss the doctrine. They refused to do so.

Some of the Baptists had now aligned themselves with the Churches of Christ. At least the four congregations, over which Askew had the oversight, had dropped the name "Missionary Baptist," and simply referred to themselves as "churches of Christ," by 1875. These changes would cause Murrell Askew much trouble.

The Association had met in September of 1875 at the Union Grove Baptist church, in the present community of North Carolina, in Lauderdale County. The Association refused to let Askew be heard on any subject. Comer said it was because "the church where he held his membership (Mt. Pleasant) sent him as a delegate and sent her letter under the name of "church of Christ" with no "Missionary Baptist" added to it.[257] The Association withdrew fellowship from the church because they retained Askew as their preacher. When they refused to discuss these matters with him, he said that he would "no longer wear the gag, and that he was now at Liberty to clear his conscience by preaching the Gospel as revealed."[258]

Sometime in late summer or early fall Mt. Pleasant Missionary Baptist Church, Askew's home church, began efforts to save face with the Baptist Associations in the area. The problem was that most of their members were in sympathy with Askew. On October 2, 1875, their conference meeting went as follows:

> The Baptist Church of Christ at Mt. Pleasant met and sat in conference Saturday before the 1st Sabbath in October 1875. Had no preaching, went into conference by choosing G. W. Thigpen moderator pro tem. After singing and prayer, we invited visiting Brothers and Sisters to seat with us.
>
> 2nd. Made way for the reception of members read. None called for references. None for new business, and after some debating chose Elder C. C. Lawrence to the pastoral care of the Church for 1876.
>
> Done in conference.
>
> G. W. Thigpen, moderator pro tem and clerk.

The Baptist having chosen Elder C. C. Lawrence and the opposite party M. Askew which the Baptist withdrew from for what we the Baptist call heterodoxy or unsound in the Baptist faith and practice which will be more fully explained in the next minutes.[259]

On November 5, 1875, they met again to try to settle the matter. This time their minutes read:

> The Baptist Church of Christ at Mt. Pleasant met and sat in conference Saturday before the 1st Sabbath in November 1875.
>
> After Divine service by Elder C. C. Lawrence and after some arguments, went into conference. We the Baptist composing the

Church at Mt. Pleasant do cordially and friendly withdraw from a portion of our brethren for heterodoxy and departing from the fundamental principle of the Baptist usage which we consider contrary to Baptist or usage and furthermore we agree in conference to take down all the names who wish to remain Baptist and to enroll them as such. Also, the names of those who wish otherwise.

Done in conference.

C. C. Lawrence moderator.

G. W. Thigpen, C.C.

On Sunday made way for the reception of members and received Brother J. T. Fulks by restoration. Done in conference.

The contents of the above minutes are this: "Whereas Elder M. Askew has been preaching doctrine that we think unscriptural and contrary to Baptist usage and whereas we Baptist withdraw from all who endorse the doctrine so taught. Done in conference.[260]

To satisfy the remainder of Baptists at Mt Pleasant they met on December 4, 1875, and recorded the following in their records:

The Baptist Church of Christ at Mt. Pleasant met and sat in conference Saturday before the 1st Sabbath in December 1875.

1st. After Divine service by Elder C. C. Lawrence, invited visiting brethren to seat with us.

2nd. Inquired about the peace of the church. Silence gave consent that she was in peace and made way for the reception of members and received none for references. None for new business. The clerk read over his list of members that wished to remain Baptist which thus far, amounted to 37; but not quite all have been seen yet. Moved for adjournment.

Done in conference.

C. C. Lawrence moderator.

G. W. Thigpen, C.C.[261]

Mt Pleasant had 78 members earlier in 1875, which was before the split, according to the Association records. Mt. Pleasant lost 41 members to the New Testament church.

The four churches over which Askew had charge did divide and adopt the name, "Church of Christ." The Union Grove church was one of these churches. It eventually became the North Carolina Church of Christ, which still thrives today (2024) with over two hundred members.

Comer said that all four churches "obligated themselves to take the Scriptures and nothing else for their rule of faith and practice, and to ignore all confessions of faith and manmade laws and contend for the apostolic faith and practice."[262]

Askew and Comer persuaded all the Baptist churches in the area to come together for a union meeting. This was held at Union Grove in 1876, probably in May or June. It was reported by Jesse Turner Wood of Cedar Plains, Morgan County, Alabama in the *Gospel Advocate* of August 10, 1876. He said that one preacher from Missouri and one from Tennessee attended this meeting. Wood said that "good feeling prevailed and much zeal was manifested on the part of many who have been heretofore called Baptists."[263] Wood further stated:

> This country east and west will furnish a repetition of the Kentuckians 40 or 50 years ago. There are a number that have gone too far to retrograde, and that too, the best of talent… There are large numbers in this country moving out of Babylon with good and substantial leaders or teachers at their head, so that the day is at hand when doubtless many will say, "why am I thus?"[264]

This upheaval continued among the Baptist ranks for the next four or five years, with Askew leading the way. The Baptists saw the problem so pressing that in their churches they began polarizing and trying to prevent our brethren from using the same facilities. An example of this was at Mt. Pleasant Baptist Church, which now had "the Gospel Party," as the reformers were called, and the Regular Baptists meeting in the same building. Askew was preaching for the "Gospel Party." Eventually, the reformers withdrew to the Salem Church building, about four miles away, and began worshipping there. Mt. Pleasant then began to be called the "Scrouge Out" church. As a footnote to this upheaval at Mt. Pleasant, the Baptists dropped Askew from their records as their minister.[265] He continued with the newly formed Church of Christ at Salem schoolhouse, about four miles south of Lexington on Mill Creek. Askew had helped to start the Salem Baptist Church at this place in 1859.[266] It is stated that 15 members of the Mt. Pleasant Baptist Church had been transferred to Salem to start a mission work. This was in William Comer's neighborhood. R. T. Lanier also lived in that vicinity. These two men became the leaders at Salem, after Askew moved to Woodland Springs, a community on the bend of the Tennessee River, about ten miles west of Florence. R. W. Officer came and preached at Askew's home, where he had recently formed a church. Officer baptized seven people.[267] Immediately after Officer left for Florence, Askew left for Savannah, Tennessee, and preached on the street corners, baptized two, and found another from the Baptists to be favorable in starting a New Testament Church. They raised between eight and nine hundred dollars toward building a building. They vowed to build the building and to be a church.[268] He crossed the Tennessee-Alabama State Line and headed southward, toward home. This road took him through the Shaw community where Poplar Springs Methodist Church was located. He preached seven or eight sermons in the Methodists house of worship and "all the prominent members pulled out of creedism."[269] Askew said that "the pastor in charge threatened heavily but shot weakly; he pledged his right arm and his blood if he did not remove all that I had done."[270] Askew said the Methodist members begged their preacher to debate him, but he refused. The preacher vowed that next Sunday he would "smash" Askew's teachings. Murrell said that he only exposed "his own ignorance and evil spirit."[271] The year 1880 had been a very busy year for Murrell. Undoubtedly, R. W. Officer had talked with Murrell Askew about work among the Indians, since Askew was one-quarter Choctaw Indian. They had been associated since the 1870s and had endured similar fates among the Baptists. It seems that Askew had laid the plans to collaborate with Officer among the Indians when Officer visited Murrell in June of 1880. [272] Officer wrote of this:

> Dear Brother: By your request, I will give to the readers of in Firm Foundation, a short article in regard to our Indian Mission. It has been four years since I induced Elder M. Askew (an Indian), to come out from Alabama, to sow the "good seed of the kingdom" among his more unfortunate and wilder brethren. Brother Askew had a good understanding of the ancient gospel, and presented it in a simple manner, but with great power.[273]

So, upon Officer's request, Askew joined him in the work in Indian Territory. Askew was skeptical of Officer's method of mission work because he did not use a missionary society to aid him in the work. Askew, who had only been severed from Baptists Missionary Societies for about six years, still trusted, to some degree, in societies. Askew's skepticism was revealed in an article that appeared three years after his death, in which he was reported as saying: "I confess I had but little confidence in its (mission work) success."[274] Others looked upon it with some suspicion and wondered why Bro. O. did not do like other missionaries over here ....[275] Officer had come from the same Baptist background as Askew, but he had completely rejected any kind of society work. He was convinced that unity would be promoted if individual congregations supported the work, instead of societies promoting it. Askew is further quoted as finally realizing the truth in Officer's method. He stated: "... but we are now convinced that we were mistaken, for we find that it does not divide, but tends to bring the churches together in mission-work."[276] Askew set up his residence in the Chickasaw Nation, which seems odd, as he was part Choctaw, not Chickasaw. He converted many Chickasaw Indians in the short time he worked there. He began teaching at Burney Institute, an Indian School near Lebanon, Oklahoma. It would make sense that he would teach school, to support his family, as he had been a schoolteacher back in Alabama. During his first year at Burney, the building partially burned.[277]

For the next two years, he taught at Burney Institute and continued to do mission work. He became ill in the late fall of 1883 and died on January 4, 1884. He was laid to rest on the school grounds, at the institute. Even in death he still left behind a legacy as described by one of Askew's old Alabama friends—N. B. Wallace:

> I received this morning the sad intelligence of the death of my dear friend and brother —Askew; and cannot let this mournful event pass without in obedience to his dying request, some expression of my sympathy with his bereaved family, and my high appreciation or his noble bearing as a Christian gentleman, and his transcendent ability as a gospel preacher. So reluctant am I to give him up, that I almost feel a disposition, if I could "Back to its mansion call the fleeting breath," but serenely his silent dust must repose in the quiet resting place, till the shrill blast of the last trumpet shall startle the slumbering millions and quicken them into life.
>
> With Bro. O. I repeat, "I would not mark. The place where the broken casket has fallen with a monument." This he did in his day, he needs "no monument's pile, no princely dome, no towering pyramid" to perpetuate his name, it is engraved in indelible characters upon the tablets of memory. This sad event brings fresh to my mind many thrilling incidents in our long labors together "in the kingdom, and patience of Jesus Christ," and these are greatly intensified with the thought that I shall see his face no more, till I too, shall have crossed the river, and stand

with him, arrayed in his robe of spotless white, before the King of kingdoms, at whoso presence the affrighted sun will give place: Then indeed will he "sing in nobler sweeter strains, his power to save," Bro. Askew had a faith and trust in the promises of his God, that enabled him to stand unmoved upon the foundation of apostles and prophets, Jesus Christ being the chief corner stone. And over many a battlefield he waved in triumph the bloodstained banner of the Prince of Peace, and though of feeble of frame and small, means, would travel from place to place, in winter's cold or summer's heat, to break the bread of life to a perishing world. Sometimes he was admonished to take more care of his health. His reply was, "The servant is not better than his Lord." Thus, he toiled on through trials and privations, making full proof of his ministry up almost to the day of his death, and we are happy in the thought that he died as he had lived. To the full assurance of faith, having drunk freely, not at the fount of Parnassus, or Helicon, but of the water of the river of life of which Jesus said, "If a man drink, he will never thirst: but it shall be in him, a well of water springing up into everlasting life." I had indulged the fond hope of seeing him once more, in the flesh, to talk of the trials by the way, and take sweet counsel together as of yore: but he has finished his work in triumph. I would not disturb his peaceful slumber and doubt not if he could speak to us from his angel home, he would say, Dear brethren, press on; it is not all or life to live, nor of death to die. I would not live always, I ask not to stay, where storm after storm rises dark o'er the way, the few cloudy mornings that dawn on us here are enough for life's woes, full enough for its cheer I trust this affliction may be sanctified to the eternal good of the living. Let us ever imitate his noble example. How humble, patient, and self-sacrificing. Bro. O., do you remember at the dear old "Oak," the discourse of our father, made on the great sacrificial atonement! What a halo of glory lit up his features as he talked of Gethsemane, Calvary, etc. Suggestive of the inspiration of Isaiah, "when wrapped in wisdom, and his hallowed lips touched with fire." May our departure be like his:

> "So, live that when thy summons comes
> to join innumerable caravan that moves
> to that mysterious realm, where each shall take;
> his chamber in the silent halls of death
> Thou go not like the quarry slave at night
> Scourged to his dungeon. But sustained and soothed
> By an unfaltering trust, approach the grave
> Like one who draws the drapery of his couch
> About him and lies down to pleasant dreams."
> N. B. Wallace.[278]

Thus ended the life of a man, who had worked among the Baptists until he studied himself into the New Testament Church. He had worn the Baptist name, but for years, before his leaving, he did not agree with the typical doctrines of the Missionary Baptist Church. His struggles with that organization show him truly to have been a "reluctant Baptist."

His work and legacy still live on in Lauderdale County, Alabama, and Savannah, Tennessee in the churches he established. Even T. B. Larimore's success among some Baptist churches in that area may have partially been due to Askew having blazed the way for him. May many generations profit from this good man's labors.

William Comer wrote of Askew's work among the Baptists in Lauderdale County:

> Since that time [September 1875], he has been preaching most of his time and is causing a general revolution in the camps. The four churches to which he preached have divided and adopted the name of the Church of Christ and have obligated themselves to take the Scriptures and nothing else for their rule of faith and practice and to ignore all confessions of faith and man-made laws and contend for the apostolic faith and practice.[279]

Macedonia

It seems likely that the few scattered members from Bluff Creek may have associated with the Macedonia Baptist Church, which was not the typical Baptist Church. This congregation had been under the leadership of Murrell Askew who was put out of the Baptist Church for preaching baptism for remission of sins, along with several other New Testament principles.[280] He had been preaching baptism for remission of sins before the Civil War. The Bevis family who became very influential in the Macedonia work were from Bluff Creek/Gravelly Springs. The connection of Bluff Creek with Macedonia has already been mentioned earlier in this book. (See chapter 4.)

The church at Macedonia is a prime example of Askew's influence among four Baptist congregations. Macedonia Baptist church in Lauderdale County was a member of the Indian Creek Baptist Association which included all four congregations that were on Askew's circuit. T. O. Bevis, who was one of the members at Macedonia told C. E. Holt how Askew turned most of the congregation away from the Baptist and they became a church of Christ. He gave the following account of the incident at Macedonia:

"Brethren," said he, "we are wrong in wearing a sectarian name, and we have some things that we call 'Baptist usage' which do us no good, but, as far as they serve as barriers between ourselves and other Christians, are evidently hurtful. Let us, then, shuck and silk ourselves of everything that we do not find in the New Testament and let us just be Christians only."[281]

Holt went on to show the congregation forty years later:

His proposition was accepted, and the church has since been known as a "church of Christ." Brother T. O. (Thomas Oswell Bevis, of Cloverdale, Ala., is a living witness to that occurrence. He was one of the brethren who "shucked" and "silked" themselves of all humanisms as tests of fellowship or conditions of church membership. He is an elder in said congregation and is pure gold. May the Lord spare him a while longer. C.E. Holt. [282]

T. O. Bevis had served as a delegate to the Indian Creek Missionary Baptists Association for the Macedonia Baptist Church in 1873. This creates a problem with a beloved North Alabama writer's statement about the establishment of the church of Christ at Macedonia. F. D. Srygley wrote in his book—*Larimore and His Boys*, concerning Macedonia's beginning:

That same year [1880] he [Larimore] went to a Baptist church in Lauderdale county, Alabama, called Macedonia, by invitation, to preach a few sermons. The entire church decided no longer to be Baptists, but Christians, nor a Baptist church, but a church of Christ. It has since been faithful in all the appointments of apostolic worship, and to this day it is a strong and prosperous church.[283]

In a case like this we are forced to take the word of the man who was a part of the change made at Macedonia and who remained a loyal member until his death. Brother Bevis' family was a part of Macedonia for many years. Some Bevis families are still members there to present time (2024).

There is no question as to whether Larimore preached at Macedonia; but rather did Larimore convert the whole church and it became a church of Christ. The answer must be, according to William Comer and Thomas Oswell Bevis, Larimore did not convert the whole church. It had already been converted at least five years before by Askew, or did he?

There is, however, a conflicting version of this story. An obituary of another Bevis— T. F. Bevis, gives some mixed information. In the obituary Brown Godwin wrote:

> On the morning of the 25th of April 1885, after an illness of eight days, while friends were ministering to his necessities, unseen angels claimed as theirs the spirit of Bro. T. F. Bevis. He was born May 19, 1 819. Joined the Missionary Baptists church about the year 1845 and lived a consistent member until he learned the good and right way. In the year 1875 he had the way expounded more perfectly to him. After listening to Bro. T. B. Larimore deliver a discourse on Christian Union, he asked permission to speak, and it was granted him; he asked his brethren to come with him and unite with us on the Bible. About fifty agreed to the proposition and they have been laboring for the advancement of Christianity from that time to this. Bro. B. was loved by all his brethren and, judging from the sadness that brooded over the community, by the world. On the day of his burial, I spoke for his congregation. (Macedonia, near Gravelly Springs, Ala.).[284]

Nothing of such a meeting was ever reported in the *Gospel Advocate*. You would think something that important would have been reported and published. Did Godwin, who was a newcomer to that community, get his facts mixed up with information on Askew and the Bevis family interaction? Could it have been that

Larimore preached at Macedonia and encouraged Askew to take a stand on what he believed, which does not seem plausible since Askew was already determined to leave the Baptists? If so, why was this not reported? It seems that T. O. Bevis, who was T. F.'s son, must be believed because he was younger and totally involved in what transpired at Macedonia in 1875.

The next preacher, other than Askew, was Brother P. J. Vandiver. He came in October 1881 and held a meeting for the church at Macedonia. He wrote of this meeting:

> "I commenced a meeting at Macedonia, Lauderdale county, Ala., near Gravelly Springs, on Saturday before the 3rd Lord's day in August, preached six discourses, resulting in ten additions, nine "from the world and one from the Freewill Baptists, and a great deal of prejudice removed. All the praise is to him that rules both in heaven and earth. I am now preaching every Sunday in Alabama and Tennessee. I have just organized a new church near Lowerville, Tennessee." P. J. Vandiver.[285]

Vandiver has already been discussed, along with his cousin John N. Vandiver, in connection with the Waterloo later work. Vandiver was a country preacher who lived in the area. He had been converted from the Baptists. He sympathized with the congregation, as he had left the Baptists, also. He knew the trials and struggles they faced daily. Thus, he was drawn to Macedonia for a meeting.

L. R. Sewell, along with John Hayes and W. H. Gresham came and held a meeting for Macedonia. The meeting began on "the third Lord's day and closed on Friday following with four additions."[286]

A note appeared in the *Gospel Advocate* concerning a meeting at Macedonia:

> T. O. Bevis, of Threet, Ala., requests us to announce that Brother J. B. Askew will commence a series of meetings on the

fourth Lord's day in September at Macedonia, Lauderdale County, Tenn. (Alabama) Everybody is invited, and all are requested to bring baskets so that dinner may be served on the ground.[287]

J. B. Askew was a grandson of Murrell Askew. It is of note that T. O. Bevis sent the request. Remember that C. E. Holt in 1921 said the Brother T. O. Bevis was an elder at Macedonia in 1921. Whether he was an elder at Macedonia at this time or not he was a leader in the church at that place.

In 1913 Brother Will Behel filled in an appointment for a homecoming with Macedonia. He described the event as follows:

> For years Brother William Gresham has had an appointment at Macedonia, Lauderdale County, Ala., the third Lord's day in May. This year he was unable to fill his appointment. He requested that I fill the appointment. Expecting to be with him on that day, anyhow, I agreed to do the best I could. An immense congregation was there, estimated at about eight hundred people. Brother Gresham told me he had planned to preach on "Acceptable Service to God." (Heb. 12: 28, 29.) I spoke on that subject. One lady confessed Christ, and she and another, who made the confession a few weeks previous, were buried with Christ in baptism after the evening service. In the afternoon I spoke on "The More Excellent Way." We took the seats out in the grove, and then one-third was not seated. The house was scarcely half sufficient to hold the crowd. And dinner — well, it was abundant. A really nice time. May God's blessings continue in those good people. William Behel.[288]

The congregation seemed to be in great shape in 1913. For a homecoming in 1913, the crowd was extremely large. Behel was overjoyed. He had only been preaching for a few years and W. H. Gresham took him underwing and helped develop him into an excellent preacher as we shall see in later parts of the Lauderdale

County history. For our time frame, this draws to a close the Macedonia work.

Since we treated Bluff Creek and Macedonia together, as they were connected familywise, we did not keep our chronology of the churches. We will now return to the natural chronology of the establishment of the various churches in Lauderdale County. We end this section with a report sent to the *Gospel Advocate* by James Paul Kimbrell of West Point, Tennessee:

> It has been some time since I reported, but I have been busy just the same; in fact, I have been almost too busy to report. I have been preaching in Lauderdale County, Ala., most of the time. I was away from home six weeks and two days, and preached every day except three, and sometimes twice a day. Despite the fact that there has been a great deal of opposition, I have had a successful six weeks' work. During that time seventy-one souls were added to the church, some of them coming from the Methodists. The last meeting I conducted was at Macedonia, fifteen miles northwest of Florence, Ala. I failed to get there on Sunday; so, we began work on Monday night and continued until the following Sunday night. The Sunday I spent there was a busy day. I preached three sermons and baptized seven people. During the week there were sixteen additions to the church. A man and his wife who had, up to that time, been almost confirmed infidels, made the confession and were baptized. He was said to be the "toughest" character in the community. He was the ringleader, and everybody spoke of him as "the belled sheep." The interest was high when the meeting closed, but the brothers thought it best to close out on account of the busy season. They were very pleased with the meeting and have engaged my services for a meeting next summer. On the second Lord's day in September, I was with the Iron City congregation. I preached for the brethren at East Florence on the fourth Lord's day, morning, and evening. I have regular appointments there and at Macedonia. While in Florence, I went out to Jackson-

burg, where Brother Hoskins was holding a meeting, and heard him deliver a sermon. Before returning on Monday, I drove out to Mars' Hill, in company with Brother W. G. Wallace, of Rogersville, and listened to a sermon by Brother Cooper, of Kentucky. Yesterday (the first Lord's day in October) I began a series of meetings at the Bradley School house, in the southern part of Wayne County. Large crowds were present at both services. I am expecting some results, as there is plenty of material to work on. After the meeting closes, I will go back to my home at West Point and will probably enter school after Christmas. J. Paul Kimbrell. Iron City, Tenn.[289]

This closes our history of Macedonia—up to 1914. Many more years of service happened there and continue even today (2024).

UNION GROVE—NORTH CAROLINA

The history of the North Carolina Church of Christ began as the Union Grove Missionary Baptist Church sometime in the mid-1850s and was established by either Aaron Askew or his son Murrell Askew. Both Askews lived in the community at that time, and both were Baptist preachers. Murrell still lived in the Stutts precinct on September 16, 1867.[290] It stands to reason that one of them or both had a hand in establishing the work at Union Grove.

The church struggled during the Civil War, as all churches in the South did. At first, they met in members' houses, but after the war, they built a union house to be used as a school during the week and a church building on weekends and nighttime. As the community built it, it was intended to be used by all religious groups, thus the name—Union Grove. A log structure was built, surrounded by woods, occupying the original grounds. Charlie (Brick) Jones deeded the land to the Baptist Church. The deed proved faulty in that no amount of money was specified as payment. Another deed was granted by Charles Brick Jones on April 11, 1882.[291] Somehow the Baptists commandeered it for their own use. By the late 1860s, the Union Grove Baptist Church had been going through a change in their religious views due to the influence of Murrell Askew. Long before he became a Baptist preacher, he had been reading material published by Tolbert Fanning a preacher among churches of Christ. In 1844, we find him subscribing to Tolbert Fanning's *Christian Review*.[292] Murrell had grown up in a very volatile time when the Baptists in Northwest Alabama were rethinking their theology, and many were becoming members of the Church of Christ. In 1830 the Muscle Shoals Baptist Association passed a "Resolution" against "Campbellites."[293] This must have influenced his later thinking of the Bible.

He was a schoolteacher before becoming a preacher.[294] Sometime between 1850 and 1854, he began to preach. Mid-year, 1854, he established the Mt. Pleasant Baptist Church in Lexington, Alabama.[295] Some people thought Askew to be a smart man because he could quote so much of the Bible.

He often told his audience, "Don't do as Askew does but do as Askew says."[296] Some of his staunch Baptist members began to question Askew's teachings. During the war (1863), his brethren had begun to rumble about his theology, which they called, "Campbellism." William Comer wrote that Askew was preaching—"that the sinner must obey all of the requirements of the gospel."

He further stated:

> " ... the sinner could not claim the promise of the pardon of sins save through obedience to the condition." ... He tried to get his accusers to discuss the subject with him, and they refused. Since that time, he has been preaching most of his time and is causing a general revolution in the camps. The four churches to which he preached have divided and adopted the name of the Church of Christ and have obligated themselves to take the Scriptures and nothing else for their rule of faith and practice and to ignore all confessions of faith and manmade laws and contend for the apostolic faith and practice. Murrell continued to preach as he understood the Bible, but many Baptists searched the Scriptures

to disagree with him. Many honest hearts saw the truth and aligned themselves with him.[297]

William Comer, who was already a member of the Church of Christ aided in getting Askew to see the truth. Comer was subscribing to the *Gospel Advocate* and shared his learning with his neighbors. He explained his actions to the *Gospel Advocate*:

> When I find a person that I think will lay down their prejudice, enough to read and investigate, I get them to read them.[298]

The *Gospel Advocate* and T.W. Brents' *Gospel Plan Of Salvation* were the two sources to which Comer referred.

He further speaks of Askew's reading this publication. Also, he mentions that other leading Missionary Baptists were now changing their views on salvation. R.T. Lanier, who was one of those honest hearts in the Baptist church, was diligently searching and would soon abandon the Baptists. He also encouraged Askew in his attempts to convert the Baptists to the New Testament church. This caused him much trouble in the Baptist ranks.

By 1874 trouble had arisen from some of his brethren, after some eleven years of peace. He was brought before the Indian Creek Association and charged with preaching "Campbellism" again (the same year he was rehired as a regular minister for the Mt. Pleasant Baptist church near Lexington.) He asked the Association to define the doctrine of "Campbellism." They told him that he was teaching that all sinners had to do was believe and obey the gospel in all its requirements, and they would be saved. They told him to stop preaching this kind of doctrine. He told them he would stop for twelve months (which would have been until the next Association meeting) if the Association would agree to discuss the doctrine. They refused to do so.

Some of the Baptists had now aligned themselves with the Churches of Christ. At least the four congregations, over which Askew had the oversight, had dropped the name "Missionary

Baptist," and simply referred to themselves as "churches of Christ," by 1875. These changes would cause Murrell Askew much trouble.

The Association had met in September of 1875 at the Union Grove Baptist church, in the present community of North Carolina, in Lauderdale County. The Association refused to let Askew be heard on any subject. Comer said it was because "the church where he held his membership (Mt. Pleasant) sent him as a delegate and sent her letter under the name of "church of Christ" with no "Missionary Baptist" added to it."[299] The Association withdrew fellowship from the church because they retained Askew as their preacher. When they refused to discuss these matters with him, he said that he would "no longer wear the gag, and that he was now at liberty to clear his conscience by preaching the Gospel as revealed."[300]

The four churches over which Askew had charge did divide and adopt the name, "Church of Christ." The Union Grove church was one of these churches. It eventually became the North Carolina Church of Christ, which still thrives today (2024) with over two hundred members.

Comer said that all four churches "obligated themselves to take the Scriptures and nothing else for their rule of faith and practice, and to ignore all confessions of faith and manmade laws and contend for the apostolic faith and practice."[301]

Askew and Comer had persuaded all the Baptist churches in the area to come together for a union meeting. The following anonymous appeal was published in the *Gospel Advocate*:

> A union meeting will be held at the Union Grove church in Lauderdale County, Ala., 14 miles northeast of Florence, commencing Friday before the third Lord's day in July [14th] next. All are cordially invited to attend who are willing to unite upon the gospel and take the Scriptures for their rule of faith and practice. Especially the ministers of the gospel are requested to attend and have a free discussion of the subjects that seem to

be as barriers to the way of all God's people uniting in one great spiritual body, therefore fulfilling the request and prayer of our blessed Savior.[302]

This meeting was held at Union Grove beginning July 14, 1876. It was reported in a lengthy report by Jesse Turner Wood of Cedar Plains, Morgan County, Alabama in the *Gospel Advocate* of August 10, 1876. He said that one preacher from Missouri and one from Tennessee attended this meeting. Wood said that "good feeling prevailed and much zeal was manifested on the part of many who have been heretofore called Baptists."[303] We quote a few lines of Wood's report:

> This country east and west will furnish a repetition of the Kentuckians 40 or 50 years ago. There are a number that have gone too far to retrograde, and that too, the best of talent... There are large numbers in this country moving out of Babylon with good and substantial leaders or teachers at their head, so that the day is at hand when doubtless many will say, "why am I thus?"[304]

A Baptist woman wrote a denial to nearly everything Wood wrote about the meeting at Union Grove. Her report was under the heading of "Alabama Correspondence." We give her report in full to show the hypocrisy and bitterness that existed among the Baptists:

> Bro. Graves: --The mass meeting was held at Union Grove church, in Indian Creek Association, Lauderdale county, Ala., beginning Friday before the 3rd Sunday in July [14th], as was expected; and we must say that we heard some strange things from the lips of those we formerly believed to be Baptist, sound in faith and practice. We attended the meeting, and though we feared all things were not as they should be, we had no idea that matters stood as they really did. We found it to be a meeting

intended for ministers of every order, to meet and discuss, or investigate, controverted points of Scripture; and we also learned that the church did not so order it. We did not arrive in time to hear much of the proceedings on Friday. We found R. Wallace Officer and M. Askew, and a minister of the Campbellite order, investigating the subject of apostacy. They did not come to any agreement but proposed to lay the subject over and fully investigate it on Saturday. As it was named no more, we suppose they just agreed to disagree, and proceed with matters of more importance. Considering the nature of the meeting, and the standing of ministers connected with it, the brethren of Indian Creek Association had resolved to take no part with them; but notice of the meeting, as given by R. Wallace Officer in The Baptist, drew brethren from a distance to wit: H. B. Wester from West Tennessee, and J. J. Wester, of Missouri, who arrived on Saturday afternoon. On Saturday R. W, Officer delivered an address. He was followed by a Campbellite. In the afternoon, the identity of the church was presented by a Campbellite named Wood. R. Wallace Officer followed, endorsing his position. Thus, an agreement seemed to exist, and all things bid fair for a union of these people, but for the interposition of Bro. H. B. Wester, who, to the astonishment of all, arose far back in the assembly, and inquired the object and nature of the meeting, and being answered, he proceeded to address the waiting crowd. His first speech, which was a perfect feast of reason and flow of soul, to all the lovers of truth, while it seemed to drive consternation into the camp of the enemy, brought consolation to many despondent hearts, who will never cease to thank and praise the great giver of all good for the timely arrival of this dear brother. O! how our hearts did burn within us, as he stood forth as a representative of that body called Missionary Baptists, and ably defended the truth against Campbellism and all other isms, proving himself to be a man, and the right man in the right place. One who was neither ashamed, or afraid to own his Lord, or to defend his cause; and while others rose up with open arms, declaring themselves ready to receive all, and denying sectarianism, he boldly took the position that he was sectarian, professed to belong to that sect everywhere spoken against, and that he was ready, willing and able, and would, by the grace of God, earnestly contend for that faith once delivered to the saints.

On Sunday morning R. Wallace Officer preached, and was followed by H. B. Wester, who presented the doctrine of the Missionary Baptist church, in contrast with others, proving by holy writ, that the Baptist church is the church of Christ; and we are happy to say that notwithstanding all the craft and cunning of the enemy during the entire discussion, his positions were not overthrown. Sunday afternoon M. Askew preached, declaring that no person was adopted into the family of God but those only who obey the Law of adoption, which is faith, repentance, confession, and baptism.

Meeting again on Monday morning 9 o'clock, the question, who, according to the Scriptures, has a right to administer the ordinance of baptism, the discussion was opened by H.B. Wester, who affirmed that none had a right to administer the ordinance but those who were legally set apart by the church of Jesus Christ; that all baptisms administered outside of her authority were null and void. He was followed by R. Wallace Officer, who took the position that all who had obeyed the law of adoption was in the church of Christ, whether he had received his baptism at the hands of Campbellites, Methodists, Presbyterians, or Baptists, and that every member who was immersed had the right, and an equal right to baptize, and that all thus baptized should commune together. He was followed by Bro. J. J. Wester of Missouri in the affirmative, and we must say that he did honor to the cause, earnestly contending for the truth as it is in Christ Jesus. Then Wood, the Campbellite, arose and endorsed R. Wallace Officer's position. He was followed by H. B. Wester, who clearly showed and proved by the Scriptures, that there was no legal authority outside of the church of Jesus Christ, his executive body, that no one had a right to administer baptism but those set apart by her, and that all acts performed outside of her authority, are illegal and invalid. The morning discussion closed with the understanding that Wood, the Campbellite, talked for an hour in the afternoon, to be followed by H. B. Wester. Wood attempted to show the Scriptural marks identifying the church of Christ but failed to show them up according to the gospel. Bro. H. B. Wester then presented the Scriptural marks of the church of Christ, plainly showing that the Missionary Baptist church, so-called, possessed these marks, and in contrasting these with the marks of Campbellites, was disturbed by Wood, who, in order to keep their falsehoods from being shown up, advanced and kept talking, and raised such confusion, that it was impossible for Bro. Wester to proceed, so the meeting closed for the day. Bro. J. J. Wester gave out an appointment for night. We went back, and enjoyed a happy hour's service, sermon by Bro. A. J. Tant, who was followed by Brethren Westers. As the enemy had gone, there was none to disturb, and all things were said in truth and love. We must say that throughout the discussion, while Bro. Wester contended for the faith, he showed all due respect for the feelings of others, and while we pray God to bless these dear brethren, we earnestly pray him to call and send forth more such laborers into vineyard. Your sister in Christ. Good Springs, Ala. Mrs. R. C. Griggs.[305]

This drew a response from Robert Wallace Officer:

BRO. GRAVES: --It is justice in me that the readers of your paper know from my pen that a letter from North Alabama of August 19th, signed by Mrs. R. C. Griggs, is a misrepresentation of my teaching: I teach no such doctrine as declared in that report; and if the people who desire to represent me to the public would tell what I say, and not what they think I may mean, there would not be so much injustice done me. Wallace Officer. Macon, Tenn. October 2, 1876.[306]

Following this appeal by Officer the Union Grove Baptist felt compelled to enter the fray, so they wrote their own statement:

Baptist Response to Meeting at Union Grove titled: Church Action

BRO. GRAVES: -- With Sister Griggs' report of the mass-meeting held with Union Grave church, Lauderdale county, Ala., commencing Friday before the 3rd Sunday in July 1876, together with Rev. R. Wallace Officer's complaint of misrepresentation before us, and contents noted, we, the Union Grove church, in conference Saturday before the second Sunday in November 1876, unanimously --

Resolve that we endorse the report of Sister R.C. Griggs, given in "THE BAPTIST" of August 19th, 1876, as being a true and correct statement of the proceedings of the mass-meeting held with said church.

Resolve that we send the same to "THE BAPTIST" for publication.

J.H. Norred, Moderator. A. McDonald, Clerk.[307]

This upheaval continued among the Baptist ranks for the next four or five years with Askew leading the way. The Baptists saw the problem so pressing that in their churches they began polarizing and trying to prevent our brethren from using the same facilities. At Union Grove Askew had converted most of the Baptists to the Church of Christ. Those Baptists who were not converted left and started another Baptist Church. Among those converted were Jack and Ann Parker. Ann was the daughter of Charles "Brick" and Sarah Jones who owned the land on which the building stood. Apparently "Brick" Jones, as he was known, along with his wife Sarah, was converted at some point before 1882. G. C. (Gilford Carroll) Thigpen was also converted at the same time. He was a charter member of the Union Grove Christian Church. Will Behel gave a description of the circumstances:

He became a member of the church in the days when Brother R. W. Officer and Brother Askew were shaking this part of the religious world with forceful, gospel preaching.[308]

Thigpen became one of the leaders in the Union Grove congregation. He managed to get students from Mars Hill College to come and speak on Sundays and even held occasional meetings for them. One such meeting was held in 1879. The meeting was reported by J. R. Bradley:

> Bro. Hudspeth and I commenced preaching at a place in Alabama, Lauderdale county, called Union Grove, which was some two or three years ago, entirely a Baptist congregation. The result of this meeting was 25 additions. I left Bro. H., there on Wednesday –went to my uncle's [house] on the Tennessee River, preached Thursday; my uncle who is above 60 years old confessed and was baptized –had one addition last night at Salem, Ala. We praise the good Lord for it all.[309]

By 1881 Bradley had a circuit of four regular congregations, which he kept for two years. Union Grove was always his standing appointment of the third Sunday of the month. He reported on the church at that place:

> The third Sunday I go to Union Grove, Ala. Here is a good place to get a large crowd on preaching days, but the brethren do not meet only when they have preaching. They say that their Lord's Day work is always "spoiled" by one of the brethren who believes and contends that the Lord has not made it binding upon us to meet every first day. Such an excuse will not please the Lord on the Day of Judgment. No, never...[310]

Another meeting was reported that same year by one of the young students from Mars Hill College. His name was William B.

McQuiddy, a preaching companion of J. R. Bradley. McQuiddy, wrote:

> Bro. J.R. Bradley and the writer closed last night a six-day meeting with the congregation at Union Grove, Lauderdale county, Ala. Nine were added to the church and the church seemed greatly encouraged and strengthened. May they ever abound in zeal and knowledge of the truth.[311]

The congregation was now steadily growing. There was a need to organize, so, a business meeting was held to incorporate to comply with the law of the state at that time. That created a need for trustees. The first entry in the original record book of the Union Grove Christian was as follows:

> The Church of Christ at Union Grove, Laud. Co., Ala., was incorporated according to Law on the 14th day of Jan. 1882 A.D. With the following named brethren as trustees for the ensuing five (5) years, viz. L. M. Fitzpatrick, Wm. H. Wood, Ben F. Thompson, G. C. Thigpen, upon the removal of Wm. H. Wood, John Stutts was chosen to fill out his term to 1887.[312]

This had to be done before the congregation could legally own property. After trustees had been appointed, Charles "Brick" and Sarah Jones sold to the trustees of the Union Grove Christian Church the land and building for the sum of ten dollars. This transaction occurred on April 11, 1882.[313]

To demonstrate the rapid growth at Union Grove we cite G. C. Thigpen's report below:

> G. C. Thigpen, Union Grove. Ala., August 25, writes: "Under the ministry of two young ministers from Mars Hill College, Lauderdale County, Alabama, the churches of this vicinity have been wonderfully blessed. The church at Union Grove was increased thirty-one-three from the Baptists, and three from the

Methodists, and the rest from the world. They went from Union Grove to Bethel, where they had twenty-three additions. To God be all the glory. They are workmen that need not be ashamed."[314]

Thigpen was one of the trustees and the most educated of all the trustees. William Behel wrote: "In his earlier years he taught school and music, was County Surveyor for a long while."[315] The other trustees seemingly turned over record keeping and reporting to him.

In 1889 William H. Gresham came and held a meeting at Union Grove which was reported by T. B. Larimore:

> Bro. W.H. Gresham, one of our Mars' Hill elders, has just closed an interesting meeting at Union Grove, near Florence —five days, ten discourses, ten accessions. Bro. G. is doing a good work in the Mars' Hill field. T. B. Larimore.[316]

Gresham returned the following year for another successful meeting. The report on that meeting was sent by W. H. Sanday. Sanday was from Rogersville, originally. His report reads:

> Preached at Gilbertsboro on the third Saturday night and Lord's day at 11 o'clock. We then decided to put off the meeting there until the third Lord's day in September. I then went to Union Grove, Ala., to help Bro. W. H. Gresham in a meeting there. There were twenty-six added to the church and two confessions. Twenty-two by confession and baptism, three from the Baptists, and one from the Methodists, and I think that part of them that were baptized were from the Methodists. The meeting was still in progress on Friday when I had to leave to fill in other appointments. Bro. Gresham and I did the preaching, except for three discourses that Bro. J. T. Underwood preached on his way home. We have warm-hearted brethren and sisters at this point, who are earnestly toiling for

the propagation of truth and the demolishing of error, and we hope to meet with them again in the near future. W. H. Sandy, Marbuts.[317]

When Sanday wrote: "We have warm-hearted brethren and sisters at this point, who are earnestly toiling for the propagation of truth and the demolishing of error." Apparently, all were not in harmony with this statement, or at least later it was not so. A letter to *Gospel Advocate* bears this out. It was written by M. W. Lefan and reads as follows:

> Should members of the church deal in whisky-making or selling? We have some contention in the church at Union Grove, some contending that it is no harm for Christians to make and sell the filthy stuff. Give us the scripture on it. M. W. Lefan. Center Star, Ala., March 30, 1894.
>
> Lipscomb's answer: Paul says (Eph. iv. 28): "Let him labor, working with his hands the thing, which is good, that he may have to give to him that needeth." A Christian man is limited to doing what is good. He cannot do that which brings evil to man. There is nothing in this land that brings more evil to men, women, and children than the use of intoxicating spirits.
>
> Paul (Rom. xiv. 21) says: "It is good neither to eat flesh, nor to drink wine, nor anything whereby thy brother stumbles, or is offended, or made weak." Oh, no; a Christian cannot help to ruin men, women, and children.[318]

This would not be Lefan's last complaint. In 1902 he would make another one.

The next mention of the work at Union Grove was puzzling. It was about a meeting held by A. P. Holtsford of Florence. A part of this report is quoted here:

> Florence, Dec. 25: I have spent the last five and a half months preaching at the following places: North Carolina; Lauderdale

county, Ala., one week, with five additions; four days at Bluewater, with good attention... A. P. Holtsford.[319]

The puzzling part is that Holtsford says that he held a meeting at North Carolina before the official records make any mention of the church being called North Carolina. Could it be that the community was already called North Carolina before the church changed its name to North Carolina and Holtsford was referring to the community, instead of the name of the congregation?

Our next report in the *Gospel Advocate* came eight years later. It was sent in by C. E. Holt of Iron City, Tennessee:

> Iron City, Aug. 13.-Our meeting at Olive Hill resulted in fifteen added to the congregation; at Union Grove, Ala., four added. We are in a good meeting at Iron City. Eight have been added to date. The crowds and interest are good. C. E. Holt.[320]

Union Grove had sponsored a meeting about a mile east of Union Grove on the road that went to Center Hill. The meeting was held in the Olive Hill schoolhouse. Years later this building would become the home of Percy D. Wright.[321] As is seen in this report, the converts became members at Union Grove.

Two years later W. H. Sanday sent a report that included information on Union Grove. He was coming to hold a meeting in October of 1899. A portion of the report is given:

> Center Star, September 5. —I have just closed a good meeting with my home church...The Lord willing, I will begin a meeting at Chewalla, Tenn., on the second Lord's day in this month; at Jacinto, Miss., on the third Lord's day; and at Union Grove, Ala., on the first Lord's day in October. There have been five additions at Union Grove since the first Lord's day in June. W. H. Sandy.[322]

Sanday was especially attached to Union Grove for a few

years. He would make several other visits over the next year or two. Sanday was followed by C. E. Holt, who held several meetings at Union Grove through the next few years. Holt was the regular preacher for the Iron City, Tennessee Church of Christ.

C. E. Holt held the next reported meeting for Union Grove, in 1901. G. C. Thigpen sent the report to the *Gospel Advocate*. His report was a concise view of the work at Union Grove at the turn of the twentieth century:

> Atlas, October 6: Brother C. E. Holt began a meeting at Union Grove on the fifth Sunday in September and continued it one week, with fifty-six additions-thirty by obedience, fifteen from the Baptists. three from the Methodists. and eight restored. It was indeed a glorious meeting. Brother Holt is a sound. forceful, logical preacher, "rightly dividing the word of truth," and greatly endeared himself to our people. He leaves us with many hearty well-wishes, and many prayers will be offered for him as he goes forward in the master's work. G. C. Thigpen.[323]

Holt held another meeting the next October. A description of the meeting is given in the following report:

> From Iron City I went to Union Grove (Atlas), Ala., and preached one week, with thirty-one additions to the church. While there I baptized two little girls —sisters —aged ten and twelve years. The little girls are very bright; they came forward at the same time and gave me their sweet little hands. It was a beautiful scene when the two little girls went down into the water and were buried —both at once and raised with their glorious Redeemer. Brother G. C. Thigpen, then, whom no better man can be found, remarked when they came up out of the water that they "looked like two little angels." There are some good brethren at Union Grove. Brother G. C. Thigpen is an elder, and right well he fills the place. I will return to Texas next summer. I have some meetings already appointed. I

can make a few more appointments than those I already have. Those who want my assistance should let me know soon. My Christian love to all the faithful in Christ Jesus. C.E. Holt.[324]

Two months later a problem arose over the unexpected. It was a box-supper.

> The brethren at Union Grove, near Stutts, Ala., gave a box supper to raise money to build a meetinghouse, A brother wants a scriptural argument on the subject, but it is very hard to give a scriptural argument on an unscriptural practice. Who ever heard of Paul's giving a box supper to raise money to build a meetinghouse? God does not need any such help. The Lord loves a cheerful giver, and one should give as he purposes in his heart. [325]

The report was sent anonymously; but Matthew W. Lefan had a falling out with G. C. Thigpen over the box-supper and he is the most likely one to write such a report. Mable Wright Parker, P. D. Wright's daughter, gave the following information from her father's diary:

> At this time, G. C. Thigpen and Matt Lefan had a disagreement. Thigpen wanted to have a box supper; to raise money to buy seats for the church, Lefan thought it was unscriptural, so along with Jim Beavers and others left the church. They then started a Sunday school at Olive Hill school house, most of them were later reconciled to North Carolina. Lefan went to Antioch Church to work with that congregation.[326]

It is stated in a history of the Antioch congregation, written by Larry Harper, that Lefan came and helped establish the congregation at that place in 1902.

In 1908 J. T. Harris comes on the scene and holds a meeting.

His first report was about the beginning of the meeting at North Carolina:

> Brother J. T. Harris is at North Carolina. Ala., in a well-attended meeting. He recently closed a meeting at Waterloo, Ala., with three baptisms.[327]

His follow-up report gave the final results of that meeting:

> On August 3, Brother J. T. Harris closed his meeting at North Carolina, Ala., with eleven additions, three baptized, seven restored. and one from the Baptists. Brother Harris is now in a meeting with the congregation at Minor Hill, Tenn.[328]

In the early 1900s, another preacher appears on the scene in Lauderdale County, Alabama. His name was William M. Behel, better known as "Uncle Will Behel." In 1909 he made an appeal for help through the pages of the *Gospel Advocate*. It is partially quoted here:

> ... Remuneration is small in new places; and if brethren do not hold a preacher up, he cannot stand long and live. I yet have five destitute places in view for meetings. Brethren, you may think this field is self-supporting. Ask Brother E. C. Fuqua; he has tried Lauderdale County. As to my character, I refer any one to the elders of the church at North Carolina, Ala. G. W. Thigpen and G. C. Thigpen, Killen, Ala., R. F. D. No. 2; or Brother C. E. Holt, Florence, Ala.[329]

It may be noted that Behel refers to the elders at North Carolina and not Union Grove. This is the second earliest reference that we have found that refers to Union Grove as North Carolina. In the trustee ledger in 1907, the congregation was addressed as Union Grove. Included on the same page are two more meetings that occurred to select trustees for five-year periods of service. The heading at the top of the ledger page is retained throughout that page. Thus in 1907, the page was titled Union Grove, even though two entries were made for North Carolina. Sometime between April 1907 and October 1909, the name changed from Union Grove Christian Church to North Carolina Church of Christ.[330] One explanation as to why the change from the Christian Church to the Church of Christ may be that in the 1906 US Religious Census, the churches of Christ were listed separately from the Christian Churches and Disciples of Christ. Up until 1906, all three groups were the same brotherhood. The division came between the instrument of music in worship and the missionary society. The church at North Carolina may have been trying to distance themselves from the Disciple group, by completely changing all parts of their old name to a new one, that seemed more Biblical.

Not much happened between 1909 and 1914. The next report in the *Gospel Advocate* clearly showed the name change at Union Grove—it was now North Carolina, as can be seen in the following report:

> West Point, August 18: On Sunday (August 16), I closed an eight-days' meeting at Shiloh Church, in Lauderdale County, Ala. Four were baptized and five restored. Great crowds attended each service. On Saturday night the brethren estimated the number present at five hundred. On Sunday night I began a meeting at North Carolina Church. in Lauderdale County. Six young people made the good confession last night and will be baptized this morning at 9:30 o'clock. The attendance is good, and we expect more results. The meeting will continue indefinitely. J. P. Kimbrell.[331]

The J. P. Kimbrell of this report was John Paul Kimbrell of West Point, Tennessee. He later got caught up in Tennessee politics and quit preaching. With this report, we close the volatile history of one of the most resilient congregations in North Alabama.

The New Hope– Salem Connection

New Hope was one of the four former Baptist churches that had been established by Askew and perhaps R. W. Officer, who preached there many times also. Officer later wrote a letter to the new Hope Church of Christ which later came into the Restoration Movement by November 1877, as is stated in Officer's letter. We give the letter in full:

LETTER TO THE CHURCH AT NEW HOPE, ALABAMA

Dear Brethren at New Hope: While I cannot be with you, maybe a few thoughts penned will not be "out of order."

The great apostle to the Gentiles said he was "not ashamed of the gospel of Christ," and gave the reason, "because," said he, "it is the power of God unto salvation; but it is the power of God unto salvation to everyone that believeth, to the Jew first and also to the Greek." Rom. i:16. As it only saves or is the power of God unto salvation to those who believe, it becomes us to see something about the means of getting faith. Hear the apostle: "For therein," i.e., in the gospel, "is the righteousness of God revealed from faith to faith: as it is written the just shall live by faith." Verse 17. Then we see faith (according to the apostle) does not only come by revelation, but the growth of faith also;

"for therein," says he, "is the righteousness revealed from faith to faith." Then the gospel is the revelation of God's power to save. Let us hear further from the apostle: "The eyes of your understanding being enlightened," says he, "that ye may know what the hope of his calling is and what the riches of the glory of his inheritance in the saints, and what is the exceeding greatness of his power toward us who believe, according to the workings of his mighty power, which he wrought in Christ when he raised him from the dead." Eph. i:18-21.

How are the eyes of our understanding enlightened? David says by the commandment; says he, "the commandment is pure, enlightening the eyes." Ps. xix:8. Then as David declares that the enlightening comes by the commandment, through which enlightening we receive a knowledge of what is the hope of his calling, the riches of his inheritance, the greatness of his power which God wrought in Christ through the resurrection, it follows that all the above-mentioned knowledge according to Paul and David, comes through the commandment, for David says we are enlightened by the commandment and Paul says being enlightened that we might know what is the hope of his calling, the glory of his inheritance, the greatness of his power, even his mighty power. It becomes us then to learn from whence and by what means cometh the commandment that we may know the means of receiving faith in his mighty power, which is the gospel, the power of God unto salvation. Jesus says (John xii:49), "The Father which sent me he gave me a commandment, what I should say and what I should speak." Then the commandment is something that is said or spoken. Let us hear from the beloved disciple, "That which was from the beginning," says he, "which we have heard, which we have seen with our eyes, and our hands have handled of the word of life, that which we have seen and heard we declare unto you, that you may have fellowship with us, and truly our fellowship is with the Father and with his son Jesus Christ." 1 John i:1-3. And in the 4th verse he says, "These things we write unto you that your joy may be full." Then what is the conclusion of the whole matter? That the gospel, which is the power of God unto salvation, which power God wrought or made manifest in Christ when he raised him from the dead, was thereby revealed to the apostles, who spake the same to the people then, in order to their fellowship with each other, with Christ and the Father, and for the same purpose it was written and left for us, that we who hear not the apostles in person, might have the same, and also that our joy may be full.

Where then is the abstract plan? It finds no room in the word of the Lord, since we get all that God offers us through speaking or writing and receive it by hearing and seeing. That then, which is not spoken written, seen, or heard must be from the devil, though the teachers of the same may be as zealous, may have as good a conscience as Saul when he killed saints, or as honest and possess as good intentions as Uzza when he touched the ark and fell, or die as happy as the Jews in the wilderness over the calf, and yet if the "blind lead the blind both shall fall into the ditch." "For not everyone that saith unto me Lord, Lord, shall enter into the kingdom of heaven, but he that doeth the will of my Father who is in heaven." Though they may have cast out demons, prophesied, and done many mighty works in the Lord's name, yet he will declare unto them, depart ye that work iniquity, for I never knew you.

May the Lord bless you in your labor of love; the Lord permitting, I will be with you on the fourth Lord's day and Saturday before in this month. I am doing very well, can walk some. Bro. R. will give you the particulars about my wound. Yours in love, R. Wallace Officer, Athens, Ala., Nov. 7, 1877.
[332]

The letter does not give any information on the congregation itself but implies several things. Officer was concerned for their spiritual welfare. He also calls the New Hope church a Church of Christ. They had rejected human creeds by 1877. Later we discover that R. T. Lanier had become a leader at Salem, which suggests that New Hope may have later merged with Salem.

Not much information has been located concerning this work. R. T. Lanier was a delegate for the New Hope Baptist Church.[333] William Comer, who lived in the vicinity and a friend of Lanier, gave a good report on the work in 1878:

> Wm. Comer writes from Lauderdale Co., Ala.: Our protracted meeting closed on the 22nd inst., after seven days' service at the church of Christ at New Hope, Ala. There were fourteen additions, eight from the world, and four from the Missionary Baptists, one of them a minister, and two from the Cumberland Presbyterian church, and a good impression made upon all that heard the word, (and the brethren strengthened and built up in the faith) which was proclaimed by Bro. Wm. Smith of Giles County, Tenn., and Bro. M. Askew of Lauderdale Co., Ala., who came out from the Missionary Baptist church and united with us upon the one foundation, which you will recollect you had notice sometime since.
>
> Our prayer to God is that the good work may go on and that you may be spared and enabled to go on and still contend for the in its purity.[334]

We believe that R. T. Lanier was the minister who came out of the Baptist during this meeting. We base that belief on T. B. Larimore's addressing Brother Lanier as "Elder Lanier," which in those days was the way ministers were addressed. Larimore wrote:

> Our dear brother, Elder R. T. Lanier, of Comer, Lauderdale County, Ala., was in "the assembly of the saints" on earth the last time on July 24, 1892.[335]

Also, Lanier was a delegate for the New Hope church to the Indian Creek Missionary Baptists Association from 1873 through 1875.[336] Many of the delegates were either ministers, elders, or deacons—as was Lanier from 1873-1875. Lanier was a close friend of Murrell Askew, during the transitional period for Askew. When Askew left the Baptist church, the New Hope Missionary Baptist Church lost 30 members.[337] New Hope and Salem had very close ties and it seems the New Hope Church of Christ may have merged with the Salem Church of Christ. That would be the reason William Comer and R. T. Lanier became leaders in the Salem Church of Christ.

R. W. Officer reported that Murrell Askew and J. R. Bradley were with him at New Hope which was in Eastern Lauderdale County, Alabama. The report was as follows:

> On the 4th Lord's day in April, I met with a congregation of brethren at New Hope Baptist church; we were closed out; a large congregation moved to the grove—we had three added. Bro Askew and Bro. Bradley were there with gospel harness all on. Last Lord's day [May 11th] I met with the brethren at Cedar Plains, in Morgan Co., Ala. One added.[338]

The above report contained the first mention of J. R. in the pages of the *Gospel Advocate*.

J. R. had somehow met Officer and Askew. These two men had both withdrawn from the Baptist church over doctrinal issues and immediately began preaching the New Testament pattern. That was the reason for their problems in the Baptist church—they had begun teaching the Bible and not Baptist doctrine. They became valuable assets in the New Testament church. Maybe J. R. identified with these men since he had been raised as a Baptist himself. Upon leaving Mars Hill, J. R.'s first preaching points were congregations that had transformed from Baptists to New Testament Christianity—such as the New Hope, Union Grove, and Salem congregations in Lauderdale County, Alabama. They had been established sometime after the Civil War. They had been converted to New Testament Christianity by Murrell Askew by the year 1875. When he left the Baptist, he took with him—

Union Grove Baptist Church (now North Carolina Church of Christ), Macedonia Baptist Church (now Macedonia Church of Christ), Salem Baptist Church (which became the mother church for other churches of Christ in the Lexington vicinity), and New Hope.[339]

While J. R. Bradley was at Mars Hill, he began to preach at several mission points in Lauderdale and Colbert counties, Alabama, and Lawrence and Giles counties, Tennessee. By 1880 he was preaching regularly at Salem, as well as other points in that vicinity. On July 14, 1880, Bradley wrote:

> Last Friday before starting to my appointment at Salem, Ala., I baptized an old gentleman, who according to his own statement is about 83 years of age. Went on to my appointment at Salem where I preached Saturday and Sunday and on Sunday, baptized five persons.[340]

Brother Wm. Comer, Comer, Ala., wrote the following report, in which he gave a good insight into the congregation at Salem:

> I can inform you that Bros. J. R Bradley, W. B. McQuiddy commenced a protracted meeting at Salem church, Lauderdale county. Ala., Saturday before the 2nd Lord's day of this month and continued up to Wednesday following with eight accessions, two from the C. P. Church. The balance from the world, all by confession and baptism. Bro. J. R. Bradley left on Lord's day evening, leaving Bro. Mc. to do the balance of the work, and well did he do it. I do not think I ever heard the gospel in its purity made any plainer. I never saw the young brother before that I know of but was made happy in making his acquaintance and am satisfied that if he still persists in the advocacy of the unadulterated word of the Lord that he will make his mark in the reformation, and we pray the blessing of God may rest upon him wherever his lot may be cast. Dear brethren, our Master's

cause is onward and upward in our vicinity. We have accessions regularly, have had several since our protracted meeting, a little over twelve months back when there were about twenty- five added; we have one-hundred and twenty-five members in our church. We have a good Bible class and meet nearly every Lord's day, investigate and partake of the emblems and are trying to advance God's cause. Our Prayer is that you may be spared long to wield your pen and influence in the glorious work.[341]

A few months later J. R. and his wife Mary moved to Comer, near Salem to better serve the church in that place. The *Gospel Advocate* reported: "Bro. J. R. Bradley's address is changed from St. Joseph, Tenn., to Comer, Ala."[342]

J. R.'s first report on Salem, after moving from Tennessee to Alabama was written as a report on his monthly preaching schedule, which included Salem:

> I have preached every Saturday and Sunday, except for two appointments, which were disappointed on account of sickness and high water. I preached the first Sunday in the month for our home congregation, at Salem, Ala. The brethren here are doing moderately good work in the vineyard of the Lord. We have a few good old faithful brethren here who are determined to do the work ....[343]

A little girl by the name of Elizabeth Lanier wrote Uncle Minor Metcalfe in the *Gospel Advocate* and gave an insight into the work at Salem. Her note was as follows:

> Dear Uncle Minor: I am a little girl, thirteen years old. My father takes the ADVOCATE, and I love to read your good letters. I am glad to say that a Bible Class was organized last Sunday at Salem. I went to church today. Bro. Turner preached. But I will close, as this is my first attempt to write. Elizabeth Lanier, Comer, Ala.[344]

Elizabeth's letter stated that a Sunday had just been organized at Salem. That would have been before April 30, 1884. This information had not been mentioned anywhere else. Later that year Dr. N. B. Wallace came and preached. He gave no results. He did, however, announce his intentions and he always kept his appointments, except when he was sick.

He reported:

> Bro. N. B. Wallace. from Athens, Ala., writes: I think the prospect is somewhat better than formerly in North Alabama, for the gospel plea. Bro. Weatherford and I have too large a field, though working constantly, we cannot do enough preaching; we get a fine hearing everywhere we can attend; we very seldom have the pleasure of being together for the lack of time, each having more than he can do. I will be off (Lord willing) for Salem, Lauderdale County, in the morning, (Saturday.)[345]

The next report came from R. T. Lanier, of Comer, Alabama, who had been a member of the New Hope Baptist Church and was converted by Askew. It reads:

> Bro. R. T. Lanier, of Comer, Ala., writes: We have had four additions at Salem this year. Three by confession and baptism, and one from the Baptists. We have no regular preacher; but we meet on Lord's day — break bread, the symbolic loaf in remembrance of our Savior.[346]

A year later N. B. Wallace from Athens came, preached, and gave a dismal report on the spiritual condition at Salem:

> Bro. J. T. Wood preached some splendid discourses for us last week, with four additions. I preached several discourses this week at Salem, Lauderdale county; the cause is about dead at that place. The cause, I suppose, is too much brandy and loving money too well. The case is now a chronic one. The prospects

are good everywhere else and have been for some time past. I see no prospect for a near reaction in their case. What a deplorable state of things. Still there are a few brethren there making some feeble efforts to live, and God grant that they may be aroused from their lethargy before it is too late. A great many professed Christians seem never to have learned that their own spiritual growth and development depend upon what they in this direction do for others. N. B. Wallace.[347]

William Comer had grown old and feeble. That, perhaps, was the reason Salem had fallen into such deplorable condition by the time Wallace had come and preached. Comer had been the rock in this congregation. He wrote of his sad condition:

Wm. Comer writes: "Dear brethren, through the mercies of our Heavenly Father, I am yet spared, although in a helpless condition, being old and infirm and a confirmed cripple and my eyesight growing very dim. I feel desirous for the welfare of our master's cause, therefore bid you God-speed in your paper, the Gospel Advocate, and the course you are pursuing. I am now over seventy-five years of age and have been a reader of the Advocate for over twenty years."[348]

Brother William Comer, who had been so vital in the work at Salem, died in October of 1889. He had been incapacitated for some time, as was stated above. We give his obituary in full:

The subject of this sketch was born in Union District, South Carolina. Was married to Miss Marv P. Williams, Feb. 7, 1832. Obeyed the gospel in Lawrence County, Tenn., in 1851, under the preaching of elder Wade Barret. Died Oct. 18, '89, aged seventy-seven years, and twenty-one days. Bro. Comer's wife preceded him to the Christian home in glory in 1882. Bro. C. has eleven children, fifty grand-children and sixty great grand-children.

He died at his son-in-law's Elder Jas Rogers, Limestone County, Ala. Our dear brother requested the writer several months before his death to go with him to his burying and write his obituary if I should outlive him. Mainly through the labor of Bro. C. the church of Christ at Salem, Lauderdale County, Ala., was started. Now a large church meets there. Bro. C. said when trying to establish the church at Salem, he wanted to live to see it built up; after it was on firm ground, he said: "now I want to live to see it live." He was a great lover of the Advocate and was a reader of it for many years. It was a great instrument in his hands in building up the cause at Salem. Let us all prepare to meet our dear brother in the sweet by and by, beyond the sunset radiant glow. This is the prayer of your brother in Christ. T. L. Weatherford.[349]

The following year Lanier sent another report on the work at Salem. Prospects, at least temporarily, were looking up, according to this brief report:

I wish to report on a meeting held at Salem by Bro. T. L. Weatherford, commencing on the second Lord's day in August and continued four days. The result was eleven added to the congregation, ten by confession and baptism and one from the Missionary Baptists. One of the ten baptized was a very old lady, she is in her 77th year. The congregation at Salem is revived and strengthened. I believe we would have had more additions if Bro. Weatherford could have remained with us a few days longer. Comer, Sept. 2, '90. R. T. Lanier.[350]

Upon Lanier's death almost two years later Larimore wrote of a terrible accident that took Brother Lanier's life. The accident occurred while he was still in the churchyard:

Our dear brother, Elder R. T. Lanier, of Comer, Lauderdale County, Ala., was in "the assembly of the saints" on earth the last time on July 24, 1892. The work and worship of the morning being ended, he was just starting home, when he was kicked by a horse, which proved fatal in a little less than thirty hours. Brother Lanier was born June 25, 1816 and passed to the other shore July 25, 1892. Many of his later years were spent in the love and service of the Lord. He was a useful, faithful Christian-true to God and man. T. B. Larimore.[351]

Within a three-year period, Salem lost both spiritual giants in the work at that place— Comer and Lanier. Both men's bodies rest within a few feet of each other, in the Barnett Cemetery, near Lexington, Alabama.

Lanier's obituary was one of the last entries into the *Gospel Advocate*, relating to the church at Salem. John T. Underwood gave a report on a meeting in September of 1893:

> Atlas, Oct. 4.: I preached five days at Salem, Lauderdale county, Ala., commencing the fourth Lord's day in July, with eight added to the one body.[352]

Following the deaths of Comer and Lanier, the congregation fell into a sharp decline. William M. Behel came in the last week of September and preached through the first week of October 1902 and baptized eleven and had one to be restored. He returned in August 1903 and baptized four. He returned in 1905 and baptized one person. In 1912 he held a week-long meeting and baptized three more.[353] This was William Behel's last entry concerning the work at Salem.

The last meeting that can be documented was held by J. T. Harris, who came and held a meeting in 1914. The report was hopeful of better days:

> Florence, Ala., July 17.-I began a meeting at Salem, near Lexington, Ala., on July 8, and preached twice each day for eight days, with large congregations at all the services. Nineteen were

baptized, three restored, and one from the Baptists. J. T. Harris. [354]

This was the last report in the *Gospel Advocate* about the work at Salem. By 1940 it had disbanded.

This brings us to our ending date of 1914 for this study. One can see the importance of the events that surrounded Murrell Askew's work. It is still lasting directly in two good country congregations in Lauderdale County and perhaps indirectly in another one. We feel compelled to give the last bit of information on the Salem—New Hope work.

Gilbert Kretzer, Jr. was born in 1920 and his first exposure to religion was at Old Salem. Gilbert said when as young teenagers he and his brothers conducted the services because they were the only male members there at Salem. This would have been in the late 1930s. The few left at Salem moved their membership to the Lock's Cross Roads congregation which had begun in 1940. Gilbert preached there for some time, and a brother of his who was about fourteen years old preached there some.

The old building at Salem was left vacant and when Center Star congregation built a house of worship in 1936, they needed benches. The benches were removed to Center Star by Melvin Campbell and Luther Parker.[355] Thus ends a work that had been so vital to the Lexington area churches of Christ.

Woodland Springs

In 1921 C. E. Holt wrote about Murrell Askew, the man who established the Woodland Springs work. He gave a very good description of the man and his faith:

> More than forty years ago there lived in Lauderdale County, Ala., a remarkable man. His name was "Murrell Askew." He was a Baptist preacher of extraordinary ability. He was for many years pastor of a large and influential church called "Macedonia," about sixteen miles from Florence. He saw, as very few men have more clearly seen, the evils of divisions among God's people. He preached the gospel as he found it written in the New Testament. This produced dissatisfaction among some of his preaching brethren.[356]

Askew was living at Woodland Springs while preaching at Macedonia. He also preached for some other locations. Holt was an admirer of Askew and his courage. When Murrell Askew traveled through Gravelly Springs from Savannah, Tennessee in 1880, he was on his way home at Woodland Springs.[357] He had moved to the Woodland Springs community sometime after 1875. Woodland Springs was located about ten or twelve miles downriver from Florence. At that time, it was part of the Colbert's Reserve. Very little information exists on the congregation at Woodland Springs. The first reference to it was made in July 1880, by Robert Wallace Officer, although he never called Askew's home Woodland Springs. Enough references later would confirm that Askew lived at Woodland Springs. R. W. Officer wrote:

> I spent most of my time with Bro. M. Askew, preaching at night at his house: Returned to Mars' Hill, Lord's day and preached for the brethren in the morning; one young man came forward and made the good confession, and went with me to Bro. Askew's 10 miles below on the Tennessee River where I preached at 7 o'clock Lord's day evening, where 7 others confessed the Lord Jesus. All were buried with the Lord, filled the grave that Jesus left empty, and arose by faith in the promise. [358]

There was no church house at Woodland Springs at the time Askew moved to Indian Territory (Oklahoma Territory) to work with R. W. Officer among the Indians. Askew had established a house church in his home. The membership grew large enough that by the time Askew moved west a meeting house was in the plans to be built. Askew had moved his family to Indian Territory by June 1881.[359]

A little more than nine years after Askew moved away from Woodland Springs a meeting was conducted by R. W. Norwood and R. M. Clark. Nora E., only daughter of James L. and Mary Davidson was born Dec. 1, 1868, near Mars Hill, Ala., where she received her earliest school training and spiritual instruction. In July 1885, she "obeyed the gospel," at Woodland, Ala., under the labors of R. W. Norwood and R. M. Clark.[360]

The next year Larimore came to Woodland Springs and preached. He wrote a short note about his visit:

While "resting up" for my St. Louis work, I am to deliver three discourses a day at Woodland, in Colbert's Reserve, twelve or fifteen miles from Mars' Hill, by way of recreation. We have some good people there, there is some good material, and I hope we may have a good meeting.[361]

John T. Underwood, a Mars Hill boy was preaching for Woodland when Larimore came. We learn this from the list of Mars Hill boys who came to the Mars Hill Reunion in 1891.[362]

John Hayes of Athens, Alabama came to Woodland with W. H. Gresham and held a gospel meeting. Hayes wrote of the meeting:

From there we went to Gravelly Springs (probably Macedonia, as there was no congregation at Gravelly Springs and Macedonia was nearby), and began the third Lord's day in July, and closed Friday following with four additions. From there, brother Hayes went to Woodland and with Bro. Grissom (Gresham) run a meeting till Wednesday following with three additions, one by obedience and two restored.[363]

Two years later an obituary was printed in the *Gospel Advocate* for one of the Woodland members by Larimore's brother-in-law —J. C. Ott:

Brother John B. Walker, of Woodland congregation, fell asleep in Jesus on March 2, 1894, at the age of 55 years. He leaves one brother (A. J. Walker), a wife, three children, and many brethren and friends to mourn his departure. Brother Walker was a man of firm character, unswerving integrity, and a devoted Christian. For eighteen years he was a faithful follower of the meek and lowly Lamb of God, and always trusted In the word to guide him. "Blessed are the dead which die in the Lord." "He that soweth to the Spirit shall of the Spirit reap life everlasting." J. C. Ott. Florence, Ala.[364]

In 1898 one of Murrell Askew's grandsons came to Woodland and held a meeting. What he found was not a pretty sight. Members had all but abandoned their service to the Lord. He wrote of the pitiable conditions:

> Willis, September 26. —I have not formerly reported my works and labors through the columns of the Gospel Advocate, yet I will give a brief report of my meetings since leaving Nashville, Tenn. Leaving Nashville sometime in May, I went to Alabama, where I held two very good meetings. One was held at Woodland. We had five additions to the one body. Here we found a few brethren and sisters "scattered abroad," who were not doing their duty to God, in that they failed to meet on Lord's day, as commanded. (Acts 20; 7.) They promised to do better. My next meeting was at Rhodesville, preaching only at night, and closing with thirteen additions, thus making a congregation of about thirty-five, who promised to keep house for the Lord. While there, I made many warm friends, among whom were Brother and Sister Sharp. They are true and tried soldiers of the cross and know how to welcome a preacher to their home. Having, then, other appointments in my native country, I took passage for my home in the Indian Territory.[365]

It appears that J. B. Askew may have come back to visit relatives and maybe to see his place of nativity. He was just a child when his large family left this community and moved to Oklahoma—formerly Indian Territory. He also mentions a meeting at Rhodesville, which is five or six miles from Woodland. There is no record of a congregation at Rhodesville; but a couple of miles east of there was the Sherrod's Valley congregation, which later relocated into Oakland. Perhaps that was the one for which Askew preached. This report was the last report to be found in the journals.

There was, however, a personal interview this writer had with a Mr. Peden, who lived in the old store and post office building at

Woodland. As a matter of fact, Mr. Peden was the only one living at Woodland Springs in 1976, when this interview took place. He showed us the spot where the church building once stood and why the building fell into disuse. He related how at some time after World War I the church building was abandoned because a Black man was shot with a mortal wound by someone in the community and he escaped to the church building. He crawled under the floor and died. After this incident, the few church members never went back in the building to worship. Some years later the abandoned building collapsed and rotted. A few rusty nails buried in the ground are all that remains of the Woodland Springs church building. Perhaps what J. B. Askew observed was a view of what was to come. The members became complacent and eventually lost their faith and stopped serving the Lord. It became easy to imagine that the church house was haunted and abandoned the building and the Lord's work at Woodland Springs.

Brush Creek—Beech Grove—Killen

Pertaining to the church in Killen, Benson observes:

> J. T. Harris conducted a tent meeting at Killen in 1911, and as a result a congregation was established there. A frame building in which to meet, about two miles off the main highway, was erected one year later. However, in 1920 a new house of worship was built about two blocks off the highway.[366]

However, while Harris did hold a meeting for the congregation in 1911 that meeting did not establish the church at that place. For the beginning of the church at Brush Creek, we must travel back to the summer of 1880, when a student from Mars Hill College came and preached on Brush Creek. We shall let that student—J. R. Bradley—tell his version of how the work began:

> J. R. Bradley writes under the date of July 14th: Last Friday before starting my appointment at Salem, Ala., I baptized an old gentleman, who according to his own statement, is about 83 years of age. Went on to my appointment at Salem where I preached Saturday and Sunday and on Sunday baptized five persons. Went from there to my uncle's [house] on the

Tennessee River, preached there Sunday evening-went from there to Brush Creek, Ala., and being compelled by the "Methodists had to go to the grove. This Brush Creek church was built by all for a free house.[367]

A few weeks later Bradley followed up with a brief report:

J. R. Bradley and M. A. Beal had twelve additions at Brush Creek, Ala., a week or two since.[368]

This time Bradley took his fellow student and close friend—M. A. Beal with him to direct the singing. Beal was referred to as a sweet singer. He was frail and died soon after graduating from Mars Hill.

A year later Brother G. C. Thigpen, an elder at the Union Grove congregation (later North Carolina), sent a report to the *Gospel Advocate* concerning a meeting at the same place on Brush Creek:

The brethren at Brush Creek, (a Methodist house) have just closed an interesting meeting of five days: resulting in five additions, four by confession and baptism, and one from the Baptists. Bro. J. R. Bradley did the preaching and did it well. During the five days he preached nine sermons and left the people of this vicinity without excuse. Twelve months ago, sectarianism locked the very door against the very man (Bro. B.) which has been so kindly thrown open during this meeting. And let me say, that the people of this community have the thanks and prayers of the brethren for their hospitality. He shunned not to declare all the counsel of God and did it in so mild and kind a way that none took offense: but all could see the truth. Sectarianism is strong here, though not so rank as it was one year ago G. C. Thigpen, Comer, Ala.[369]

In this meeting, it appears that things were getting on good footing on Brush Creek. This little struggling group endured hardships in the beech grove on Brush Creek road for many years. John D. Cox, who was born in 1907, grew up in this congregation. He wrote of their little meeting place:

> My earliest memory of attending a "big meeting" is that of a series of "open air" services under the stately poplars and spreading beech trees on the lot where stood the little white church building known as Beech Grove. On the other side of the meeting house a rippling brook rushed on its way to Brush Creek just across the road.[370]

During the summers, in fair weather, the congregation held services under a brush arbor. During bad weather, they would meet in the union house (claimed by the Methodists). Remember that Bradley said that the building had been built "by all for a free house." The congregation was disorganized for several years and did not meet on a regular basis. They would meet when a preacher would come and hold a meeting. During one of these meetings, E. C. Fuqua came to Brush Creek and held a meeting. This would have been before the Fall of 1906 because Fuqua had moved to Georgia to work by that time.[371] Fuqua remained in the Georgia work until he moved to Colorado by November 1908.[372]

Willis Lucius Cox and his wife, the parents of John D. Cox, were baptized into Christ during Fuqua's meeting on Brush Creek.[373] The baptizing place was just below the Shoal Creek bridge before Wilson Dam was completed and formed Wilson Lake.[374]

The little band had grown indifferent and accomplished but very little. Then came J. T. Harris. He gave a very good account of his 1911 meeting and spoke of the disorganized situation on Brush Creek:

Brother J. T. Harris writes: "On September 6, I closed a very interesting tent meeting at a point about two miles north of Killen, Lauderdale County, Ala. The Interest was good from the very start. It was estimated that the audiences at night numbered from five hundred to seven hundred. Twenty-eight were baptized. One united with us from the Methodists, and about ten were restored, making about forty additions in all. I found several brethren in the neighborhood who had not met for worship for many years; and these, with the ones who obeyed the gospel during the meeting, about fifty in all, agreed that they would go to meeting and keep house for the Lord. They will use the tent till they can build a house, which they hope to have done by cold weather. I do not think I ever saw more interest manifested in a meeting."[375]

Harris said the congregation would meet in the tent until they could build a house of worship. He also pictured the disorganization of the Brush Creek congregation. They were a church and had been since Bradley's meetings; but had stopped, at some point, meeting regularly. Harris helped reorganize them into a properly organized congregation. This meeting rekindled the fire they had in the beginning. Harris returned and held a tent meeting in 1912.[376] He would return for a Sunday meeting in 1915.[377] By 1913 John T. Underwood was preaching on regular appointments for Beech Grove. In August he reported six baptisms on one of his visits.[378] In 1914 he sent another report on one of his visits to Beach Creek:

> John T. Underwood reports nine additions, including four baptisms, at Brush Creek, near Florence, Ala., at a regular appointment. Five were restored.[379]

J. T. Harris continued to come and conduct meetings for many years at Beech Grove. Even though this last report is well beyond our time frame of 1914 we are compelled to insert it. It reads as follows:

> J. T. Harris writes from Lawrenceburg, Tenn., March 15: "Last Lord's day I filled my regular appointment at Beech Grove, near Killen, Ala., and baptized a very intelligent young married lady." [380]

In this report, we see that the congregation was still meeting at Beech Grove. John D. Cox gave a vivid picture of the way classes were conducted in his early childhood:

> Five classes assembled in the small meeting house at Beech Grove. There were no classrooms. I have a vivid memory of the "card class." Impressions for good were permanently stamped upon my tender heart as a child. I shall be eternally grateful to the godly women who taught me in this class although I cannot recall the names of all of them. Occasionally the teacher would reward us for "perfect attendance" or memory work by giving us a small New Testament or an attractive little book containing a Bible story or some story emphasizing a moral. I received a booklet about Daniel in the den of lions. I read it over and over until its pages were loose and the beautifully colored backs fell off. This experience has kept the "arguments" of those who contend that it is wrong to reward children for attendance at a Bible Class or for completing a special assignment in memory work, etc. from impressing me. So long as the award is appropriate to the achievement, it may influence the child for good for years to come.[381]

It will be noticed that even though the building was small there were five different classes conducted in the building. Cox wrote of the transition to the town of Killen:

As time passed, it became obvious that a congregation was needed in the community of Killen. This was becoming the "population center" for that section of the county. Most of the members of the Beech Grove congregation lived in Killen. This seemed to make it practical to move the meeting place from Beech Grove to Killen. Some who lived nearer to Beech Grove were displeased; others preferred to keep the church there for "sentiment's sake." But the good of the cause of Christ as a whole, in that area was considered and the decision was reached to sell the little Beech Grove meeting house and erect a building in Killen. A few of those who lived in the Brush Creek community found it convenient to begin worshipping at Lone Cedar, a few miles away.

My father gave a beautiful lot to the church and furnished much of the lumber from his forest. Soon a neat, white building was completed. But no classrooms were provided in the new building. Several classes still had to meet in the auditorium. The confusion of voices and the din of noise caused by so many classes being "taught" at one time made the words that were spoken by the various teachers sound like scrambled eggs look!
[382]

This is our final look at the Brush Creek—Beech Grove—Killen work.

Our beloved friend and brother in Christ, Major William Robert Dean had been working on a congregational history of the Killen congregation. We had been looking forward to its completion; but unfortunately, he was called to be with our Lord on May 26, 2022, before finishing it. Maybe someone will take up where he left off his work and complete it.

Sherrod Valley— Oakland Work

Oakland church of Christ originated in the early 1900s. Sherrod Valley Church of Christ was its original name. The meeting place was Sherrod Valley School, a public school that allowed the church to meet there. We have information that in 1901 there was an all-day singing at the Church of Christ and in 1923 or 1924 Percy Wright, Jr., at age five, led singing at the Church of Christ. On September 11, 1928, Percy Wright Sr. and B. L. Johnson bought the Sherrod Valley building and two acres of land for $250.00. This building became the meeting place for Sherrod Valley Church of Christ. A preacher was only available one or two Sundays a month so on the other Sundays the Lord's Supper was observed and classes were held. In 1952 a new building was built about three miles east of the Sherrod Valley building and the name was changed to Oakland Church of Christ. The land was donated by T. A. Smith. Oakland meets there today. An addition of four classrooms was added about 10–12 years later and a fellowship addition was completed in 2010. Adjoining land was purchased that same year.

We realize we have deviated from our timetable ending at the end of 1914, but was necessary to include this work as its beginning was before 1914. Not much material has been found for the first thirty years of its existence.[383]

THE CHURCH IN THE CITY OF FLORENCE

Early Efforts in Florence

In the earliest days of the Restoration Movement, Ephraim D. Moore and James E. Matthews preached in the vicinity of Florence, Alabama; but no reports were sent addressing any kind of work in Florence proper. We can only speculate that neither of the men ever preached in Florence.

Tolbert Fanning had made a visit in 1842, while on his way to Columbus, Mississippi. He preached in the Methodist meeting house with no visible results. He only gave a short reference to it in Campbell's *Millennial Harbinger*:

> Before reaching this place [Russellville, Alabama], I called at Florence, in Lauderdale county, Ala., and addressed large assembly in the Methodist meetinghouse twice.[384]

Following this report, it would be two more years before any effort to preach in Florence would be mentioned in any journal.

James Matthew Hackworth sent a report on the three viable works in Lauderdale County in August of 1844. In the latter section of his report, he made an appeal to Fanning to come to Florence for a meeting. He wrote:

> At Bluff Creek, (a place with which you are well acquainted,) there are about 18 or 20 excellent and intelligent Brethren, (not organized.) We have added to the good cause since last fall, at different points, about 25. We direct all our efforts, not at the animal, but at the intellectual powers of man. We are not fond of Brethren created in a storm. If we could compensate your labors, we would be pleased to have them for a time at Florence and Bluff Creek, this summer. The Review is a good work, may it prosper. Yours in hope, James M. Hackworth.[385]

Fanning had published his intended stop-over in Florence in his *Christian Review*. It was in answer to Hackworth's letter:

> Note— "The Lord willing and I live," I expect to be in Florence, Ala., on Saturday, November 2d., 1844, and remain over Lord's day. Will the friends procure a place for the meeting and let it be known? Besides preaching the Gospel, I expect to present the objects of "Franklin College." As I cannot visit Bluff Creek, I hope the Brethren will meet me in Florence. T. Fanning.[386]

In October of 1844 Tolbert Fanning began a tour southward from Nashville, which included his old childhood neighborhood of Northwest Alabama. His report is the second mention of any preaching in Florence, as he had been there and preached two years prior. The report read as follows:

> Friday, November 1, 1844, we journeyed to the neighborhood, of Florence, in Lawrence (Lauderdale) county, Ala., and spent the night with our faithful friends in the family of Jno. Chisholm, Esq.
>
> Saturday, Nov. 2d, we reached Florence, where we met our brethren, Ligon, McDonald, Dunn, Hackworth, Young, Hous-

ton, and many others of our brethren and old acquaintances. The Methodists were kind enough to open their house of worship, and we addressed the citizens for three days, on the first principles of Christianity. The men of. the world listened attentively, though few partisans were inclined to know the truth. There was much prejudice against the church of God, mainly from the influence of the party preachers and the unbecoming conduct of false friends. One manoeuvre I can but mention: From various circumstances, it was obvious the members of the Presbyterian church were either forbidden by the pastor or had mutually agreed not to attend. They were evidently fearful to trust themselves, in hearing of the truth. But a Rev. gentleman, Mr. Slack, D. D., who was supposed to have great learning, and who felt himself well-grounded in his traditional, attended and heard for all the rest, and reported to the timid lambs of Mr. Vancort's flock, as seemed to him best calculated to satisfy them with their sect. I heard one of the members say, "Dr. S. knows all about it"-meaning thereby, that he understood all we teach, and was better capable of judging of the truth than the common people, and his version of the matter was to satisfy all who were not to be trusted to hear for themselves.

A word or two in reference to this course. In the first place, it was not true that the Doctor had investigated the subject of Christianity, and understood our teaching, as was supposed; and in the second place, he acted as no independent man, who knows the truth, will act. We, frequently and respectfully, invited those who had objections, to make them known, and we pledged ourselves to answer them; but this be sternly refused to do, yet he insinuated to his brethren, and other gentlemen in private, that the "doctrine was very bad," even "worse than he had before thought." Thus, it will be seen our opposers are covert, and such as will not show themselves in open day. May the Lord enable us to bear opposition as good soldiers of Jesus Christ!

While at Florence, we had the opportunity of presenting a

great amount of truth, and we doubt not, fruit will be seen in the good world. But one, however, had the nobility to confess the authority. Mr. and Mrs. Jno. Simpson were most kind in their attentions to Mrs. F. and myself.[387]

The John Chisholm family, mentioned above, were members at the Old Cypress meeting house, which was located about two miles due west of the Chisholm homesite. Fanning had known the Chisholms since childhood. It was near this site that Fanning had been converted by the preaching of B. F. Hall baptized by James E. Matthews, in the fall of 1826.

These two reports of Fanning's visits to Florence are the only reports of any preaching in the city of Florence until after the Civil War.

Popular Street

Poplar Street

The first efforts to establish a congregation within the boundaries of Florence began as early as 1880. T. B. Larimore's school provided young preachers to preach in the area around Mars Hill College. Some of them came to Florence and attempted to establish a congregation. The very first bona fide attempt was not made by Larimore, but instead, by one of his teachers—E. A. Elam. Elam wrote of his work in Florence:

> Dear Bro. J. M. Barnes: I thus address you, for all brethren in the Lord are dear to me. I have heard so much of you and have read so many good pieces from your pen that I love you, though I have never seen you. Therefore, though a young man, I use this familiar address.
>
> My object in writing to you is to send you five dollars for old Bro. Nathan W. Smith. I know you called on the good sisters, for the sufficient amount to buy him a horse, yet I know you will accept this, especially since I send it in the name of some good sisters. They are not aware of it, however, yet I send it in their name. I send it in the name of the sisters, for it was from them

and two brothers that I received it. I would not overlook these two brethren, for they contributed their share to this sum, I think.

From about the first of November 1879, I have preached every Sunday, with few exceptions, for a small congregation, consisting of two brethren and nineteen sisters, in Florence, Ala. I have walked every time a distance of four miles. Last Lord's day I received from them nine dollars with which to hire a horse. I think I can continue to walk, especially since the mud is drying up. Bro. Smith is old and cannot walk to fill his appointments. So, saving four of the nine dollars to have the shoes of my faithful pony exchanged for new ones, I am desirous that Bro. Smith shall have the remainder of it in the names of those who gave it to me.

Our two brothers and most of the sisters (I am indeed sorry that all do not feel the vast importance of attending weekly meetings) constitute a faithful little band of disciples. They have the moral courage to stand out on the "Bible-alone" side in the midst of very strong prejudice. Some of the young sisters have been told by their fashionable friends that they had withdrawn from society and excluded themselves from the world, because they possessed true heroism and firmness enough to choose rather to serve the Lord than to attend balls and other places of fashionable amusements. If they continue, they will not be excluded from the society of heaven... I remain yours in the hope of salvation through Jesus Christ, E. A. Elam.[388]

Srygley, in his *Larimore and His Boys,* described Elam as thus:

E. A. Elam, of Fosterville, Tenn., graduated at Burritt College, and went to Mars' Hill to teach with the determined purpose to preach whenever the opportunity offered. The attendance being too small to require all of his time teaching, arrangements were made for him to spend part of his time studying the Bible to further prepare himself for his chosen work of preaching.

Possessed of a strong intellect, a thorough education, a converted and consecrated heart and a soul abounding in desires for the salvation of all men, he made rapid progress in the study of the Bible and soon began to preach with great ability and remarkable success. He gave up teaching entirely and devoted himself unreservedly to preaching.[389]

Our next glimpse was about Robert Wallace Officer's intention to preach in Florence. Someone published the following in the *Gospel Advocate*:

R. Wallace Officer will be at Temperance Oak, 4th Lord's day in May, and at Mars' Hill College, Ala., and on the 5th, and if a house can be provided in Florence, he will preach there, or anywhere in that part of the county they may direct, from Tuesday till Saturday, at night.[390]

Officer came and gave this report:

Bro. (T. C.) Biles made the good confession, and I baptized him at Mars' Hill. He went to Florence and began preaching in the City Hall. His congregations grew through the week at night... Yours in hope, R. W. Officer, Lewisburg, Tenn., June 7th, 1880. [391]

It seems, that because of the report of having a sick child back at home; Officer never got to preach in Florence on that trip; but in his stead T. C. Biles, the newly converted Methodist preacher went and preached. This was borne out in Officer's report.

T. B. Larimore believed that a congregation in Florence could thrive. He wrote a typical Larimore description of the city of Florence in his own magnanimous way:

Believing Florence, Ala. to be second to no place known to me, as a home for good people among good people, it will afford me great pleasure to render all assistance in my power to all worthy persons seeking a home in this pleasant, prosperous, rapidly growing city, crowning an undulating plateau overlooking the limpid, majestic, matchless Tennessee. T. B. Larimore, Florence, Alabama, April 7, 1887.[392]

With the city being as Larimore believed it to be: why did it take so long to get a permanent work within the city? We do not know the answer to this burning question.

The *Florence Gazette* carried, possibly, the first reference to Larimore's preaching in the city of Florence. It reported that Larimore was to preach in the public schoolhouse at 11:00 am. Page 3 of the *Gazette* was dedicated to local events and especially religious notes. It reported:

> Reverend T. B. Larimore on last Sunday morning preached — as he always does — an excellent sermon at the public schoolhouse to a large and highly pleased congregation.[393]

The congregation met wherever it could secure a meeting place. They even met in private houses when no other place could be found. They met in Mrs. Susan Thrasher's residence for a while as is born out in a report about her intentions of moving and her residence was for sale "Intending to move from Florence, I offer my residence on the corner of Court and Tuscaloosa Streets for sale..."[394] Sister Thrasher was a charter member of the congregation in Florence and used her residence for a meeting place until the group grew too large to meet in her house. In June 1886, the *Florence Gazette* reported — "Rev. T. B. Larimore will preach in Morrison Hall tomorrow morning at 10 ½ o'clock."[395] In July, the *Gazette* published:

> Mrs. Susan Thrasher has bought part of the lot of Mr. James W. Jordan on Tuscaloosa Street and presented it to the Christian denomination who will soon erect a church thereon.[396]

In November it was announced that plans were being made to build the house of worship. The *Gospel Advocate* published the following:

> We are glad to be able to announce with certainty that a house of worship will soon be built in our town, by the Christian denomination. The vacant lot of Mrs. Susan Y. Thrasher —on the corner of Seminary and Tuscaloosa streets, has been bought for that purpose, the church is to be built, fronting, on Seminary. It is the intention to erect a neat, but plain edifice. There are a number of members of this church among our best townspeople; and the number will be increased when a regular house of worship is provided. The book of subscription has been started, with several very liberal contributions; and can be found at the banking house of Messrs. Young & White, by persons who desire to aid on this good cause. Florence Ala., Gazette.[397]

Larimore had sent the above clipping from the *Gazette* to the *Gospel Advocate* stating that the church in Florence to raise their own money in Florence and that there would be no begging other churches for help.

Larimore began to get serious about the work in Florence. We give some information concerning Larimore's preaching in Florence. He was intending to preach at the following Sunday (April 25, 1886) —morning and evening, at Ludike's Hall in Florence.[398] The rent was $4.00 per month.[399] On May 1, 1887, it was reported that Larimore had been conducting a series of meetings that week.[400] As the budding congregation had no regular house of worship; they rented Odd Fellows Hall for the year 1887.[401] The rent was $7.50 per month.[402]

Florence was now the topic of planting a permanent work in the city and Larimore was all set to see that one was established there. The *Gospel Advocate* published an announcement about Larimore and the coming Florence work:

> Bros. T. B. Larimore, and Meeks, of Jackson, Tennessee, a brother of R. P. Meeks, made us a brief but pleasant call one day last week. Bro. Larimore is now working earnestly to firmly establish the cause in Florence, Ala. See his article in reference to building a church house there. He desires to have the church grow up with that fast-growing town. In this week's paper you will see an account of the vast improvements that the Florence Mining, Land & Manufacturing company are making. This company is composed largely of Nashville men, whom we consider good, reliable business men.[403]

The above report stated Larimore's intentions to the establish a permanent work in the city of Florence. His plan coincided with the planned growth of the city. Once the brethren knew Larimore was going to be involved with the establishing a congregation in Florence, they fell in line with him.

The *Florence Herald* published an article about the soon to be Poplar Street church building and it was republished in the *Gospel Advocate* in the following words:

> The members of the Christian church are having plans drawn up for a new church building, which will be quite an ornament to the city. The building will be of brick, with stone foundations and is handsomely designed. A tower on the left will be one hundred feet high and will add much to the appearance of the building. The main building is 84x50 feet, with an audience room 50x50 feet. In the rear of the rostrum, there are two dressing rooms, a study and a baptistry. The church will be built on Tombigbee and Poplar streets. Active work will be begun inside of one month. The work will probably be contracted. Mr. F. L. Rosseau, the architect, designed the building.[404]

It took only three years for Larimore's dream of having a permanent work in Florence to become reality. That took many hours of teaching the word and many honest souls that wanted to be part of heaven's population someday.

By May the building was still being finished. G. A. Reynolds, who would become the first elder at Poplar Street, was also a gospel preacher. He visited the office of the *Gospel Advocate* and Lipscomb gave the following comment:

> Bro. G. A. Reynolds, of Florence, Ala., enlivened us with his presence one day last week. He reports the cause moving steadily forward at Florence and hopes that they will have their new house of worship done by the first of July. He thinks now would be an excellent time to make an effort to firmly establish the ancient gospel at Tuscumbia. He had one addition there at his last appointment.[405]

Reynolds expressed the expectations of the members in Florence. Having their own place of worship was about to be realized. This article also gave a glimpse of the infant work in Tuscumbia, Alabama.

In September, the *Florence Times* reported that the house was finished by September 27, 1890, because an article appeared in the *Florence Herald*, stating that the building was completed.[406] It was reported as completed by Larimore in a private letter to Lipscomb. The good news was revealed:

> In a private letter just to hand our beloved brother, T. B. Larimore, says: "Florence, Ala., house finished. 'They say' it is the largest and the best house in 'the coming city of the South.' However, that may be, it is a very conservative estimate, to say, its 'protracted meeting' seating capacity is 700; its commercial value $7,000; the range of its bell seven miles—that it is, in all respect, good enough for us. Never a dollar raised by any kind of a 'shindig.'"[407]

According to Larimore, at the time of its completion, it was the largest church building in Florence. Its seating capacity and the cost were the talk of the town. Just a few days later Larimore was engaged in a meeting in the new building, as was published in the *Gospel Advocate*:

> By the time this appears in print he (Larimore) will be in the midst of a glorious meeting at Florence, Alabama, and immediately after that meeting closes, he will begin at Dallas, Tex. Thank the Lord for his recovery, brethren, and pray for the success of his meetings.[408]

Larimore had suffered exhaustion and had been recuperating. He so much wanted to preach the first meeting in the new building, that he risked his fragile health. G. A. Reynolds wrote of the meeting also:

> Our meeting has been going on one week. Sixteen persons have made the good confession, seventeen have united by commendation, making thirty-three in all. The good work will be continued. Bro. Larimore is doing some of the best preaching we have heard from him. Large audiences gather nightly to hear the word of life. We thank the Lord for the good work. G. A. Reynolds. [409]

About one year later Larimore made a sad report about a young lady who was the first in three things in the new building. Larimore gave the details:

> A request has just reached me from our bereaved brother and sister McPeters, of Florence, Ala., to write, for the Advocate, a notice of the death of their devoted daughter—our dear sister—Lula. She was the first to make the good confession, the first to be baptized and the first to wear a shroud, in our new church-house in Florence, where the latter years of her brief life were spent. Our dear, departed sister was born, Jan. 10, 1873. On

Oct. 7,' 90, she made the good confession; on Oct. 8,' 90, she was baptized; on Oct. 9,' 91, she ceased to breathe the breath of life; on Oct. 10,' 91, she was buried in the beautiful Florence cemetery... T. B. Larimore.[410]

A little less than a year another young life departed from the congregation. She was the daughter of a prominent family at Poplar Street. She was the daughter of J. B. White, one of the deacons at Poplar Street. Larimore wrote:

> Miss Lula McPeters was the first to make "the good confession," and the first to be baptized, in our new Florence (Ala.) church house; and the first to ascend from the Florence flock to "the upper fold'" after that house-the house in which she was "born again" and from which she was buried, was built. Miss Irma White was second in all these solemn scenes and important events. Who, next? None on earth can tell. Let. us, therefore, all be ready, "every day and every hour:" for We "know neither the day nor the hour" when we shall be called hence... T. B. Larimore.[411]

There was a string of deaths of the A. P. Holtsford family in about three- and one-half years. It began with the death of A. P. and M. B. Holtsford's infant son John Henry, who died in March 1893.[412] Then his sister-in-law America, wife of Hiram S. Holtsford, died in December 1893.[413] Then July 6, 1896, his baby boy —Earl Roy died.[414]

Larimore held a meeting in September 1894 that lasted for ten days. By the second day, he had already baptized three persons.[415] In March 1896 he held a meeting at Poplar Street which was to last until interest ran out.[416] This was typical of Larimore. He usually held at least one meeting there; and sometimes two meetings in one year. The work at Poplar Street was on a firm foundation in Florence. Larimore's protégée, Fletcher Douglas Srygley came and held a meeting that began on the third Sunday of October 1898.[417] Srygley wrote of the meeting:

> I spent the last two weeks of October in a meeting at Florence, Ala. The audiences were small in daytime, except Sundays, but fairly good on Sundays and at night. The auditorium in which the meetings were held will seat from four hundred to five hundred people, and on the second Sunday night of the meeting it was full. The attention was all that a speaker could wish, but the results were unsatisfactory in number of additions. Only one person was baptized. Florence has been a "boom town," and religion has been on a "boom" basis. While the town was on a "boom," people neglected the details of practical business in efforts to promote the growth of the city and get rich fast and easy by speculative schemes on an inflated basis; but when the "boom" collapsed, every man settled down to practical, conservative methods and gave strict attention to the details of his daily business. On that basis the people have prospered, and, as a result, the city has had a steady and healthful growth. On a "boom" basis in religion Christians try to build up the church and do great things. In such efforts they sometimes forget and often neglect the simple individual duties of practical Christianity in daily life. The church does not prosper, because Christians do not grow in grace and in the knowledge of our Lord and Savior Jesus Christ on such a basis. If Christians will attend strictly to their individual duties in daily life and each do his part personally in religious work and worship, the church will grow and prosper as a result of such religious worship and service. What is needed in Florence and everywhere else to promote the growth and prosperity of the church is the development of Christian character in each member of the church by faithful performance of individual duty. I tried to make this clear in a series of sermons addressed especially to Christians, but how far I succeeded remains to be seen. Brother A. P. Holtsford, with whom I made my home, is a faithful preacher, whom I have

known for twenty years. He is also a good carpenter and a reliable contractor. He has done a good work for the Lord in Florence and has also preached extensively in other parts of Alabama and in contiguous States. As a carpenter and a contractor, he has the confidence of the people, and he has built many good houses in the city. Brother Ed. Fuqua, a young preacher from Tennessee, recently moved to Florence and he will be a valuable addition to the Christian forces in that city and contiguous country. He is also a carpenter, and he proposes to work at his trade and preach as he has opportunity. Brother Matheny also lives in the city, works in the cotton factory, and preaches as he has opportunity. Mars' Hill, the home of T. B. Larimore, is only four miles away, and the high esteem in which he is universally held opens to him a wide field in Florence and contiguous country if he can see his way to cultivate it. Brother Gresham also lives at Mars' Hill and does much preaching in the contiguous country. All these preachers, except Brother Larimore, who was preaching in Missouri, rendered valuable assistance in the meeting. The outlook for New Testament Christianity is not discouraging if every Christian will do his duty. In the town of Florence there are probably one hundred and fifty persons and, in that county, at least one thousand people who have renounced all denominations and determined to be nothing but Christians, belong to nothing but the church, which is the body of Christ, and preach and practice nothing but. what Christians and churches preached and practiced in New Testament times under the leadership of inspired men. F. D. Srygley.[418]

Srygley was disappointed with the meeting, as most preachers would be because he was accustomed to having many responses. He did, however, give a fairly accurate picture of Florence after the "boom" of growth had ended. It shows how spiritual interest had subsided with the economic "boom" came to an end. Not much was reported in the *Gospel Advocate* about the Poplar Street work for the next three years. Interest had shifted more to the East Florence work. This meeting was also reported in the *Florence Times*.[419]

In May 1899 S. R. Hawkins came and held a meeting at Poplar Street. The *Florence Times* gave the following account:

> Evangelist S. R. Hawkins began a meeting at the Christian Church last Sunday (May 14). The interest is growing. Mr. Hawkins comes well recommended.[420]

Later that year T. B. Larimore held his annual meeting at Poplar Street. No notice of this meeting was found in *Gospel Advocate*; however, a report was published in the *Florence Times*. It read:

> Elder T. B. Larimore is conducting a series of meetings in the Christian Church here. The meeting will continue until Sunday night, at least. Remember the preaching by T.B. Larimore at 7:30 every evening and 11:00 and 3:30 also on Sunday.[421]

Nothing else was reported in the *Gospel Advocate* for that year. In 1900 J. J. Castleberry, who had former connections with the missionary society, came to Poplar Street for a meeting. It was reported in the *Florence Times*. He began on October 14, 1900.[422] Nothing of note was reported. In July Castleberry had held a meeting for the East Florence congregation with 115 additions.[423] Apparently, the congregation at Poplar Street thought they might have similar results. Apparently, that was not the case. That meeting was never published in the *Gospel Advocate*.

Castleberry's preaching in Florence brought forth the following letter in the *Gospel Advocate*:

> In the Gospel Advocate of September 6, 1900, I noticed the following sentence in a report of a meeting held by Brother J. J. Castleberry, at Florence, Ala.: "Brother Castleberry is a young

man, but did his work well, contending earnestly for the old apostolic doctrine, without addition or subtraction." While it is far from my intention to detract anything from Brother Castleberry, yet I happen to know that he was employed by the State Board last year, and is yet in full sympathy with it, if not actually engaged by it. I do not know that he is not engaged by it again this year. I write this so that some may know how he stands. Several persons have called my attention to the article and said he was not "sound." It is but fair to us who contend for the faith once delivered to the saints and to the church of Christ that the positions of preachers be known. If you could, it would be well to always state the attitude of preachers on these questions which gender strife. A. P. Johnson, Huntingdon, Tenn.[424]

Castleberry never came back to Florence and preached, after this was published. The seeds were sown and would bring forth fruit fourteen years later.

In 1901 George A. Klingman, an anti-society preacher, came and held his first meeting at Poplar Street. It was first reported in the *Florence Times*:

> Elder George A. Klingman will preach "to men only" in the auditorium next Sunday afternoon at 3:00 o'clock on "Sin and its Consequences."[425]

The *Florence Times* published another note on the 25th. "Reverend Klingman will preach in the auditorium at 3 o'clock on "Infidelity."" The *Florence Times* published another note in the same issue on page 1, concerning the lessons presented by Klingman:

> Reverend Mr. Clingman (Klingman) conducted a delightful men's meeting Sunday afternoon in the YMCA auditorium. A large number of men were present and enjoyed the service, which was conducted in a chaste and more elevating manner.

May the Master send more such men into the field. Next Sunday at 3 o'clock he will again address the men. His subject will be "Infidelity." All men are cordially invited, especially those who have doubts or unsettled convictions about the Divinity.[426]

Klingman wrote a short note on the meeting, and it was published in the *Gospel Advocate*:

Brother George A. Klingman writes from Florence, Ala.: "The meeting here is progressing nicely. There have been six additions up to date, all baptisms. Pray for me, that I may 'preach the word' faithfully and with boldness in love..."[427]

Up until this time Poplar Street had no regular preacher. They had enjoyed the preaching of different preachers such as T. B. Larimore. George A. Reynolds, A. P. Holtsford, and W. H. Gresham, and perhaps from time to time a visitor passing through the area. Then there were the meetings held by out-of-town preachers. J. Paul Slayden was their first full-time minister. He came from Columbia, Tennessee in 1901. The *Florence Times* published this advertisement:

Reverend J. Paul Slayden of Columbia, Tennessee will spend a few days in Florence and will preach in the Christian Church Sunday morning and evening. Members desiring him to locate here should encourage him by their presence.[428]

In February, this note was followed up with a brief statement — "Elder Slayden recently of Columbia, Tennessee, is now in charge of the Christian Church of this place."[429] Slayden remained in Florence until December of 1902.

In 1902 George A. Klingman returned to Florence to hold another meeting. The *Gospel Advocate* reported:

> Brother George A. Klingman is holding a fine meeting at Florence, Ala. At last reports there had been ten additions.[430]

Klingman had by now won the hearts of the people and over the course of the next several years, would return for several more meetings.

The next meeting reported was Larimore's meeting. On December 20 Larimore came home to hold his Christmas season meeting at Poplar Street. On the 21st he began preaching. At the close of the first sermon Dr. Bramlett, a prominent physician, of Florence, Ala., was baptized. The meeting closed on December 28. ...[431]

By the middle of the year the congregation decided to hire Percy Hiram Hooten of Lewisburg, Tennessee as their full-time minister. He was a young minister who came from a family of preachers. His grandfather, John Hooten, had preached in the area in the beginning years of our Restoration Movement in Lauderdale County. The following note appeared in the *Gospel Advocate* in July of 1904:

> We are informed that the labors of Brother P. H. Hooten in Florence, Ala., are very acceptable to the church there. The brethren of Florence have a splendid brick church house, and by continuing in welldoing they will accomplish still greater good. [432]

Within a year Hooten contracted Typhoid fever and died. In early July he was reported as being sick and by the end of the month, he died. John Bose of Florence made the report of his sickness.[433] On the afternoon of July 20, 1905, he died. His death was reported in the *Nashville American* on July 21, 1905. It read:

> Elder Percy H. Hooten, pastor of the Christian Church, died this afternoon. He was thirty-three years of age and a young

minister of great promise. He came to Florence two years ago from Petersburg, Tenn. His ministry has been most successful, and he was universally popular with his congregation and with the townspeople at large. Previous to becoming a minister Mr. Hooten was in the drug business in Nashville, where he was educated. The remains will be shipped to his former home at Lewisburg, Tenn. He leaves a widow (formerly Miss Carney, of Ashland City, Tenn.), and one child.[434]

The *Nashville Banner* reported Hooten's death the same day as the *Nashville American* did. It read:

Elder P. H. Hooten, pastor of the Christian Church, who has been seriously ill for several weeks of typho-malarial fever, died on Wednesday afternoon at three o'clock. Mrs. Hooten, his wife, is seriously ill. Elder Hooten's remains were taken to Lewisburg, Tenn., his former home. for interment to-day.[435]

E. G. Sewell combined both reports and published them in the *Gospel Advocate* with the following words:

We desire to express our most sincere sympathies to the bereaved family of Brother Hooten. Our loss of preachers has certainly been heavy for the last few weeks. Someone will, doubtless, prepare and send to the Gospel Advocate a suitable notice of our departed brother. E.G.S.[436]

Sewell's request for a decent obituary was answered. It came forth from the pen of a future Pulitzer Prize winner—T. S. Stribling of Florence, Alabama. Stribling's obituary on Hooten was published in the *Gospel Advocate*.[437] These various reports of Hooten's death illustrate what an impact Hooten made not only on the brotherhood but the entire south. His death was a great loss to the church at Poplar Street and the church in general.

By the end of December C. E. Holt had been hired as the full-time minister at Poplar Street. Holt would impact the church in Florence, as well as elsewhere. He was a solid and strong preacher. His coming to Florence was published in two short statements a week apart, in the *Gospel Advocate*: "Brother C. E. Holt changes his address from Iron City, Tenn., to Florence, Ala."[438] This report was followed by: "Brother C. E. Holt's address is now at 543 North Cherry street, Florence, Ala."[439] It would be a little more than two months before Holt's first report on the Florence work was published. It was a generic report:

> Brother C. E. Holt writes from Florence, Ala., under date of February 23: "Our work at Florence is moving along very encouragingly. One confession at our regular service on last Sunday."[440]

J. C. McQuiddy visited Poplar Street and gave a report on Holt and the work at Poplar Street. It was published in the *Gospel Advocate*:

> J. C. McQuiddy was in Florence, Ala., last week, and reports the church there as being in a good working condition, and that Brother C. E. Holt's work is much appreciated by the church. [441]

Poplar Street apparently was supporting E. C. Fuqua in establishing some other works, including a work in North Florence. They had supported the establishment of the East Florence work in this manner. The first notice was brief but informative. It read: "Brother E. C. Fuqua's meeting at North Florence, Ala., resulted in three additions."[442]

Holt gave a more detailed account later that month on the Poplar Street work along with Fuqua's work:

> Under date of July 11, Brother C. E. Holt writes from Florence, Ala.: "Our work at Florence moves steadily on.

Audiences are good at every service. We use the literature published by the McQuiddy Printing Company. There is none better. Brother Fuqua is now in a good meeting at Guin, Ala."
[443]

Many reports to the *Gospel Advocate* were made about Holt's work over the next several years. The following report was sent in September:

Brother C. E. Holt began a meeting with the church at Florence, Ala., on Sunday, September 2, which is well attended. When last heard, there had been two additions. At the prayer meeting just before the meeting began there was one addition.[444]

To illustrate the involvement with establishing a permanent work in North Florence we give the following:

Brother C. E. Holt began a mission meeting at Seven Points, North Florence, Ala., on Thursday evening, November 8.[445]

It has already been stated that E. C. Fuqua had been working some, in North Florence and now Holt holds a meeting there. The North Florence work will be discussed in more detail later.

The year 1907 was a promising year. It began with several reports over the next year. The work at Poplar Street, under Holt, was flourishing, as is illustrated by reports such as the following: "Brother C. E. Holt reports two additions to the congregation at Florence, Ala., on Sunday, January 20."[446] Followed up by the second report for the year:

Brother C. E. Holt writes from Florence, Ala., under date of February 4: "At our regular service on grows in attendance, yesterday there was one confession, and one at the service at East Florence. I am now preaching for both congregations. Prospects for good results are encouraging."[447]

And by the end of February, another report came forth:

> Brother C. E. Holt baptized three persons at Florence, Ala., recently. The work there seems to be in quite a prosperous condition.[448]

The additions kept coming and Holt kept reporting. One was reported as occurring in March and one in early May.[449]

In June W. D. Campbell held a meeting for the entire month. The report stated:

> After having continued over four Lord's days, Brother W. D. Campbell's meeting with the congregation at Florence, Ala., closed with sixteen additions. The brethren were delighted with Brother Campbell's work.[450]

During July Holt held an extended meeting at East Florence. Poplar Street continued to be very supportive of the work in East Florence.

We should show the work of individuals at Poplar Street. The report below will illustrate this very clearly. A letter from C. M. Southhall, an elder in the congregation and owner of a very successful drugstore, states:

> Florence, Ala., September 21, 1907.-Dear Brother Elam: Having sent you one hundred dollars for the school, I felt that I had done my part. After seeing Brother Slater's proposition to be one of a hundred brethren to raise ten thousand dollars and realizing the difficulty of interesting that number to that extent and also the vast good that such would doubtless accomplish, I will joyfully give another hundred, if it be necessary, to raise the amount. I am praying for success. C. M. Southall.[451]

This shows the willingness of people who have the means to support many good works, such as the school in Nashville. Others did their part as their talents allowed. Holt illustrates this in an obituary:

> Sister Lucy Myers, daughter of Brother C. A. and Sister Nettie Myers, after seventy-nine days of great suffering, passed from scenes of mortality to the land of perpetual health. To scenes of fadeless beauty and of glory and light supernal. Sister Myers lived on earth twenty-one years. She was always good. I baptized her when she was a little girl, at one of our meetings at Iron City, Tenn. She was beautiful and kind and good in the superlative degree. She was one of the best lady teachers in our Bible school of Florence, Ala., where she spent the last two years of her pilgrimage on earth ... C. E. Holt.[452]

The above articles not only show how the members worked by using their abilities; but that the women did their part, same as their male counterparts.

Holt's next report gave a bright picture of the Florence work. He also speaks of the work in Sheffield. We include what he says concerning some preachers of that day is worth our attention:

> Brother C. E. Holt writes from Florence, Ala., under the date of March 30: "Our work at this place is progressing nicely. Two persons have recently been baptized, and prospects are bright for continued prosperity. Our Bible-school work is growing. We use the helps furnished by the McQuiddy Printing Company. I would be glad to see these most excellent aids to Bible study in every congregation in the world. I preach for the congregation at Sheffield, Ala., on every Lord's-day afternoon at three o'clock. I contemplate a protracted effort there in the very near future. It is a regrettable fact that the work in Sheffield has been somewhat crippled by a corrupt preacher. Churches should be exceedingly careful along these lines. All men who have the 'gift of gab' are not suitable for preachers. A preacher should be a clean man. Unfortunately, some preachers are intellectually and education-

ally strong, but morally weak, Churches too often seek for the former qualification without giving much attention to the latter."[453]

At times Holt was very busy. Here is a sample of a Sunday in his life:

Brother C. E. Holt, of Florence, Ala., writes, under the date of October 19: "Our work in this city is moving along very smoothly and prosperously. Yesterday was a very busy day with me. I preached three times, baptized five persons, and performed a marriage ceremony. Success to the Gospel Advocate."[454]

In early March 1909 Holt spoke of the congregation's condition as being stronger than ever before. The Bible school was growing in numbers and interest.[455] Brother C. E. Holt, of Florence, Ala., writes:

The congregation in this city is in good condition, probably better than at any other period in its history. Our Bible school is growing in numbers and interest.[456]

In April Holt reported that the work in Florence, and especially at Poplar Street, was doing fine:

Brother C. E. Holt writes from Florence, Ala.: "Our work in this city is progressing nicely." Two additions recently-one baptized and one from the Methodists. The attendance at our Bible school has increased about sixty per cent since the first of the year. The prayer meetings are growing in interest and attendance. On last Wednesday night (April 7) we had edifying talks by Brethren Southall, Campbell, and White. There was one baptism at the close of the service."[457]

In July Isaac Hoskins of Gallatin, Tennessee came and held a three weeks' meeting. Holt described this meeting:

> Brother C. E. Holt, of Florence, Ala., writes: "Our three weeks' meeting at this place closed on Sunday evening, June 20, with twenty-eight accessions. Brother I. C. Hoskins, of Gallatin, Tenn., did the preaching, and Brother R. A. Zahn, of Louisville, Ky., led the song service. Both the preaching and the singing were perfectly satisfactory, and the church rejoices."[458]

By the end of the year, Holt gave a lengthy re-cap of his work at Poplar Street, under the title "The Work In Florence, Alabama." It was published in the *Gospel Advocate*:

> Since the latter part of the year 1905 I have been with the first church of Christ in Florence, Ala. We speak of our congregation in this way, calling it the "First Church," because it was the first congregation after the New Testament order established in the city. The second congregation was established several years after the establishment of the first and is located in the eastern part of the city. Brother J. T. Harris, of Minor Hill, Tenn., will locate in Florence, and will preach for this latter congregation during the year 1910. Brother Harris will be a very valuable addition to our preaching force in North Alabama.
>
> During the four years which I have labored with the First Church everything connected with the work has been exceedingly pleasant. There has not been a jar or discord to mar the peace, happiness, and prosperity of the congregation. There has been a steady, healthful growth, numerically, financially, and spiritually. During the time I have been here we have had Brethren W. D. Campbell, of Detroit, Mich., and I. C. Hoskins, of Gallatin, Tenn., to assist us in protracted meetings. Both these brethren did good, faithful work, and will do any congregation good and faithful service with which they may labor. In our Bible school we use the printed helps published by the

McQuiddy Printing Company, of Nashville, Tenn. There are no helps in existence better than these. They are as true to the "old landmarks" as the needle is to the pole. Every congregation in the world should use them.

We use "Gospel Praise" in our song service, and we like it more and more. The longer we use it, the better we like it.

I do not think there is a congregation in the world which is nearer to the New Testament model than the congregation of which I write.

Our contributions are made on the first day of the week. We follow this plan: At the beginning of the year, we first ascertain the amount (or about the amount) of money necessary for all expenses. We then ask the members to state the amount each one feels able and willing to give for the work. With few exceptions, the members state what they will pay each Lord's day. We take up no collections in any other way.

For the year 1910 we have promised eighteen hundred dollars for the local work. Of course, we will give liberally to mission work in other fields. I am just entering on my fifth year in the work here, and the outlook is far brighter than in any former year.

We have a very efficient eldership. C. M. Southall, J. B. White, and W. E. Sharp are our elders. Our membership is a little more than four hundred.

We greet all the churches of Christ in all parts of the world and pray that they may "keep the unity of the Spirit in the bond of peace" and prosper as never before. Florence, Ala.[459]

Another report followed a week later:

Brother C. E. Holt, of Florence, Ala., writes, under date of December 13: "There was one more baptism at our regular service on yesterday-my own dear little daughter, my baby, eleven years old. My whole family, one son and four daughters, are now in the kingdom. Surely, I should be one of the happiest men in the world, and I am. May the Lord bless the Gospel Advocate force."[460]

Then another followed a week after that:

Brother C. E. Holt, of Florence, Ala., writes: "We have had two more baptisms at the First church of Christ, this city, since last report. The work is progressing nicely."[461]

Things kept moving along in a pleasing way. Holt made only two reports to the *Gospel Advocate* during 1910. He did, however, give a history of the Poplar Street congregation, especially the period covering his work for that congregation. The title of the article was "The Florence Church":

The church of Christ in Florence, Ala., has been in existence about twenty-five years. It had a hard struggle the first years of its existence, the denominational spirit among the people being the dominating religious force in the city. Sectarianism was firmly established here when Brother T. B. Larimore, then a young man, began his great work at Mars' Hill four miles from the city. His school was patronized by brethren throughout the United States and Canada and was a great force in planting primitive Christianity in Alabama and in the States adjoining.

I began work with this church in 1905. and have been asked to remain another year, the year 1911. The work has been exceedingly pleasant and we think it is very prosperous. We have two houses, one in the heart of the city and one in the eastern part, Brother J. T. Harris laboring at the latter place. Brother Harris is a true yokefellow and one of the best men I ever knew. Both of us do considerable work in the country around Florence. Our worship is strictly after the New Testament pattern-the teaching of the apostles, the fellowship, the breaking of bread, and the prayers.

Notwithstanding the fact that we strive to reproduce the

true worship as given by the Holy Spirit and recorded in the New Testament, it has been reported to some Texas college president and an editor in the Lone Star State, that the Florence church, myself included, has gone "digressive"-yes, gone "digressive." This is certainly news to us which comes from the great Southwest.

Someone says we are "digressive" because we use printed helps published by the McQuiddy Printing Company, of Nashville, Tenn., in studying the Bible. Well, if this is our sin, we plead guilty. We use those helps and are glad that we have them. No sounder teaching than is found in those helps. We use a song book-"Gospel Praise"-published by the same company. without any instrumental accompaniment. We do not have instrumental music, nor do we favor the use of instruments in the song service. We have never contributed one cent to a missionary society nor to any other kind of a society, but work exclusively through the church, the local congregation. We use no methods of raising money but the Bible plan, all making freewill offerings on the first day of the week as the Lord prospers them. This is the way we are "digressive." Such reports would be treated as they deserve, with silent contempt, but for the fact that certain evil-minded sons, full of the spirit of envy, want to cripple our work and influence by surreptitiously circulating false reports. Brethren, visit with us and see how "digressive" we are. Our work speaks for itself.

Brother J. T. Harris, of Florence, Ala., under date of November 15. 1910, makes the following statement: "It has been reported that Brother C. E. Holt, my coworker, is "digressive." I have known Brother Holt for a number of years. have been very closely and intimately associated with him all this year, have heard him preach many sermons, and have talked with him a great many times about the evil of innovations and departures from the truth, and I know that such reports are absolutely untrue." ED.[462]

For the months of March and April 1911, Holt reported in the *Gospel Advocate* that four more baptisms occurred at Poplar Street.[463] George Klingman returned in October to conduct a three-week meeting. Holt reported on the meeting:

> Brother C. E. Holt writes from Florence, Ala.: "Brethren G. A. Klingman and R. A. Zahn have been with us three weeks. The preaching and singing are good. Two have been added to date. We are hoping for others..."[464]

Holt resigned from Poplar Street in December and wrote a farewell message in the *Gospel Advocate*; unfortunately, it was published a couple of weeks late. It was not published until Holt was already at work in Montgomery. He reveals more facts on the work in Florence as follows:

> An intermingling of joy and sorrow was the chief feature of our meeting on the last Lord's day of 1911. For six years and three months I have been associated as minister with the church of Christ in Florence, Ala. Our work has been pleasant and, in some respects, marvelously successful. The condition of the congregation is healthy and strong. Not only has the congregation supported the local work, but, in addition to this, it has given Brother J. T. Harris six hundred dollars for general evangelistic work for two years and will continue to assist in his support. Brother Harris has been very successful. He is one of the best men in the world, and one of the best evangelists. For two years Brother Harris and I have labored together! as local evangelist and he as general evangelist-in perfect harmony. Our friendship is like that of David and Jonathan. It is much greater than that of Damon and Pythias. Any congregation is fortunate when it secures Brother Harris for a meeting. Our elders, or bishops, are men of sterling worth. Brethren Southall and White are pillars in the temple. Associated with them are some of the best men in the brotherhood. when we take a retrospective view

of the work in Florence our struggles and triumphs, we thank God and take courage.

I am now working with the Catoma Street church of Christ in Montgomery, Ala. This is a very fine body of Christians, and, with God's help, we expect great results when I gave up my work in Florence, it was my purpose to do general evangelistic work. I am very much in love with this line of work, having engaged it therein for many years before taking up the work in Florence. But I am in the hands of our Heavenly Father, to be used by him in the greatest work which was ever given man to do. I pray that I may be a faithful soldier in his army. Brother J. M. Barnes, than whom a greater and better man cannot be found, is with us in our work in Montgomery. To the indefatigable energy and unsurpassed loyalty of Brother Barnes is due, largely, the success of the cause in Central and Southern Alabama. He is a man of towering strength, of faith and courage, and fights valiantly, yet lovingly, for what he believes is the truth on all questions pertaining to the spiritual welfare of Zion. I sincerely trust that the new year holds many good things in store for us all.

Brother I. C. Hoskins succeeds me in Florence. and I bespeak for him a pleasant and profitable year.[465]

Hoskins would arrive in Florence in January 1912. He was the son-in-law of Brother I. B. Grubbs, a longtime teacher at the College of the Bible. He would remain in Florence until the year 1919. Hoskins had hardly arrived in Florence until false reports began to surface that Poplar Street was a "digressive" church. This had stemmed from an earlier attempt by prominent church leaders in Texas to label the Florence church and Holt as "digressive."

Holt felt compelled to defend his reputation and that of the church at Poplar Street—where he had labored for seven years. He had the grit to stand up to any who questioned his faithfulness. He was by far, no liberal, and brethren across the country knew that. He wrote the following in defense to the *Gospel Advocate*:

> I want to say to the readers of the Gospel Advocate that the church of Christ at Florence, Ala., where Brother I. C. Hoskins preaches, and for which I preached six years, is not "digressive," as has been falsely reported. It is the best church in North Alabama and is sound in the faith. The church there is perfectly loyal—has no musical instruments in the worship nor any societies through which to do the Lord's work. It is an active, working church. This may be the reason it is so greatly misrepresented by some who "say, and do not." It should be so.[466]

The attacks upon the soundness of the work in Florence did not hinder its efforts to continue evangelizing. Hoskins soon began arranging appointments to preach in the surrounding communities. The next report reveals this fact:

> Brother Isaac C. Hoskins is conducting a series of Bible studies each Tuesday evening at Florence, Ala. Of the church there he writes: "Audiences are growing and we are hopeful because the outlook is brighter."[467]

He had only been in Florence about four months at the time of his first report about his holding gospel meetings in the local congregations. In the fall of that year, he reported a meeting at Poplar Street in which there were fourteen baptisms, two restorations, and five by placing membership. R. A. Zahn led the singing. Robert A. Zahn married Helen Lulie Klingman, the sister of George Klingman. Klingman was Hoskins' brother-in-law. Helen was the author of the song— "There Is A Sea," which has appeared in many of our hymnals through the years.

Hoskins and his wife had become very ill in the January of 1913. He was unable to stand and preach for most of three months. He wrote concerning this troublesome period of illness:

> Florence, Ala., March 2.-A cheerful message sent with a heart full of gratitude to our Heavenly Father that, after being unable

to preach since the first Lord's day in January, I today had the blessed privilege of speaking to the people, though I had to remain seated a part of the time. Mrs. Hoskins and I have been walking together "in the valley." Isaac C. Hoskins.[468]

One of the editors at the *Gospel Advocate* wrote a follow-up statement in April concerning Hoskins' health:

We are rejoiced to learn that Brother Isaac C. Hoskins, of Florence, Ala., is improving in health. He was a visitor at the Sheffield meeting last week.[469]

In November of that year, Hoskins' brother-in-law—George A. Klingman came to Florence to visit him and his family Hoskins.[470]

By January Hoskins was back full steam in his work. A report in the *Gospel Advocate* confirmed that:

Isaac Hoskins is busy in the Master's service at Florence, Ala. Here is his latest report: "We had fine audiences yesterday; indeed, the outlook is very encouraging. On Saturday afternoon (January 17) I began giving a series of biblical studies of the New Testament church, using two charts-one of the Bible, the other of the church. Fine interest manifested therein."[471]

By the fall of 1914 Isaac Hoskins was doing very well. His brother-in-law George A. Klingman conducted a successful meeting at Poplar Street, and Hoskins rendered assistance. Hoskins wrote:

Florence. October 26.-The meeting at this place began on October 4 and closed on October 25. Brother G. A. Klingman did the preaching and Brother R. A. Zahn led the singing. There were three sermons each Lord's day (one of them at the courthouse) and two each week day, except the first Saturday, when there was but one. Seventeen were baptized and three backsliders returned. There were four from the Methodists. two from the Episcopalians. and one from the Presbyterians. Brother Klingman's doctrinal sermons on conversion and on the church and his plea for unity on the one foundation were at once powerful. tender, and scriptural. The exposition of Psalms on week days were spiritual feasts. The singing was splendidly led. This was an excellent meeting. Isaac C. Hoskins.[472]

This brings us to the close of our time frame—1914 at Poplar Street. But much more work is still to be done in other parts of the county before we close the Lauderdale County work.

Lexington The Early Work

On September 14, 1883, J. R. Bradley came near Lexington, Alabama, in Lauderdale County, to a new church house called Chapel Hill. The meeting house was built by brother James McPeters. J. R. said that Professor A.D. Ray was "an excellent teacher" and taught there. He also said that Professor Ray and his daughters greatly aided the meeting with their good singing. He said that Ray's daughters "are fine singers." The meeting continued through Wednesday, September 19, 1883. There was only one addition during this effort. This Lexington work would struggle to survive until the early 1900s when it finally would get on firm footing.[473]

This was possibly the first time the gospel had been preached in that very community, however Murrell Askew lived in that community and was preaching the gospel of Christ also. This was the first documented report of any work having been done there. Eris Bonner Benson quoted H. C. Warren and Henry B. Romine:

> In 1915 the church at Lexington was established by H. C. Warren and J. C. Bullington. Although some members were already there, they had not been meeting to worship.[474]

What should have been said in this situation is that Warren and Bullington organized a church there. They said there were members already there in Lexington, but not meeting like they should.

Thomas L. Weatherford of Limestone County, Alabama and a graduate of Mars Hill Bible College came near the Lexington community and held a meeting in November 1892. He wrote the following:

> O'Neal, Nov. 29, '92: ...5th Lord's day in October preached near Lexington, Ala., with two additions, one from the Baptists and one from the Cumberland Presbyterians... T. L. Weatherford. [475]

Weatherford was a preaching companion of J. R. Bradley's. They were fellow students at Mars Hill and preached together in many gospel meetings.

The next communication came from Lexington:

> Brother Lipscomb: When Jesus Christ washed the feet of his disciples, and said unto them, "If I, your Lord, and Master, have washed your feet, ye ought also to wash one another's feet," what did he lack of making "foot washing" an ordinance? If the early disciples ought to wash one another's feet, why ought not we? What is the proper explanation of John xiii. 14, 15? Please answer in Gospel Advocate. J.P. Jones. Lexington, Ala., August 17, 1893.[476]

Lipscomb gave an answer. No more came on that subject. Lipscomb apparently to the satisfaction of Jones. Jones did, however, communicate with Lipscomb again. His next communication was rather amusing; We give the full report:

> Brother J. P. Jones, of Lexington, Ala., calls for help in these words: A Primitive Baptist preacher in this country is firing into

the disciples of Christ with all the venom that a depraved nature can bring to bear. Among other things he tells everywhere he goes that Alexander Campbell and another fellow both got drunk, and that while intoxicated Campbell baptized, the other fellow and then be baptized Campbell, and that started the Campbellite Church. Dr. Blake, in his "Old Log House" says that Alexander Campbell was once a minister in the Baptist Church, but was excluded from that denomination but does not say for what reason. The Cumberland Presbyterians are using that on us. Please give me the exact history of Alexander Campbell's life and transactions as instigator of the current reformation.[477]

Jones said that even the Presbyterians were using that warped tail to frustrate the work of our brethren. Lipscomb responded as usual and denied the charge against Campbell. Jones, currently, had been preparing to preach the gospel. He possibly had already preached his first sermon by that time because he preached his second sermon at Porter Springs in October. W. H. Sanday wrote of this event:

> Rogersville, Oct. 30.-Brother J. P. Jones, of Lexington, Ala., preached his second discourse in life for us last Lord's day, at Porter's Springs, and I must say that he did well for a new beginner. He seems to be the right man for the work he has chosen, for he shuns not to declare the whole counsel of God. Dr. Jones is sound to the core, and I think the core is sound too. Brethren, give him a helping hand, and enable him to devote more of his time to the ministry ... W. H. Sanday.[478]

By 1894 Dr. J. P. Jones was serving as a minister in the Lexington area. He performed a wedding in November 1893. The announcement was as follows:

Dr. J. P. Jones The undersigned solemnized the rite of matrimony on the 11th of this month between Mr. J. T. McPeters and Miss Lou Davis, at the residence of the bride's parents. J. P. Jones, Lexington, Ala., Nov. 12.[479]

Brother Frank Morrow held a meeting at Lexington, Ala. in 1909. It was reported in a very succinct message.[480] At the end of the meeting, a sister Belle Green sent a report to the *Gospel Advocate*:

> Sister Belle Green writes from Lexington, Ala., under date of July 12: "Brother Frank Morrow has just closed a series of meetings at this place, with one baptism. On yesterday he preached two able discourses at Grassy."[481]

Frank Morrow was a successful local preacher who came to Lexington and reinforced Christianity in that place.

Finally, a preacher comes to Lexington to try and solidify the work—in the person of J. Petty Ezell. He wrote of his endeavor:

> Brother J. P. Ezell has encouraged the little congregation at Lexington, Ala., to meet regularly on the first day of the week and to worship "as it is written."[482]

This states that there was a congregation in Lexington—they just were not meeting regularly. Ezell was also a local preacher from just east of Rogersville. Another minister came and held a meeting in the summer of 1912. He was G. T. Kay. He wrote that he had "fine interest" during the meeting. The result was four baptisms.[483]

To further prove a church was already there is shown by the following two reports by J. T. Harris. In his first report, Harris wrote:

> Lexington, October 13. On last Friday night I closed a two-weeks' meeting at Minor Hill, Tenn., resulting in fourteen added to Christ. Last January they had the misfortune to lose their house, but they have rebuilt, and the congregation seems to be getting along nicely. I began at this place last Lord's day and am preaching to large audiences. J. T. Harris.[484]

He said he was preaching to large audiences. That sounds as though there were many members present. Denominational members usually did not turn out in large crowds.

In his second report, he gave the results:

> Florence, November 3. Since my last report I have held two meetings. The first was at Lexington, beginning on the second Lord's day and closing on the third Lord's day in October, with one addition from the Methodists ... J. T. Harris.[485]

We know there was a group of Christians in that community before Warren and Bullington organized the church in Lexington. It is interesting that Warren's and Burlington's work was not reported in the *Gospel Advocate*. The congregation did not have their own meeting house until 1917. This closes our history of the early work at Lexington, Alabama.

Antioch

In about 1900 a church was established at Antioch. While working with the new church its preacher, William M. Behel, walked from Lone Cedar, a distance of about twelve miles. In addition to preaching once a month for several months at the church for about eight years, John Campbell conducted four meetings for the church.[486]

Larry Harper, a former minister at Antioch (1968–1971), wrote a brief history while some of the charter members were still living. He wrote:

> A very small group began to assemble in an old log house and brush arbor located somewhere between where Doyce Parker and James Faust now live. Bill Williams was one of the first to help form the church. He came from the Pleasant Valley community and began teaching Bible classes.[487]

A problem already discussed in the Union Grove history reveals that the Matthew W. Lefan family was dissatisfied with the way the elders at Union Grove raised money to finish the church building at that place. The problem was over the unexpected. It was a box supper. In January of 1902, Lefan sent a question to

David Lipscomb of the *Gospel Advocate* inquiring about the priority of raising money to make repairs to their church building by having a box-supper. The question was:

> Brother Lipscomb: Is it right for the members of a church to have a box supper to get money to repair their church house? Please answer through the Gospel Advocate. Stutts, Ala. M. W. LeFan.
>
> The only way approved in the Scriptures for raising money for any purpose is for each to labor, working with his hands that which is good, that he may have to give to any worthy work. All cajoling of persons to give by appeal to their appetites or fleshly feelings is sinful. All should give in the name of Jesus Christ, in his place as he would give, in a direct Manner, doubtful.[488]

Lefan could not put that to rest in his mind, so he reacted. An anonymous letter was sent to the *Gospel Advocate* and was published in December of 1902, concerning this matter. It read:

> The brethren at Union Grove, near Stutts, Ala., gave a box supper to raise money to build a meetinghouse, A brother wants a scriptural argument on the subject, but it is very hard to give a scriptural argument on an unscriptural practice. Who ever heard of Paul's giving a box supper to raise money to build a meetinghouse? God does not need any such help. The Lord loves a cheerful giver, and one should give as he purposes in his heart. [489]

Though the report was sent anonymously, the Union Grove members knew that it was Lefan who wrote it. Matthew W. Lefan had a falling out with G. C. Thigpen over the box supper and by the end of the year had taken his family to help in start the Antioch work. Mable Wright Parker, P. D. Wright's daughter gave the following information from her father's diary:

At this time, G. C. Thigpen and Matt Lefan had a disagreement. Thigpen wanted to have a box supper; to raise money to buy seats for the church, Lefan thought it was unscriptural, so along with Jim Beavers and others left the church. They then started a Sunday school at Olive Hill school house, most of them were later reconciled to North Carolina. Lefan went to Antioch Church to work with that congregation.[490]

It is stated in a history of the Antioch congregation, written by Larry Harper, that Lefan came and helped establish the congregation at that place in 1902.[491] Harper also told of Lefan bringing the communion basket all the way from his home, in the North Carolina community, to Antioch.[492]

From interviews that Harper conducted with older members, it was learned that the infant congregation continued to meet in the old house, and for meetings, they would meet under brusharbors. This continued for about three years. As other families moved into the community the congregation grew numerically, as well as spiritually.

As the community grew larger there was a need for a schoolhouse and a building for the church. In 1906 the government decided to sell an old government school building. Richard Hamner bought the building for $500 and in the fall, tore the building down, hauled the lumber back to Antioch, and built a building. This building burned. Later another building was built.[493]

Bro. Will Behel preached in a meeting at Antioch in August 1905 and baptized three persons. He came back in 1906 and baptized three more. He had begun preaching once a month in about 1908. He recorded one baptism on June 29, 1909; two in 1911; and two in 1913.[494] He traveled by buggy or horseback.[495] Often, he preached, receiving no money in return.[496]

The only meetings reported in the *Gospel Advocate* within our time frame were—one conducted by J. T. Harris in 1912 and two by William Behel. Harris sent two reports on the meeting he held. His first report spoke of his beginning the meeting:

> J. T. Harris, Town Creek, Ala., 6 baptisms, 1 from Methodists, 1 took membership. Now at Antioch, Lauderdale County, Ala.[497]

A week later he reported the results of that meeting:

> J. T. Harris, Antioch, Lauderdale County, Ala., 2 baptisms, 2 restorations. Now in a tent meeting at Killen, Ala.[498]

The following year William Behel reports on two meetings. The first was a brief line in a larger report:

> St. Joseph, Tenn., August 26. This summer's work so far is as follows: At Antioch, Ala., two baptized; Cherry Hill, Tenn., five baptized; Littleville, Ala., four baptized, four from the Baptists; Frankfort, Ala., six baptized, one restored; at Macedonia, Ala., seven baptized, one from the Baptists. I will begin near Barton, Ala., on August 31. William Behel.[499]

His second report was of the same nature:

> St. Joseph, Tenn., October 11. I send a message for the "cheerful" page, reporting my summer's work. I held meetings as follows: At Cherry Hill, Tenn., with five additions; Littleville, Ala., eight; Frankfort, Ala., seven; Lone Cedar, Ala., seven; North Carolina, Ala., ten; Barton, Ala., none; Antioch, Ala., two; Shiloh, Ala., fifteen; Macedonia. Ala., ten; Tharp town, Ala., five. This last meeting closed too soon on account of my daughter's being sick and my having to come home. The brethren there say they will build a house of worship, although there are but fifteen members. I am at home now but have a few more meetings yet promised. William Behel.[500]

From Antioch records, we learn of meetings and baptisms not recorded in the *Gospel Advocate* or any other brotherhood paper. The following are the earliest baptisms at Antioch:

> During the first meeting at Antioch Richard Hamner, Sam Glass, Jim Smith and Holley Hamner were baptized - about 1907. Some of the dates of baptisms we have been able to find— Bro. Rufus Smith- 1908- by E.O. Coffman— Sis. Florence Glover- 1908- by Will Behel—Sis. Lizzie Jones- 1910- by Billy Harrison.[501]

As we stated in the beginning, the information for Antioch was very scanty. Without the Harper-McCafferty history, most of Antioch's past would have been lost.

Burcham Valley—
New Hope

Another church was established, not more than six miles from Stoney Point, during the 1870s. William B. Young, the younger brother to George P. Young, had gone to school at Bethany College. During the summer recess of 1875, he returned to Bethabara (Bethelberry) community, which was his home. He traveled to Burcham Valley, due west of modern-day Central Heights, and preached in Burcham Valley Schoolhouse. As a result of Young's preaching, the Concordia Church of Christ was formed with eight members. Within the next week, another three were added to the number.[502] This congregation would later form the nucleus for modern-day New Hope Church of Christ, which is the congregation from which E. H. Ijams came forth. The countryside around Burcham Valley and Stoney Point was filled with people seeking the truth.

Young reported this meeting to two brotherhood journals—*The Christian Standard* and the *Gospel Advocate*. His *Christian Standard* report was referred to above and was a repeat of the *Gospel Advocate* article. His *Gospel Advocate* report is given in full:

W. B. Young writes from Florence Ala., Sept. 5th: "The good cause is advancing in North Alabama. In Lauderdale County on

Burcham creek. In the midst of strong sectarian prejudice, I made an appointment and was prevented both by rain and a Methodist revival to commence my meeting at the time; however, on the Thursday following the fourth Lord's day in August, my series of discourses began and on the fifth Lord's day an aged gentleman who heard and saw the truth said, 'The meeting had driven a stake into the M. E. Church which they never could pull out.' On Monday a church of Christ was organized in the vicinity with eight members; the name of which place is Concordia Church.

On Thursday, three persons obeyed the Gospel and went on their way rejoicing in the truth. Many more are disposed to turn to the Lord, and I pray ere twelve months roll away there will be thirty-five or forty members in Concordia Church.

They have decided to begin building in Dec. or Jan. a good house of worship. Then the cause will be on a firm footing in that community. My thanks for the kindness of sister Cook and many other kind hearts who long have waited for church privileges."[503]

He had suggested that his converts had made plans to build a house of worship. We do not know if the house was ever built. There is no official record of it ever existing. These first converts continued to worship near the Burcham Valley School, but they were not properly organized until after 1898. In 1898 William M. Behel came and preached—baptizing twelve precious souls into Christ. This brought the total number of members to twenty. The other eight were already living in the valley and probably were some that had been converted by Young in 1875. No doubt some of Young's earlier members were still around when Behel came and gathered the flock together. Behel wrote of this meeting:

... Before there was a congregation at New Hope, I was in that community the meeting which resulted in the building of the New Hope house of worship.[504]

Benson in his thesis referenced this meeting:

> The church at New Hope was established by W. M. Behel in 1898 on the banks of Burcham Creek, about a half mile from the place where a building was later erected. The church was begun by a meeting in which twelve persons were baptized, bringing the number of members to twenty. Before the place of worship was completed, the church met in the home of a member. Before the building was ready for use, there were thirty members. The first elders of the church were Joe Ijams and Bud Phillips. When the building was destroyed by a storm in March 1913, the members met in Beulah school house until the meetinghouse was rebuilt in the fall of the same year...[505]

Behel also came back and held a meeting in 1903. He baptized six persons on July 12, 1903, whose names were Hattie Whitten, Willie Whitten, Daisy Harris, Katie Harris, and two persons whose last name was Fulmer.[506] In the heading above these names, Behel had written—Burcham Mills, Alabama, or New Hope.

J. T. Harris came to New Hope and held a gospel meeting in August of 1912. He wrote that they were having "large audiences."[507] That was all that was written in the *Gospel Advocate* concerning that meeting.

> Brother J. T. Harris is preaching to large audiences at New Hope, nine miles from Florence, Ala.

He returned and held a meeting in October of 1914. His report was more informative on this occasion. He wrote:

Florence, November 3.-Since my last report I have held two meetings. The first was at Lexington, beginning on the second Lord's day and closing on the third Lord's day in October, with one addition from the Methodists. The second was at New Hope, about nine miles west of Florence, beginning on the fourth Lord's day in October and closing on the first Lord's-day in November, with five baptized. J. T. Harris.[508]

This is the only information we have found on the earliest days of New Hope Church of Christ on Burcham Creek near the Central Heights community. Thus, we close our history for the New Hope congregation.

JACKSONBURG

The Church of Christ that meets at Jacksonburg can trace its roots back to the summer of 1898 or 98. In 1916 Fuqua said this: "Jacksonburg is one of the congregations established by myself some seventeen years ago (1898–9)."[509] Mr. John Allen, Mr. C. D. Griffith, and Mr. S. P. Clemmons had organized a Union Sunday School.[510] The brief history of the Jacksonburg congregation gives a few helpful facts:

> They met, for a while, in the train depot at Jacksonburg. And several attended this worship service. Some of these folks were members of denominational groups. At some point, Mr. Clemmons retained Brother E.C. Fuqua to hold a meeting. During that meeting Mr. John Zahnd was baptized. He was the father of Sister John Abston and Brother Walter Zahnd. Also baptized during the meeting was Mrs. Segretain who had moved to the United States from France and had been a member of the Catholic church.[511]

During this meeting, Brother Fuqua discovered that the church had not been observing the Lord's Supper. Fuqua talked to Mr. Clemmons about it, and Clemmons began providing the communion for members. Soon after this meeting was held, the ticket agent at the Florence Depot sent for the key and began locking the building.[512] Some thought he might have been a member of a denomination and apparently not too happy that the Church of Christ was using the depot to meet.

In 1907 Will Behel held a meeting at Jacksonburg. He wrote: "I am now in a meeting at Jacksonburg, Ala., with one baptism to date. I expect to begin a meeting at Pleasant Valley, Ala., on August 17."[513] This was the earliest reference to Jacksonburg in the journals. The most we can glean from this is that Jacksonburg was having some semblance of gospel meetings, perhaps on a regular basis, and that one had been baptized early in the meeting. Behel followed up with a report on the whole meeting and revealed the meeting lasted ten days with only the one baptism.
[514]

It seemed that the Jacksonburg area was a difficult place for a struggling church. But persistence pays off—they did not give in to obstacles—they began to grow.

This fact was confirmed by Will Behel in a report on the Lauderdale County work in 1908. He stated: "Jacksonburg has an energetic congregation, the result of Brother E. C. Fuqua's preaching there."[515] He reported later in September that the Jacksonburg meeting closed with two baptisms.[516]

The next report in the *Gospel Advocate* was six years later but it contained more information on the church at Jacksonburg than all the other reports combined. We give the report in its entirety:

> Florence, October 3. I am glad to report the very successful meeting recently held at Jacksonburg, in Lauderdale County, which began on September 7 and closed on September 29. The preaching was done by Brother Isaac C. Hoskins, local evangelist at Florence, which announcement is a guarantee to the brotherhood that the simple gospel story was presented in beauty, love, and power. The immediate results were thirty-seven added to the one body—five restored to their "first love," two Methodists and

one Baptist that claimed scriptural baptism, twenty-nine by primary obedience. Many of those baptized were formerly Methodists and Catholics members of leading families, who are greatly rejoicing that they have found "the way of the Lord more perfectly." The meeting was held in a schoolhouse, in which this little band has promised to meet on the first day of the week to keep house for the Lord. Let us pray that these newborn babes in Christ may grow and develop into strong Christian characters and win many more souls to the true and living way. L. T. Farrar.
[517]

From the above report, we learn several things about the Jacksonburg church.

1. The meeting lasted 22 days.
2. The preaching was conducted by Isaac C. Hoskins—the evangelist for the Poplar Street congregation in Florence. [Hoskins was minister for Poplar Street from 1911 until 1919.]
3. 37 were added to the church at Jacksonburg.
4. The congregation was worshipping in a schoolhouse.
[518]

From the church's own history, the following information is given:

The community built a new school house sometime between 1908 and 1912. Soon after the new building was erected, Brother E. C. Holt began preaching once a month and the first elders of Jacksonburg were appointed. The first elders were John Zahnd, A. C. Delano, and T. F. Blackburn. In 1916, Brother Isaac C. Hoskins held a meeting that lasted nearly a month during which thirty men and women were baptized into Christ. Others who preached during these early years were L. T. Farris (Farrar), Thornton Crews, Gilbert Schaffer, and E. O. Coffman, who traveled by train from Lawrenceburg once a month to preach.[519]

L. T. Farrar's report was the last report that fell within our timeline, but we feel compelled to give two more reports beyond the established time. These two reports reflect, somewhat upon the prior years:

> Florence, September 20.-The meeting at Jacksonburg, eight miles north of Florence, closed yesterday afternoon at the water. During the meeting there were fourteen sermons, sixteen baptized and five restored. Everybody is enthusiastic. The interest manifested throughout was fine. I was at Jacksonburg one year ago, when thirty-seven were brought in during the three weeks of night meetings. Isaac C. Hoskins.[520]

This report shows that the congregation is on an upward swing—showing that it is finally established firmly on the Bible. It continued to grow spiritually and numerically.

The next report has already been discussed at the beginning of this history. In it, Fuqua claimed he established the Jacksonburg congregation,[521] and that was confirmed above by Will Behel in 1906: "Jacksonburg has an energetic congregation, the result of Brother E. C. Fuqua's preaching there."[522]

This closes the part of Jacksonburg's history by the beginning of World War I. We now move to our next congregation.

Pine Hill

The only written document for the establishment of the Pine Hill congregation is taken from Eris Bonner Benson's history of the Churches of Christ in Lauderdale County:

> In about 1900 Billy Dowdy, D. H. Bevis, Joe Perkins, and Forest Bevis established the church at Pine Hill. W. M. Behel, a minister named Hutton (Jerome Mansel Hutton), C. E. Holt, Joe Holt, Gollyheir (Joseph N. Gallaher), and Si Darby were some of the early preachers who conducted meetings for the church. The church met in a school house for thirty-five years, but later moved into its own building.[523]

The exact date was speculative at most. The information on Pine Hill's early days is almost nonexistent. The oldest record is a photograph of the old school-church building in 1917. It was believed to have been taken on some occasion such as an all-day dinner/singing. In an interview many years ago with Brother George McCorkle, he informed me that he revived the Pine Hill church because it had almost ceased meeting.[524] Fred Bevis was the earliest song leader for the church.[525]

Threet—Hendrix Chapel

W. H. Owens established the church at Hendrix Chapel in 1916 by conducting a tent meeting. Ministers named Owens, McCorkle, Whittier, and Gainer have conducted meetings for the church, and in one meeting about fifty persons were converted. Before a building was erected in 1918, the church met in a tent and under a "brush arbor." Owens preached for the church for about four years and McCorkle preached for about two years ....[526]

While this account has been used as an authoritative source for decades in Lauderdale County, the above version of how Hendrix Chapel was established seems to be in error. Benson's thesis relied heavily upon personal interviews rather than written documentation.

Some years before the date given by Benson, a brother Thomas Oswell Bevis lived at Threet but was a member at Macedonia which was about five miles away. He was portrayed as a very strong Christian, and perhaps one of the leaders at Macedonia. He had been a strong Baptist but was converted by Murrell Askew, who himself had recently quit the Baptist Church.[527] He saw the need for a congregation at Threet, later Threet's Crossroads. He would have been a prime suspect in why William Behel came and preached the first meeting at Threet in 1906.[528] He baptized eleven during this meeting.[529] It was reported in the *Gospel Advocate* that Behel came again and held a meeting at Threet in 1907. It read:

> Brother William Behel, of R. F. D. No.1, St. Joseph, Tenn., preached at Threet, Ala., on the first Lord's day in this month, with one baptized and one restored.[530]

During that meeting, he baptized ten persons.[531] Behel in his next report said that that was the first meeting in that place:

> St. Joseph, September 13. I will report my summer's work in Lauderdale County, Ala. My first meeting at Waterloo, which resulted in twelve additions, has already been reported. I preached ten days at Jacksonburg, with one baptism; eight days at Lone Cedar, with one restoration and one baptism; nine days at Pleasant Valley, with one reclaimed; seven days at Threet, with two restorations and six baptisms. Last year I conducted the first meetings there, with twelve additions. I think a strong church will be built up there in the near future. Already the idea of a house in which to worship is being considered. May the good work continue. Sectarian opposition is great.[532]

Behel made it clear that the year before (1906) he conducted the first meeting there: "Last year I conducted the first meetings there, with twelve additions."[533] Our brethren think that a church is not a church until it is set in order. That is not the case. See Acts 14:23 "And when they had ordained them elders in every church, and had prayed with fasting, they commended them to the Lord, on whom they believed."[534] There were churches before elders in them. Such was the case at Threet; it was just a very weak little band.

Behel came and held another meeting in 1908, as was

reported: "My next meeting was at Threet, Ala., with Brother J. M. Hutton, and resulted in three baptisms."[535] This Brother Hutton was Jerome Mansel Hutton of Walnut Grove, Hardin County, Tennessee. Behel reported that Threet had become a congregation that year:

> A congregation of about thirty persons has lately been planted at Threet; and while they are not working as they should. I am quite sure they will soon.[536]

Behel acknowledged that the church was still weak. He had tried to make them into a properly functioning church but apparently, they were not mature enough to worship as a viable congregation. He came back in 1909. On this visit, he tried something new:

> From August 1 to August 7, I labored at Threet, with no visible results, save that I succeeded, I think, in inducing this small congregation to work and worship with the congregation at Macedonia, which is also a small congregation; and I think a good, strong congregation is better than two small ones, especially where sect opposition is as strong as it is around Threet. [537]

So, for four years consecutively Behel held meetings at Threet, and he referred to them as a church. Apparently Behel thought the opposition from the denominations was too strong for the fledgling church for them to stay in that community and struggle. So, he advises them to unite with Macedonia. We do not know if they followed his advice—even Behel was not sure if they did. He stated: "... save that I succeeded, I think, in inducing this small congregation to work and worship with the congregation at Macedonia."[538]

All of this was about seven years before W. H. Owens came and set the church in order. The work at Threet survived and relocated when a new building was erected at a new location about a quarter mile from the old schoolhouse. The congregation was renamed Hendrix Chapel and remains so today (2024). It is a spiritually healthy congregation, even though it is in a more remote part of Lauderdale County. They keep a good number in their membership.

Shiloh

Preaching had been done long before William Behel gave his report in 1905. Larimore had preached at Green Hill long before Behel's report. His first report came in October 1879 to the *Gospel Advocate*. T. B. Larimore wrote from Florence, Ala., Oct. 30th, 1879:

> Last Lord's day, with our Bible pupils, some of our literary pupils, two of our teachers, and an audience variously estimated at from six hundred to one thousand, I spent a few hours at an elegant church home recently erected by my friend, Mr. McCluskey, on the military road, twelve miles in the direction of Nashville from Mars' Hill, my services having been secured for the occasion before the foundation of the house was laid. Preached two discourses, with only one accession. A few years ago, ten, at most very few, in this country, were willing to hear a simple gospel preacher tell saints and sinners what to do to be saved. Now, "come over and help us," wells up from the bosoms of many, and it is not unusual for the largest house to be distressingly small in view of the fruitless demand for seats. Truth will prevail.[539]

The *Florence Gazette* published an article in the last of October 1879 about a meeting Larimore held in Green Hill, Lauderdale County, Alabama. It was reprinted in the *Gospel Advocate* the first week of November. It was follows:

> At Green Hill, last Sunday, there was the largest crowd gathered together that we have ever seen in Lauderdale County outside of Florence; the crowd was variously estimated from 800 to 1,000. The occasion was the preaching by Rev. T. B. Larimore at Mr. McCluskey's new Chapel. The house, which is a large one, was literally filled with ladies, and a great many were left outside. Dinner was spread on the ground by the neighbors, and all invited to help themselves. Preaching was heard morning and evening. The Florence Gazette.[540]

One can easily see that Behel was not the first to preach in that area. However, Behel seems to be the one to have organized the little band into a functioning church. Eris Bonner Benson provides the date for the establishment of the church at Shiloh as 1902.[541] However, the date was likely 1905. William Behel wrote a brief autobiography just weeks before his death. This is his story:

> I held a meeting booked to be held in a denominational church building. Upon my arrival there, I saw several little "squads" of folks here and there talking and it was visible they were not in the best of humor. I hitched my horse and walked to where one of these "squads" were standing and imagine my surprise when told that the preacher in charge had forbidden my using either the building or the lot on which it stood. Surprised! And why? Because several of the members of that denomination's members of that place had invited me repeatedly to hold a meeting there. I ask the preacher, (he was present and a house full seated) if I could use the house for that particular service only, as the crowd was already assembled. He said, "No, but do not think hard of me about it. This was done by the order of the

General Conference." I replied, "If you had been a member of The Church of Christ you would not have been driven to do that which you could not conscientiously do; viz., refuse to let me preach just one sermon here." It hurt the man so much that I halfway wished I had not said that, but I offered no apology. And as angry group of folks at a religious gathering as you ever saw was there, mostly for, but some few, against me. I saw that some fighting was likely to take place if something was not done soon. I jumped upon a stump and announced that preaching would begin in thirty minutes in Mrs. Dial's yard, a good Methodist, about one fourth mile away by her invitation. I started. Everybody except the preacher followed and we left him locking the door. I was offered a place for an arbor just across the road from that forbidden land. I gratefully accepted and requested the people to meet me Monday morning and build an "arbor." On our arrival a man sent me word not to build the arbor, stating that his wife and daughter would not let him stay at home if he let me preach on his land. There I was, expecting a congregation for preaching and now, no place to preach. The question arose, "Now what will you do"? "Wait until 11:00 o'clock and we will see", I replied. The hour and the congregation arrived. I laid my hat on the side of the Military Road, remarking that I owned as much of that road as any man in the county, you make seats on the bank of the road, and I stood in the road and there I preached the second sermon of a successful meeting. A citizen whose wife was a Christian at the close of this sermon offered me his new tool shed to preach in long as I desired. I accepted the offer thankfully. Thus began a two-week meeting with sixty-two additions, the major part, of which had been Methodists. This was in 1905, and there is at present a congregation worshipping there regularly. The house of worship then built was named "Shiloh," because of the hard fight we had to establish that congregation.[542]

Behel gave the date as 1905. His baptismal records harmonize with this year—1905. His first entry for Shiloh was on September 13, 1905. He continued until September 24.[543] There were no other entries earlier for Shiloh, even though he had several congregations documented with baptisms before 1905.

The little band of Christians went to work almost immediately in securing a permanent place of worship. In October of that year, Pugh Houston House and wife Martha gave and deeded two acres of land for the purpose of building a house of worship on October 7, 1905.[544] The congregation went immediately building the church house. By December, a report came out in the *Florence Herald* about the construction of the new church building.[545] April 1906 *The Florence Herald* printed another article on Shiloh. This time it was about the dedication of the new building. It read as follows:

> After a few weeks silence, because of lack of news, I shall again ask for space in that welcome visitor, The Florence Herald—Mr. A. T. Clemmons and son, J.P., together with a number of others from here, attended preaching at the new church house, recently built, west of Greenhill. It will be remembered that W. Behel conducted a successful meeting in that locality. On April 22, he preached the first sermon in the new house. The honor of naming the new house was conferred upon him, and it will be known as "Shiloh." A large crowd was present. Preaching there Sunday April 29th, at 3 p.m.: subject, "The Lord's Supper."[546]

Behel held a meeting in August 1906. He baptized five in that meeting. He returned in 1907 and held an eleven-day meeting in which he baptized three persons. He had already baptized two earlier in April of that year.[547] In 1908 Behel wrote a summary of his work and the following is a portion of this report:

> It may be of interest to the readers to give a brief statement of the cause in Lauderdale County. There are but few congregations in this county where I have not preached. My work is

almost entirely where no other gospel preaching is done .... Pleasant Valley, Oliver, Antioch, North Carolina, and Shiloh are doing as well as one could reasonably expect. Lone Cedar is somewhat lethargic but is improving. William Behel.[548]

Behel did not hold the meeting in 1909; but a young preacher student from Potter Bible College in Bowling Green, Kentucky came and held the annual meeting. The first week of October 1909 the *Gospel Advocate* published this note:

> On August 22: Brother J. P. Ezell, a Potter Bible College student, preached at Lone Cedar to a large audience. On August 22 I began a meeting at Shiloh, and to date (August 27) have had the pleasure of hearing fifteen persons confess Christ, twelve of whom will be baptized on next Lord's-day afternoon, and three have been restored.[549]

Ezell was a North Alabama boy. He was being trained to be a preacher. Apparently, the college did its job well; he became a very well loved and respected preacher and was known throughout the country. He had twelve baptisms and three restorations at Shiloh during that meeting. His appearance at Shiloh was long remembered.

Behel returned to Shiloh in 1910 and preached in the regularly scheduled meeting. He reported in the *Gospel Advocate*: "On the third Sunday night I began at Shiloh and continued until Saturday following. and closed with nine additions."[550] That would have been from July 17th through the 23rd of July. He apparently preached one lesson before the actual meeting began; because in his baptismal record book for 1910, he baptized one person at Shiloh.[551] He returned that October and baptized five more into Christ.[552]

In 1911 William Behel held the October meeting at Shiloh and baptized eleven into Christ.[553] For some unknown reason Behel never reported this meeting—as a matter of fact, he never reported that years' work. He could have been very ill during that year, or some other pressing occurrence may have arisen. Whatever the reason he never reported that year's work.

The records are silent on Behel's work and on the congregation at Shiloh for the year 1912. This is a mystery. Did Behel become ill or did something else hinder his work for that year? He was very active for the next year (1913). He gave a summary:

> St. Joseph, Tenn., October 11. I send a message for the "cheerful" page, reporting my summer's work. I held meetings as follows: At Cherry Hill, Tenn., with five additions; Littleville, Ala., eight; Frankfort, Ala., seven; Lone Cedar, Ala., seven; North Carolina, Ala., ten; Barton, Ala., none; Antioch, Ala., two; Shiloh, Ala., fifteen; Macedonia. Ala., ten; Tharp town, Ala., five. This last meeting closed too soon on account of my daughter"s being sick and my having to come home. The brethren there say they will build a house of worship, although there are but fifteen members. I am at home now but have a few meetings I have promised. William Behel.[554]

Here Behel gave his summer schedule. That was probably due to his running a large farm to support his family and summer was what was known in farm terms as "laying by" or when crops need little or no attention until harvest time. That period gave farmer-preachers an opportunity to preach in extended meetings. In the above report, he gave a statement about his Shiloh meeting. He wrote that fifteen were added to the church at that place. His baptismal record book shows sixteen baptized and one restored during that meeting and Behel listed all their names.[555] This could be a case of his having relied upon his memory for the *Gospel Advocate* report rather than his record book.

The year 1914 was a busy year for Shiloh. On Tuesday, July 15, 1914, Behel came and held a week-long meeting. The result was ten persons added to the church at Shiloh. In August J. Paul

Kimbrell came and to Shiloh held an eight-day meeting. His report on the Shiloh meeting is as follows:

> West Point, August 18. On Sunday (August 16), I closed an eight-days meeting at Shiloh Church, in Lauderdale County, Ala. Four were baptized and five restored. Great crowds attended each service. On Saturday night the brethren estimated the number present at five hundred.[556]

Kimbrell was a young preacher who lived in West Point, Tennessee. He lived there all his life. This writer, when a small boy, remembers him at his residence sitting in his rocking chair. He had a long flowing grey beard. With Kimbrell's report this brings us to the end of 1914 which is our ending date for our North Alabama history. Shiloh is still a thriving active congregation to this present day—2024.

Rogersville

It seems that J. T. Harris was the first preacher among the churches of Christ to have preached in Rogersville. Listen to him as he speaks of a series of meetings at that place:

> My last meeting for the year was at Rogersville, Ala., beginning on the second Lord's day in October and closing on the night of the third Lord's day. While there were no additions, I consider this one of the best meetings that I have been in this year; for, if I have been correctly informed, this was the first series of sermons ever preached by one of our brethren there. The Cumberland Presbyterians voluntarily offered us the use of their house; they also attended the meetings and seemed to be well pleased with the preaching. The Lord willing, I will hold a meeting there, next fall. I have baptized eighty-seven people this year. J. T. Harris.[557]

Even though Harris was not successful in baptizing anyone, during that meeting he felt that a work could be established there. He stated that the Cumberland Presbyterians allowed him the use of their building. The Cumberland house of worship would become the regular meeting place for the Rogersville church when it was established. This was the seed planting for future visits by Harris. There were some folks living in Rogersville who were members at Oliver. They may have requested Harris to come and preach a meeting for them in Rogersville, in hopes that a congregation could be established there. For some reason, Harris was not discouraged. He said he intended to return the next fall. Even W. H. Sanday, who lived in Rogersville, was a member at Oliver. Sanday soon began to preach and would eventually preach in meetings at both Oliver and Rogersville.

J. T. Harris returned in the Fall of the following year. He reported:

> Minor Hill, October 11. On the second Sunday in October, I began a meeting at Rogersville, Ala., in the Presbyterian meetinghouse, which continued eight days. There were six baptisms, one was restored, and one abandoned her Baptist name and decided to be a Christian only.[558]

From this meeting, the group became a congregation and from that time forward it was referred to as a church. Remember it was a church but still not organized with elders and deacons. The congregation continued to meet in the Presbyterian meetinghouse and did so until they built their own building in 1914. Some of its early members were:

> Robert Lanier, Joe Bullington, W. L. Stults, who was a former sheriff of Lauderdale County, C. C. Ezell, Ira Bedingfield, Henry B. Romine, M. G. Moore, and H. C. Warren, the song leader. J. D. Longshore, who has served as tax assessor of the county, was also a song leader. His son, H. K. Longshore, a member of the church of Christ, was later probate judge of the county.[559]

Harris returned in 1908 but never reported the results. We know he came because the *Gospel Advocate* said he was in a meeting at Rogersville. It read simply: "He (Harris) is now in a meeting at Rogersville, Ala."[560]

In 1909 Brother Thomas C. King of Etheridge came and held a successful meeting at Rogersville. His report was published in the *Gospel Advocate*:

> Brother Thomas C. King recently closed a good meeting at Rogersville. Ala., with seven baptized. There are now thirty-seven disciples at Rogersville who meet every Sunday afternoon, in the Presbyterian meetinghouse. to worship the Lord. These brethren own a nice lot on which they hope to build a house in which to worship at an early day. Brother King's meeting was held in the Presbyterian meetinghouse.[561]

He gave great spiritual strength to this newly established church. He said that there were thirty-seven disciples in Rogersville at the close of his meeting. He had helped add seven of those precious souls during that meeting. He returned the next year and held another meeting which was reported in the *Gospel Advocate*:

> Brother Thomas C. King, of Etheridge, Tenn., is in a meeting at Rogersville, Ala. He is preaching in the Presbyterian meeting-house. He recently closed his sixth meeting with the Etheridge congregation, with six baptized and three from the Baptists.[562]

The *Gospel Advocate* gave a final report on that meeting: "Brother T. C. King recently closed a good meeting at Rogersville, Ala., with two baptized."[563]

By 1911 the Rogersville congregation had become concerned about a work among the Black population around Rogersville and arranged for S. W. Womack to come and help establish a Black congregation in the Rogersville area. This would result in the Southside congregation. Brother Womack reported the following:

> I am now in Rogersville. Ala., engaged in a mission meeting supported by the white church here. This is a new field among us. The meeting opened with a large attendance. There are no colored[sic] members here. Brother J. A. Harding has just closed a good meeting here for the white church. I am thankful to Brother Harding for his kind words of commendation to the church at Rogersville, and I pray that the Lord will help me to be watchful and live up to it. S. W. Womack.[564]

Womack said that the Black church in Rogersville was supported by the "white church here." This is the earliest account of a white church taking interest in establishing a black work in Lauderdale County. He also mentions that J. A. Harding had just closed a meeting with the white church in Rogersville. This meeting was not reported in the *Gospel Advocate*, except for Womack's mentioning of it. So, we know that there was a meeting by Harding in 1911 and know nothing of the results.

In 1912 Brother R. S. King came and held a very successful meeting He had twenty-three additions to the church at Rogersville and one came from the Baptists.[565] He returned with another successful meeting the following year. The *Gospel Advocate* gave the report:

> Brother R. S. King's meeting at Rogersville, Ala., resulted in thirty-eight additions-thirty-four baptized, four restored-and two thousand dollars raised for a church building. Brother King says: "The fruits of this meeting show the value of good Sunday schools. The most of these additions were young people from three Sunday schools College Hill, Rogersville, and Oliver." Brother King is now on his way to Oxford, Ala., where he is to assume the position of superintendent of schools.[566]

So, from this report we can glean a useful fact—Sunday Schools played an important role in the strengthening of the church. King, it seems, took an important role in these Sunday

Schools, as he was an educator, as well as a minister. It was a sad thing for the Rogersville church that he was leaving the area to head up the schools in Oxford, Alabama. R. S. King also spoke of money being raised to build a new meeting house. This contradicts local lore that said the first house of worship to be owned by the Rogersville church was built in 1909/1910. The building had not been built when R. S. King held his last meeting for Rogersville in 1913.

T. C. King came back for a meeting in August 1914. Here he speaks of a new house of worship being "just built." The report read:

> Athens, Ala., August 15.-The meeting at Rogersville, Ala., closed on August 11, with four baptisms. The brethren had just built them a good meetinghouse and the church is able to do a good work. I am now at Mount Carmel, near Rogersville, in a good meeting. Seven have been baptized to date, August 15. Thomas C. King.[567]

The above reports are the "who done its" These are the accurate records, and they must be followed. That is the only way a true history can be reconstructed. This is the last report for our time frame. Rogersville is a strong congregation numerically and spiritually. They have helped many other works—nationally and internationally. They are still a shining light in the community. We close the early history of the Rogersville Church of Christ.

Lone Cedar

The church at Lone Cedar was started in about 1910 by William M. Behel[568] [Incorrectly given by someone going solely on memory instead of documentation]. A date that has not been proven is how many histories of Lone Cedar begin. William M. Behel is the main character in the story of Lone Cedar. We begin with an introduction to him and his work. Before his conversion, Behel and his future wife rode mules to hear T. B. Larimore preach at the church at Mars Hill. Larimore baptized them in Cox's Creek near the church building, on August 17, 1888. Some years after his baptism Behel decided to preach. Not long afterwards he realized a church needed to be established in his community. Dates for its establishment are "all over the board." Some give the date as late as 1910.[569] Others give it as 1906, 1908, or some other date. The reason for this confusion is that William Behel never told the exact date in any of his writings. We can, however, surmise an approximate date from his baptismal records and a note from the *Gospel Advocate*.

First, let us start with how the congregation got its name. Back in the 1960s, there were congregational singings at many congregations out in the county. One of those singings at Center Hill Church of Christ Fred Hamner (affectionately known as

"Uncle Fred") got up to lead a song and for some reason, he told a story first. He told us how Lone Cedar got its name. He was just a lad at the time but old enough to help work on the building. He said when the last work was finished: "Uncle Will Behel walked to the door as he was dusting his hands—looked out the door and saw one lone cedar tree standing near the front of the building. He exclaimed to the workers—Well boys we are going to call her 'Lone Cedar.'" So, the building was built after the congregation was established. William Behel kept good records of the baptisms he performed. In his records, the baptisms at Lone Cedar began on December 23, 1900. The names of the first three baptized at Lone Cedar were May Behel, Mary E. Peden, and Mollie Peden.[570] That indicates that the building was already built and named. His records began with 1900 and go through the 1920s.

The second thing that aids in establishing an approximate date is an article written about Behel's daughter—May. Someone wrote a note in the *Gospel Advocate* about her teaching Sunday School classes. It was under the heading:

> What a Little Miss Can Do. — In making some inquiry as to the progress of our Sunday school, I learned that a very intelligent little lady, Miss May Behel, at the early age of fifteen years, is teaching the Bible class at Lone Cedar, Ala. Miss May was baptized into the Christian faith on December 23, 1900. She deserves great success in her work. A Reader, Mar's Hill, Ala. [571]

The building was obviously built in 1900 from the above evidence. We see that not long after the church was started, a building was erected which served as a schoolhouse and church. It faced the old Jackson Highway. When the new highway was completed, the building was turned around so it would face the new highway.[572] From this information, the church could have been established as early as 1899. The best time for the beginning is the summer of 1900. That would have been the season for gospel meetings.

Behel did not preach regularly at Lone Cedar as is shown by the baptismal records. He baptized seven persons in 1901; two in 1904; three in 1905 and several restored. The records run thus through his entire preaching career. His first report on Lone Cedar to the *Gospel Advocate* was made in 1907. His report was noticeably short. It was only three lines:

> Brother William Behel, R. F. D. No. 5, Florence, Ala., reports one confession at the regular service at Lone Cedar, eleven miles from Florence, on the third Lord's day in this month.[573]

His reports came sporadically on the Lone Cedar work. This report was rather short for one of his reports. This may have been because he was still concerned about the congregation's spiritual growth, as will be noted later. His second report was not very much longer than his first. It read:

> St. Joseph, September 13. I will report my summer's work in Lauderdale County, Ala. My first meeting at Waterloo, which resulted in twelve additions, has already been reported. I preached ten days at Jacksonburg, with one baptism: eight days at Lone Cedar, with one restoration and one baptism... William Behel.[574]

His preaching for eight days brought only one baptism and one restoration. This was not typical of Behel's meetings. In 1908 he described Lone Cedar as "lethargic." He wrote: "Lone Cedar is somewhat lethargic. but is improving."[575] That, to say the least, was not very complementary. Perhaps that was the reason Behel did not report much on that work.

Behel's address, at this time, was St. Joseph, Tennessee, route one; but he lived seven or eight miles south of the Tennessee state line. This writer was a substitute mail carrier on that route for about a year during 1968–1969. His house was not more than three hundred yards from the Lone Cedar church building.

Another report came from Lone Cedar in September 1908. Behel reported of his plans to begin a meeting at Lone Cedar on October 1, 1908.[576] Unfortunately for us, nothing useful was contained in the report. Mention this only to show that he intended to hold the meeting, but the meeting was never reported in any brotherhood journal. We do, however, have his baptismal records. He preached on the Sunday prior to the beginning of the meeting and baptized one and restored one. He then extended the meeting because he baptized two more on the 11th of October.[577]

The work at Lone Cedar must have been a little disappointing for Behel because of the low number of souls being gleaned for the Master at that place. It would be four years before a report containing any reference to Lone Cedar would appear in the *Gospel Advocate*. However, in Behel's baptismal records, he held a meeting in August 1909, with five baptisms.[578] He did send a report in to the *Gospel Advocate*. We give the following:

> From August 15 to August 20, I preached the word at Lone Cedar, and baptized seven persons. On August 22 Brother J. P. Ezell, a Potter Bible College student, preached at Lone Cedar to a large audience. William Behel.[579]

It is interesting that Behel wrote of J. Petty Ezell having preached at Lone Cedar. Ezell was a Rogersville native and later became a very popular preacher throughout the South. After this meeting, Behel recorded nothing for Lone Cedar until 1913. In that meeting of 1913, he recorded six baptisms and one restoration.[580] In the *Gospel Advocate,* he wrote that there were seven additions. He combined the baptisms and the restoration into one statistic.[581]

Then came Behel's final report within our set time frame.

This report gave a ray of hope for the future of Lone Cedar. We give the report in full:

> St. Joseph, Tenn., April 30. Yesterday was a busy day with me. I preached at three different places, traveling about twenty miles, and baptized a very intelligent young man. At the night service, at Lone Cedar, I secured a promise from the congregation to begin keeping house for the Lord, and I am looking for an advance on the line of duty there. The three points referred to are in Alabama. There is much work in the rural districts in North Alabama. The "field is ripe unto the harvest," but laborers are few. William Behel.[582]

Behel gave an unexpected picture of the church at Lone Cedar. The church had apparently stopped meeting on a regular basis or had stopped all together, but then they agreed to "keep house." He must have gotten a little joy writing "they agreed to begin keeping house" again. Things turned around at Lone Cedar. In 2024 Lone Cedar is one of the largest rural congregations with over two hundred members.

Pleasant Valley

The church at Pleasant Valley was established sometime before October 1904. [A word of caution—there is a congregation east of Rogersville and in Limestone County, very close to the Lauderdale County line— not to be confused with the congregation under discussion]. The community was originally known as Frog Pond, as a pond was located near the school building in which the church worshipped at first. W. D. Craig came and held a meeting for a month beginning in July and ending in August. A report on this meeting was sent to the *Gospel Advocate*. It was short but to the point:

> I held a meeting at Pleasant Valley Church, in Lauderdale County, beginning on July 7 and closing on August 7. The brethren seemed encouraged and aroused to greater zeal and there appeared to be fine interest and good attention. but there were no additions. Sheffield, Alabama. W. D. Craig.[583]

This report reveals that the church had already been established at that place before Craig came. Even though there were no additions the church was edified. It is important for a congregation to have edification in order to grow and be spiritually sound.

Craig apparently did that because he wrote: "The brethren seemed encouraged and aroused to greater zeal."

The next reported meeting came when William Behel held a meeting in September 1906. It was not reported in the *Gospel Advocate* but was recorded in Behel's baptismal records. He baptized four and had two restorations.[584] Behel made plans to return in August 1907 for another meeting. This time he reported his intentions for the meeting: "I expect to begin a meeting at Pleasant Valley, Ala., on August 17th."[585] His records show him having one restoration on August 21st.[586] Later he reported on his summer's work:

> St. Joseph, September 13.-I will report my summer's work in Lauderdale County, Ala...nine days at Pleasant Valley, with one reclaimed;[587]

Note that this report was only on his Lauderdale County work. The reason for this explanation is that there is a Pleasant Valley congregation just over the Limestone County line and east of Rogersville—often confused with Pleasant Valley near Center Star, Lauderdale County.

In 1908 William G. Harrison from the Hopewell community, Colbert County, came and started a meeting and it was finished by J. Petty Ezell. We give the report in full due to some interesting facts contained therein:

> Killen, August 22. On Sunday, August 2, Brother William Harrison closed a meeting with the congregation at Antioch, with eleven additions—eight by baptism and three by restoration. On Sunday night he began a meeting at Pleasant Valley and preached until Wednesday night, when he had to leave to meet an appointment at another place. Brother Petty Ezell continued the meeting until the following Wednesday night, with seven baptized, one restored, and one from the Baptists. This was Brother Ezell's first meeting, and these seven persons were the

first he ever baptized. We had services only at night, as Brother Ezell was teaching at the same place. Brother Harrison and Brother Ezell are both young men, and both expect to enter the Potter Bible College in October. J. W. Williams.[588]

This was Ezell's first meeting. We learn that he was teaching in the Pleasant Valley School, which was the same building as the church. This meeting was the first time that Ezell had ever baptized anyone. We also learn that both Harrison and Ezell were planning to attend Potter Bible College in Bowling Green, Kentucky. Ezell followed through with his plans and Harrison went to Nashville Bible School (now Lipscomb University).

J. T. Harris came to Pleasant Valley in 1909 and held a meeting. The *Gospel Advocate* published the following:

Brother J. T. Harris recently held meetings at the following places in Alabama: At Oliver, with six baptized and two restored; Pleasant Valley, with three restored. He is now in a meeting at Bunker Hill, Giles County, Tenn.[589]

From this report, we learn that there was a gospel meeting at Pleasant Valley and who conducted it. That is about all we can learn from reports such as this one. They are brief and to the point—no reporting on conditions or events at the places where the meetings are held.

J. Petty Ezell, who grew up in the Rogersville area, held a meeting at Pleasant Valley, where he was teaching school. The report gave a brief statement:

Brother J. Petty Ezell recently closed an eight days' meeting at Pleasant Valley, Lauderdale County, Ala., with two baptisms. [590]

The last official report on the church at Pleasant Valley came from the pen of W. G. (Uncle Billy) Harrison. It states:

Sheffield, Route 1, November 13. I present herewith a brief summary of my summer's work. I was at Pleasant Valley. in Lauderdale County, July 19-26, with two reclaimed; Antioch, in Lauderdale County, from July 26 to August 2, with six baptized... W. G. Harrison.[591]

Uncle Billy Harrison, as he was affectionately known, preached often for Pleasant Valley through many years. He lived in Colbert County. On Sunday mornings he would leave the Hopewell community and travel eastward along the south side of the river until he got within about two miles of where Wheeler Dam is situated today (2024). He kept an old wooden boat tied up at his crossing place—he would get into the boat and paddle across the river near the road that led to Pleasant Valley. Someone would meet him with a horse, and they would travel to the church building where he remained until he had finished the service. He would then be taken to his boat, and he would paddle back across the river and make the long journey home.[592] During meetings, he would stay with the Watsons or the Yanceys. With the above information, we bring the story of Pleasant Valley to a close.

ROMINE

We know that Thomas L. Weatherford (a former "Larimore Boy") was coming into that community and preaching because he performed at least one marriage there on September 13, 1890. It was reported to the *Gospel Advocate*. It read as follows:

> Married, near Rogersville, Ala., Feb. 13, Brother Butler Wallace and Sister Malissa Rominenes. T. L. Weatherford.[593]

Thus, the earliest report from the Romine-Goose Flat community came as a wedding report. It was sent by the minister Tom Weatherford. There were two errors in the report—the names of the bride and groom were misspelled. Bular Wallace is the correct name for the groom, not Butler. The bride's maiden name is "Romine" not "Rominenes"[594] The *Gospel Advocate* made many errors with people's names, due to the hand-written notes sent to them. From this note, we see that Weatherford, who lived sixteen miles away in Limestone County was known in this community and most likely by his preaching at the Romine Schoolhouse. The above wedding more than likely occurred during a gospel meeting. Sixteen miles was a very long journey to make just for a wedding, especially in those days.

The following history is taken from a Romine directory:

> In this community, geese from all around would come to a certain flat place every day (you could always see geese there). Therefore, the community became known as "Goose Flat."
>
> In the early 1900's, a school was built on some land donated by Bennet Romine. It was a wood structure built by men of the community. School was held there during the week and church services on Sunday. The congregation of the church that met there was called Goose Flat Church of Christ. Folks walked or came in wagons or buggies to church. There was no electricity. A good well supplied plenty of water to drink for the people as well as the horses and mules. There were plenty of oak trees around to hitch the horses to while services were going on.
>
> Every year on the second Sunday in August (this time of year was chosen because by now people had "laid by" their crops and had time to come), a gospel meeting was held. They had preaching followed by dinner on the ground at noon then a singing in the afternoon. The meeting lasted a week. When they had baptisms, they were done in a nearby creek. The building was always full during the meetings. The windows were open and lots of people stood outside by the windows. The preacher and his family stayed with members of the congregation during the meeting.[595]

In 1914 the church was finally organized with elders and deacons. This transpired when Tom Polk was holding a gospel meeting. Eris Bonner Benson said that Polk established the church at Romine, but he likely meant organized rather than established. [596] The church had been established several years before and most probably by T. L. Weatherford, who had been preaching in the Romine community since the 1890s.

We searched for any information sent to the *Gospel Advocate* under the name—T. L. Weatherford, W. H. Sanday, and under Goose Flat and Romine. There was no more information than what is presented in this short essay. That brings our history of the Romine Church of Christ confined to our timetable. After 1914 several articles relating to Romine appear in the *Gospel Advocate*—but that is for another time.

This brings us to the close of the history of Lauderdale County, Alabama.

At the of time this writing there were more than seventy churches of Christ in this county. That is why more congregations were discussed in Lauderdale County than in the other counties. We have tried to keep these works in chronological order, so, with the counties.

Endnotes

[1] Donald Townsley, *Gospel Guardian* (February 8, 1973), 614.
[2] *Gospel Advocate* (January 1860), 32.
[3] Donald Townsley, *Gospel Guardian* (February 8, 1973), 614.
[4] *Gospel Advocate* (January 1860), 32.
[5] *Gospel Luminary* (October–November 1831), 52.
[6] B. F. Hall, *Handwritten Autobiography*, 57.
[7] *Christian Messenger* (November 25, 1826), 24.
[8] B. F. Hall, *Handwritten Autobiography*, 57.
[9] *Millennial Harbinger* (November 1843), 511–14.
[10] B. F. Hall, *Handwritten Autobiography*, 45
[11] B. F. Hall, *Handwritten Autobiography*, 57.
[12] *Firm Foundation* (March 1885), 19–20.
[13] B. F. Hall, *Handwritten Autobiography*, (the next page after p. 57, had no number, because Hall intended for it, along with another half page to be inserted after Fanning's baptism).
[14] *Christian Messenger* (July 25, 1827), 213.
[15] *Christian Messenger* (November 1827), 16–17.
[16] *Christian Messenger* (December 1828), 42.
[17] *Christian Reformer* (August 1829), 379.
[18] *Christian Messenger* (December 1830), 284–85.

[19] *Gospel Luminary* (October–November 1831), 52.

[20] *Alexander Campbell's Subscription Ledger 1830–1836*, 309.

[21] B. F. Riley, *History of the Baptists of Alabama* (Birmingham: Roberts and Sons, 1875), 75.

[22] Hosea Holcomb, *A History of the Rise and Progress of the Baptists in Alabama* (Philadelphia: King and Laird, 1840), 206.

[23] *Christian Messenger* (December 1831), 280.

[24] *Christian Messenger* (December 1830), 285.

[25] *Christian Messenger* (January 1832), 27.

[26] *Christian Messenger* (December 1832), 376–77.

[27] *Christian Messenger* (September 1833), 279; 285.

[28] *Christian Messenger* (September 1833), 287.

[29] *Gospel Luminary* (October–November 1831), 52.

[30] *Christian Messenger* (January 1833), p. 32).

[31] *Christian Messenger* (August 1834), 256.

[32] *Alexander Campbell's Subscription Ledger 1830–1836*, 309.

[33] *Marriage Book–1835*, (Lauderdale County Courthouse, Florence, Alabama), 607.

[34] *Christian Messenger* (June 1836), 92.

[35] *Christian Messenger* (November 1836), 173.

[36] *Bible Advocate* (December 1842), 78.

[37] *Bible Advocate* (November 1843), 64.

[38] *Christian Messenger* (July 1830), 214.

[39] *Christian Review* (December 1844), 265.

[40] *Millennial Harbinger* (April 1842), 186.

[41] *Christian Messenger* (May 1844), 29.

[42] Bethelberry Church Records, 9–10.

[43] Confirmed in a conversation with E. H. Ijams on March 15, 1979.

[44] Bethelberry Church Records, 1.

[45] *Deed Book, 1853*, (Lauderdale County Courthouse, Florence, Alabama), 612.

[46] *Gospel Advocate* (December 1856), 375; (October 1858), 320.
[47] *Christian Review* (May 1845), 113.
[48] *Christian Review* (September 1845), 206–8.
[49] *Christian Review* (December 1846), 268.
[50] *Christian Register*, (only one issue ever published, 1848), preface.
[51] *Deed Book, 1853* (Lauderdale County Courthouse, Florence, Alabama), 612.
[52] *Christian Register* (1848), preface.
[53] J. H. Dunn's personal letter, May 11, 1849. Found in the Gresham family papers of which a copy is in the library at Heritage Christian University.
[54] *Christian Magazine* (October 1851), 317.
[55] *Christian Magazine* (September 1850), 288.
[56] *Christian Magazine* (February 1852), 63.
[57] *Christian Magazine* (June 1852), 188.
[58] *Christian Magazine* (September 1852), 287.
[59] *Gospel Advocate* (December 1860), 375—6.
[60] *Christian Magazine* (June 1852), 173.
[61] *Deed Book, 1853* (Lauderdale County Courthouse, Florence, Alabama), 612.
[62] *Deed Book, 1853* (Lauderdale County Courthouse, Florence, Alabama), 612.
[63] *Gospel Advocate* (December 1856), 375.
[64] *Gospel Advocate* (December 1856), 375.
[65] *Gospel Advocate* (October 1860), 319.
[66] *Gospel Advocate* (December 1860), 376.
[67] *Gospel Advocate* (December 1860), 376.
[68] *Gospel Advocate* (October 1860), 319.
[69] *Gospel Advocate* (October 1860), 319.
[70] *Millennial Harbinger* (May 1845), 195.
[71] 1860 U.S. Census of Lauderdale County, Alabama.
[72] *Church Book*, Title page.

[73] F. D. Srygley, *Smiles and Tears: or Larimore and His Boys*. (Nashville, TN: Gospel Advocate Company, 1989), 136–37.

[74] *Gospel Advocate* (June 26, 1906), 469.

[75] *Gospel Advocate* (June 28, 1877), 409.

[76] Srygley, *Larimore And His Boys*, 155.

[77] *Gospel Advocate* (July 18, 1883), 458.

[78] *Gospel Advocate* (July 18, 1883), 458.

[79] *Gospel Advocate* (July 8, 1885), 423.

[80] Deed to Stoney Point Church, *Deed Book, 1886*, (Lauderdale County Courthouse, Florence, Alabama), 383.

[81] *Gospel Advocate* (July 15, 1885), 439.

[82] *Gospel Advocate* (December 10, 1891), 780.

[83] *Deed Book, 1853*, (Lauderdale County Courthouse, Florence, Alabama), 612.

[84] *Gospel Advocate* (September 10, 1903), 589.

[85] *Gospel Advocate* (June 26, 1906), 469.

[86] *Gospel Advocate* (June 4, 1908), 364.

[87] *Gospel Advocate* (November 5, 1908), 709.

[88] *Gospel Advocate* (September 2, 1909), 1112.

[89] *Gospel Advocate* (October 6, 1910), 1116-7.

[90] *Gospel Advocate* (October 13, 1910), 1140.

[91] *Gospel Advocate* (August 22, 1888), 14.

[92] B. F. Hall, *Unpublished Journal*, 47.

[93] Marshall D'Spain's Will, Lauderdale County, *Will Book 1824-1825*.

[94] *Christian Messenger* (December 1832), 380.

[95] *Christian Messenger* (July 1834), 224.

[96] *Christian Messenger* (August 1834), 256.

[97] *Christian Messenger* (January 1836), 16.

[98] *Christian Register*, (1848), inside cover page.

[99] The Mansell W. Matthews Papers in Texas Christian University library, Fort Worth, Texas.

[100] *Gospel Advocate* (December 1860), 364.

[101] *Gospel Advocate* (October 8, 1884), 651.

[102] *Gospel Advocate* (November 26, 1884), 757.

[103] *Gospel Advocate* (November 4, 1880), 712.
[104] *Gospel Advocate* (October 8, 1884), 651.
[105] *Gospel Advocate* (May 28, 1890), 346.
[106] *Gospel Advocate* (October 8, 1890), 642.
[107] *Gospel Advocate* (August 4, 1898), 496.
[108] *Gospel Advocate* (July 6, 1899), 429.
[109] *Gospel Advocate* (July 5, 1900), 417.
[110] *Gospel Advocate* (September 12, 1901), 588.
[111] *Gospel Advocate* (October 29, 1903), 689.
[112] *Gospel Advocate* (October 1, 1903), 636.
[113] *Gospel Advocate* (February 7, 1907), 85.
[114] *Gospel Advocate* (October 17. 1907), 669.
[115] *Gospel Advocate* (August 22, 1907), 533.
[116] *Gospel Advocate* (October 17. 1907), 661.
[117] Revelation 2: 10.
[118] *Gospel Advocate* (June 4, 1908), 364.
[119] *Gospel Advocate* (July 23, 1908), 462.
[120] *Gospel Advocate* (August 6, 1908), 501.
[121] *Gospel Advocate* (March 4, 1909), 272.
[122] *Gospel Advocate* (July 15, 1909), 871.
[123] *Gospel Advocate* (July 15, 1909), 880.
[124] *Gospel Advocate* (February 23, 1911), 246.
[125] *Gospel Advocate* (October 24, 1912), 1173.
[126] *Gospel Advocate* (March 13, 1913), 261.
[127] *Deed Book 1827*, Lauderdale County, Alabama, 103.
[128] *Apostolic Times* (June 11, 1874), front page.
[129] *Gospel Advocate* (December 10, 1891), 779.
[130] *Christian Messenger* (December 1831), 280–281; *Gospel Luminary* (October-November 1831), 52.
[131] *Deed Book 1832*, Lauderdale County, Alabama, 326.
[132] *Campbell's Subscription Book*, 309.
[133] Deed Book 1848, 372–373.
[134] Deed Book 1848, 373.
[135] *Christian Review* (August 1844), 191.
[136] *Christian Review* (May 1845), 119.

[137] *Christian Review* (May 1845), 112.
[138] *Christian Register*, (1848), 38.
[139] *Christian Review* (August 1844), 191.
[140] *Official Records*—SERIES I—m, VOL. XLIX/1 [S# 103, pp. 355] March 22–April 24, 1865).
[141] *Gospel Advocate* (June 17, 1869), 658.
[142] *Gospel Advocate* (November 4, 1880), 712.
[143] Holcomb, *History of the Rise and Progress of the Baptists in Alabama*, 208–209.
[144] *Christian Review* (August 1844), 191.
[145] *Christian Register* (1848), inside cover page.
[146] *Gospel Advocate* (January 4, 1894), 12.
[147] Charles Beavers, Interview, 2010.
[148] *Gospel Advocate* (October 24, 1867), 859.
[149] *Deed Book* 1867, Lauderdale County Courthouse, Florence, Alabama, 580–581.
[150] Srygley, *Larimore and His Boys*, 98.
[151] Srygley, *Larimore and His Boys*, 34.
[152] *Gospel Advocate* (August 19, 1869), 784–785.
[153] F. B. Srygley, *Letters and Sermons*, vol II, (Nashville: McQuiddy Printing, 1910), 44.
[154] *Gospel Advocate* (August 31, 1871), 798–799.
[155] *Gospel Advocate* (October 9, 1879), 646.
[156] *Gospel Advocate* (October 23, 1879), 683.
[157] *Gospel Advocate* (July 1, 1880), 423.
[158] *Gospel Advocate* (February 20, 1884), 119.
[159] *Gospel Advocate* (September 17, 1884), 603.
[160] *Gospel Advocate* (May 26, 1886), 331.
[161] *Gospel Advocate* (May 26, 1886), 331.
[162] *Gospel Advocate* (March 25, 1891), 186.
[163] *Gospel Advocate* (October 14. 1891), 649–650.
[164] *Gospel Advocate* (December 10, 1891), 780.
[165] *Gospel Advocate* (September 15, 1892), 583.
[166] *Gospel Advocate* (October 13, 1892), 648.
[167] *Gospel Advocate* (July 6, 1893), 430.

[168] *Gospel Advocate* (August 2, 1894), 486.
[169] *Gospel Advocate* (August 26, 1897), 530.
[170] *Gospel Advocate* (August 30, 1894), 550.
[171] *Gospel Advocate* (June 30, 1898), 406.
[172] *Gospel Advocate* (September 1, 1898), 549.
[173] *Gospel Advocate* (October 6, 1898), 640.
[174] *Gospel Advocate* (February 15, 1940), 147.
[175] *Gospel Advocate* (December 24, 1903), 819.
[176] A Flyer titled "An Appeal."; *Gospel Advocate* (August 30, 1903), 285.
[177] *Gospel Advocate* (November 5, 1903), 709.
[178] *Gospel Advocate* (September 3, 1903), 575.
[179] *Florence Times* (August 15, 1904).
[180] J. C. Ott, *Diary* (August 1904).
[181] *Gospel Advocate* (March 14, 1907), 169.
[182] *Gospel Advocate* (July 18, 1907), 451.
[183] Srygley, *Larimore and His Boys*, 221.
[184] *Gospel Advocate* (October 24, 1907), 685.
[185] *Gospel Advocate* (November 9, 1911), 1302.
[186] *Gospel Advocate* (July 31, 1913), 733.
[187] *Gospel Advocate* (October 8, 1914), 1060.
[188] *Gospel Advocate* (October 22, 1914), 1110.
[189] Srygley, *Larimore and His Boys*, 94–95.
[190] J. M. Pickens, Jr., *Letter to Richard L. James*, 1936.
[191] Mrs. T. B. Larimore, *T. B. Larimore's Life, Letters, and Sermons* (Nashville, Tenn: Gospel Advocate Company, 1955), 107–113.
[192] Basil Overton was one of the writer's teachers at International Bible College.
[193] Holcomb, *History of the Rise and Progress of the Baptists in Alabama*, 206.
[194] Eris Bonner Benson, "The Church of Christ in Lauderdale County, Alabama" (Thesis, Alabama Polytechnic Institute, 1949), 27; M. V. Freeman gave this information to Eris Bonner Benson.

[195] *Bethelberry Church Book*, 9.
[196] Srygley, *Larimore and His Boys*, 34.
[197] Srygley, *Larimore and His Boys*, 184–185.
[198] Srygley, *Larimore and His Boys*, 184–185.
[199] Srygley, *Larimore and His Boys*, 34–35.
[200] *Bethelberry Church Book*, 3.
[201] *Bethelberry Church Book*, 3.
[202] *Gospel Advocate* (September 17, 1868), 899.
[203] *Bethelberry Church Book*, 9.
[204] *Bethelberry Church Book*, 17.
[205] *Bethelberry Church Book*, 17.
[206] *Deed Book, 1888,* Lauderdale County, Alabama, 350.
[207] *Bethelberry Church Book*, 17.
[208] Bethelberry Church Book, 11–12.
[209] *Gospel Advocate* (October 5, 1871), 924.
[210] *Gospel Advocate* (April 4, 1883), 212.
[211] *Gospel Advocate* (July 18, 1883), 458.
[212] Srygley, *Larimore and His Boys*, 35.
[213] *Gospel Advocate* (November 21, 1878), 731.
[214] *Bethelberry Church Book*, 21, 23.
[215] *Gospel Advocate* (November 5, 1890), 706.
[216] *Gospel Advocate* (January 4, 1894), 12.
[217] *Gospel Advocate* (August 26, 1926), 800.
[218] *Gospel Advocate* (April 22, 1880), 266.
[219] *Gospel Advocate* (March 24, 1881), 182.
[220] Interview with Sister Plot in 1993, Rogersville, Alabama.
[221] Benson, "The Church of Christ in Lauderdale County, Alabama" 27–28; Interview, December 17, 1948, with H. C. Warren and Henry B. Romine, Rogersville, Alabama.
[222] *Deed Book, February 25, 1870,* Lauderdale County Courthouse, Florence, Alabama, 215.
[223] *Gospel Advocate* (September 14, 1871), 851.
[224] *Gospel Advocate* (August 16, 1877), 507.
[225] Benson, "The Church of Christ in Lauderdale County,

Alabama." 27–28; Personal interview, December 17, 1948, with H. C. Warren and Henry B. Romine, Rogersville, Alabama.

[226] *Gospel Advocate* (July 1, 1880), 423.
[227] *Gospel Advocate* (September 26, 1888), 3.
[228] *Gospel Advocate* (October 12, 1893), 652.
[229] *Gospel Advocate* (November 9, 1893), 716.
[230] (*Gospel Advocate* (October 3, 1895), 636.
[231] William Lindsey McDonald, *A Walk Through the Past* (Florence, Alabama, 1997), 150.
[232] *Oliver Church Record Book* (1938), 1.
[233] *Gospel Advocate* (February 14, 1935), 168.
[234] *Gospel Advocate* (August 23, 1906), 540.
[235] *Gospel Advocate* (December 27, 1906), 832.
[236] *Gospel Advocate* (August 1, 1907), 485.
[237] *Gospel Advocate* (August 15, 1907), 517.
[238] *Gospel Advocate* (September 24, 1908), 613.
[239] *Gospel Advocate* (October 22, 1908), 677.
[240] *Gospel Advocate* (December 11, 1913), 1224.
[241] *Gospel Advocate* (January 22, 1914), 112.
[242] Indian Creek Baptist Association Records, 1875.
[243] Holcomb, *History of the Baptist in Alabama*, 208.
[244] *Marriage Book 5, 1841–1852*, Lauderdale County Courthouse, Florence, Alabama.
[245] Percy D. Wright's Handwritten Journal.
[246] *Christian Review*, (Vol. 1. 2), 24.
[247] B.F. Riley, *History of the Baptists of Alabama* (1895), 79.
[248] *US Agricultural Census, Lauderdale County, Alabama, 1850*, 567.
[249] "Organizational Minutes," Mt. Pleasant Baptist Church, (1854), p.1).
[250] *General U.S. Census of 1850*, Lauderdale County, Alabama, Entry Number 814.
[251] *US Census 1860*, 25.
[252] *Return of Qualified Voters Registry* (1867).

[253] "Mt. Pleasant Organizational Minutes," Mt. Pleasant Baptist Church.

[254] Wm. Comer, *Gospel Advocate* (May 11, 1876), 454.

[255] Wm. Comer, *Gospel Advocate* (December 9, 1875), 1174.

[256] Wm. Comer, *Gospel Advocate* (December 9, 1875), 1174.

[257] Wm. Comer, *Gospel Advocate* (May 11, 1876), 454.

[258] Wm. Comer, *Gospel Advocate* (May 11, 1876), 454.

[259] Mt Pleasant Baptist Church, Lexington, Alabama, (October 2, 1875), 125.

[260] Mt Pleasant Baptist Church, Lexington, Alabama, (November 6, 1875), 126.

[261] Mt Pleasant Baptist Church, Lexington, Alabama, (December 4, 1875), 127.

[262] Wm. Comer, *Gospel Advocate* (May 11, 1876), 454.

[263] J.T. Wood, *Gospel Advocate* (August 10, 1876), 378.

[264] J.T. Wood, *Gospel Advocate* (August 10, 1876), 378.

[265] *Mt. Pleasant 150th Year Celebration*, 5.

[266] *Mt. Pleasant Record Book*, 1859.

[267] R.W. Officer, *Gospel Advocate* (July 1, 1880), 423.

[268] "Askew to Comer," *Gospel Advocate* (November 4, 1880), 712.

[269] "Askew to Comer," *Gospel Advocate* (November 4, 1880), 712.

[270] "Askew to Comer," *Gospel Advocate* (November 4, 1880), 712.

[271] "Askew to Comer," *Gospel Advocate* (November 4, 1880), 712

[272] R.W. Officer, *Gospel Advocate* (July 1, 1880), 423.

[273] *Firm Foundation* (February 1885), 11.

[274] *Octographic Review* (January 4, 1887), 3

[275] R.W. Officer, *Gospel Advocate* (July 1, 1880), 423.

[276] R. W. Officer, *Octographic Review*, January 4, 1887), 3.

[277] B. C. Burney, "Chickasaw Academic Leaflet," (May 1881, Vol. 1. 111), 121.

[278] *Gospel Advocate* (February 13, 1884), 99.

[279] *Gospel Advocate* (May 11, 1876), 454–455.
[280] *Gospel Advocate* (May 11, 1876), 454.
[281] *Gospel Advocate* (March 17, 1921), 252.
[282] *Gospel Advocate* (March 17, 1921), 252.
[283] Srygley, *Larimore and His Boys*, 198.
[284] *Gospel Advocate* (June 17, 1885), 378.
[285] *Gospel Advocate* (October 13, 1881), 646.
[286] *Gospel Advocate* (August 11, 1892), 505.
[287] *Gospel Advocate* (September 25, 1902), 613.
[288] *Gospel Advocate* (June 5, 1913), 533.
[289] *Gospel Advocate* (October 22, 1914), 1110.
[290] *US Return Qualified Voters Register*, Entry 134.
[291] "Jones to Union Grove Christian Church," *Deed Book 24*, Lauderdale County Court House, 493.
[292] *Christian Review*, (Vol. 1, No. 2), 24.
[293] Riley, *History of the Baptists Of Alabama* (1895), 79.
[294] *US Census* 1850.
[295] *Organizational Minutes*, Mt. Pleasant Baptist Church, (1854), 1.
[296] Nathan Wright, Interview, 2011.
[297] Wm. Comer, *Gospel Advocate* (May 11, 1876), 454.
[298] Wm. Comer, *Gospel Advocate* (December 9, 1875), 1174.
[299] Wm. Comer, *Gospel Advocate* (May 11, 1876), 454.
[300] Wm. Comer, *Gospel Advocate* (May 11, 1876), 454.
[301] Wm. Comer, *Gospel Advocate* (May 11, 1876), 454.
[302] *Gospel Advocate* (May 11, 1876), 455.
[303] J.T. Wood, *Gospel Advocate* (August 10, 1876), 378.
[304] J.T. Wood, *Gospel Advocate* (August 10, 1876), 378.
[305] J. R. Graves, ed., *The Baptist*, (August 19, 1876), 580.
[306] *The Baptist*, Oct. 14, 1876), 707.
[307] *The Baptist*, (Jan. 13, 1877), 84.
[308] *Gospel Advocate* (May 27, 1920), 536.
[309] *Gospel Advocate* (September 18, 1879), 603.
[310] *Gospel Advocate* (May 5, 1881), 280.
[311] *Gospel Advocate* (Sept. 29, 1881), 611.

[312] *Record Book* (beginning January 11, 1882), 1.
[313] "Jones to Union Grove Christian Church," *Deed Book 24*, Lauderdale County Court House, 493.
[314] *Gospel Advocate* (September 3, 1884), 570.
[315] *Gospel Advocate* (May 27, 1920), 536.
[316] *Gospel Advocate* (August 14, 1889), 526.
[317] *Gospel Advocate* (September 3, 1890), 563.
[318] *Gospel Advocate* (May 10, 1891), 289.
[319] *Gospel Advocate* (January 4, 1894), 12.
[320] *Gospel Advocate* (August 26, 1897), 541.
[321] Interview with Nathan Wright, Percy's son, in 2010.
[322] *Gospel Advocate* (September 14, 1899), 588.
[323] *Gospel Advocate* (October 17, 1901), 668.
[324] *Firm Foundation* (October 28, 1902), 3.
[325] *Gospel Advocate* (December 11, 1902), 789.
[326] Compiled by Mable Wright Parker, Typed by Ethel Michael, (May 12, 1968).
[327] *Gospel Advocate* (August 6, 1908), 501.
[328] *Gospel Advocate* (August 13, 1908), 517.
[329] *Gospel Advocate* (October 7, 1909), 1280.
[330] *Union Grove/North Carolina Trustees Ledger* (April 1907–April 1917).
[331] *Gospel Advocate* (August 27, 1914), 920.
[332] *Gospel Advocate* (February 14, 1878, p. 104).
[333] *Indian Creek Missionary Baptist Association Minutes* (1873-1875).
[334] *Gospel Advocate* (August 29, 1878), 541.
[335] *Gospel Advocate* (September 10, 1890), 578.
[336] *Indian Creek Baptist Association Records* (1875).
[337] *Indian Creek Baptist Association Records* (1875).
[338] *Gospel Advocate* (June 12, 1879), 370.
[339] Wm. Comer, *Gospel Advocate* (May 11, 1876), 454.
[340] *Gospel Advocate* (July 22, 1880), 447.
[341] *Gospel Advocate* (October 28, 1880), 696.
[342] *Gospel Advocate* (February 10, 1881), 91.

[343] *Gospel Advocate* (May 5, 1881), 280.
[344] *Gospel Advocate* (April 30, 1884), 284. [The Brother Turner was H. H. Turner, a student at Mars Hill—CWK].
[345] *Gospel Advocate* (July 2, 1884), 420.
[346] *Gospel Advocate* (August 29, 1885), 535.
[347] *Gospel Advocate* (August 11, 1886), 510.
[348] *Gospel Advocate* (April 11, 1888), 10.
[349] *Gospel Advocate* (November 6, 1889), 718.
[350] *Gospel Advocate* (September 10, 1890), 578.
[351] *Gospel Advocate* (August 11, 1892), 509.
[352] *Gospel Advocate* (October 12, 1893), 652.
[353] Wm. M. Behel's Baptismal Records for 1902–1912.
[354] *Gospel Advocate* (July 23, 1914), 796.
[355] Interview with Melvin Campbell, (1972).
[356] *Gospel Advocate* (March 17, 1921), 252.
[357] *Gospel Advocate* (November 4, 1880), 712.
[358] *Gospel Advocate* (July 1, 1880), 423.
[359] *Gospel Advocate* (June 23, 1881), 392.
[360] *Gospel Advocate* (November 26, 1890), 761.
[361] *Gospel Advocate* (October 14, 1891), 648.
[362] *Gospel Advocate* (August 19, 1891), 516.
[363] *Gospel Advocate* (August 11, 1892), 505.
[364] *Gospel Advocate* (April 5, 1894), 214).
[365] *Gospel Advocate* (October 6, 1898, p. 640).
[366] Warren and Romine, interview, (December 17, 1948); Benson, 39–40.
[367] *Gospel Advocate* (July 22, 1880), 477.
[368] *Gospel Advocate* (August 26, 1880), 556.
[369] *Gospel Advocate* (November 1, 1881), 711.
[370] John D. Cox, *A Word Fitly Spoken* (Nashville, TN: Gospel Advocate Company, 1963), 22.
[371] *Gospel Advocate* (December 27, 1906), 831.
[372] *Gospel Advocate* (November 19, 1908), 741.
[373] Cox, *A Word Fitly Spoken*, 11.
[374] Cox, *A Word Fitly Spoken*, 25.

[375] *Gospel Advocate* (September 21, 1911), 1073.
[376] *Gospel Advocate* (September 26, 1912), 1078.
[377] *Gospel Advocate* (April 29, 1915), 420.
[378] *Gospel Advocate* (August 21, 1913), 805.
[379] *Gospel Advocate* (November 12, 1914), 1188.
[380] *Gospel Advocate* (March 24, 1921), 285.
[381] Cox, *A Word Fitly Spoken*, 24.
[382] Cox, *A Word Fitly Spoken*, 26.
[383] Material compiled in a booklet by Joan McFall in 2016. Miss McFall is a lifelong member at Oakland.
[384] *Millennial Harbinger* (April 1842), p. 186.
[385] *Christian Review* (August 1844), 191.
[386] *Christian Review* (August 1844), 191.
[387] *Christian Review* (December 1844), 265–266.
[388] *Gospel Advocate* (April 8, 1880), 233.
[389] Srygley, *Larimore and His Boys*, 167.
[390] *Gospel Advocate* (May 6, 1880), 299.
[391] *Gospel Advocate* (July 1, 1880), 423.
[392] *Gospel Advocate* (April 20, 1887), 243.
[393] *Florence Gazette*, March 13, 1886), 3.
[394] *The Banner* (April 1, 1886), 1.
[395] *Florence Gazette* (June 12, 1886), 3.
[396] *Florence Gazette* (July 10, 1886), 3.
[397] *Florence Gazette* (October 23, 1886), 3; *Gospel Advocate* (November 17, 1886), 730.
[398] *The Banner* (April 22, 1887), 1.
[399] *Poplar Street's Christian Church Record Book*, 7–13.
[400] *Florence Gazette* (May 1, 1886), 3.
[401] *Florence Gazette* (January 1, 1887), 3.
[402] *Poplar Street's Christian Church Record Book*, 7–13.
[403] *Gospel Advocate* (April 20, 1887), 254.
[404] *Gospel Advocate* (March 5, 1890), 145.
[405] *Gospel Advocate* (May 14, 1890), 314.
[406] *Florence Herald*, (January 14, 1891).
[407] *Gospel Advocate* (October 8, 1890), 650.

[408] *Gospel Advocate* (October 22, 1890), 674.
[409] *Gospel Advocate* (October 22, 1890), 674.
[410] *Gospel Advocate* (November 19, 1891), 734.
[411] *Gospel Advocate* (October 27, 1892), 684.
[412] *Gospel Advocate* (March 16, 1893), 168.
[413] *Gospel Advocate* (January 4, 1894), 13.
[414] *Gospel Advocate* (August 6, 1896), 512.
[415] *Gospel Advocate* (September 13, 1894), 578.
[416] *Gospel Advocate* (December 24, 1896), 824.
[417] *Gospel Advocate* (October 6, 1898), 633.
[418] *Gospel Advocate* (November 17, 1898), 725.
[419] *The Florence Times* (September 30, 1898), 3; (October 21, 1898), 3.
[420] *The Florence Times* (May 19, 1899), 5.
[421] *The Florence Times* (October 20, 1899), 1.
[422] *The Florence Times* (October 12, 1900), 8.
[423] *Gospel Advocate* (September 6, 1900), 572.
[424] *Gospel Advocate* (October 4, 1900), 629.
[425] *The Florence Times* (October 18, 1901), 8.
[426] *The Florence Times* (October 18, 1901), 1.
[427] *Gospel Advocate* (October 24, 1901), 677.
[428] *The Florence Times* (November 29, 1901), 8.
[429] *The Florence Times* (February 21, 1902), 1.
[430] *Gospel Advocate* (November 13, 1902), 725.
[431] *Gospel Advocate* (January 1, 1903), 5.
[432] *Gospel Advocate* (July 21, 1904), 457.
[433] *Gospel Advocate* (July 6, 1905), 421.
[434] *Nashville American* (July 21, 1905); *Gospel Advocate* (July 27, 1905), 469.
[435] Reprinted in *Gospel Advocate* (July 27, 1905), 469.
[436] *Gospel Advocate* (July 27, 1905), 469.
[437] *Gospel Advocate* (August 3, 1905), 491.
[438] *Gospel Advocate* (December 21, 1905), 805.
[439] *Gospel Advocate* (December 28, 1905), 821.
[440] *Gospel Advocate* (March 1, 1906), 133.

[441] *Gospel Advocate* (March 22, 1906), 181.
[442] *Gospel Advocate* (July 5, 1906), 421.
[443] *Gospel Advocate* (July 19, 1906), 453.
[444] *Gospel Advocate* (September 13, 1906), 581.
[445] *Gospel Advocate* (November 15, 1906), 725.
[446] *Gospel Advocate* (January 31, 1907), 69.
[447] *Gospel Advocate* (February 14, 1907), 101.
[448] *Gospel Advocate* (February 28, 1907), 133.
[449] *Gospel Advocate* (April 4, 1907), 213; *Gospel Advocate* (May 9, 1907), 293.
[450] *Gospel Advocate* (July 4, 1907), 421.
[451] *Gospel Advocate* (October 10, 1907), 641.
[452] *Gospel Advocate* (April 23, 1908), 270.
[453] C. E. Holt, *Gospel Advocate* (April 9, 1908), 229.
[454] *Gospel Advocate* (October 29, 1908), 693.
[455] *Gospel Advocate* (March 11, 1909), 305 [17].
[456] *Gospel Advocate* (March 11, 1909), 305 [17].
[457] *Gospel Advocate* (April 8, 1909), 464 [16].
[458] *Gospel Advocate* (July 1, 1909), 616 [16].
[459] *Gospel Advocate* (December 16, 1909), 1598.
[460] *Gospel Advocate* (December 23, 1909), 1616.
[461] *Gospel Advocate* (December 30, 1909), 1648.
[462] *Gospel Advocate* (December 1, 1910), 1342–1343.
[463] *Gospel Advocate* (March 2, 1911), 272; *Gospel Advocate* (April 20, 1911), 468.
[464] *Gospel Advocate* (November 9, 1911), 1297.
[465] *Gospel Advocate* (January 11, 1912), 59.
[466] *Gospel Advocate* (March 28, 1912), 400.
[467] *Gospel Advocate* (April 25, 1912), 528.
[468] *Gospel Advocate* (March 6, 1913), 229.
[469] *Gospel Advocate* (April 10, 1913), 348.
[470] *Gospel Advocate* (November 20, 1913), 1128.
[471] *Gospel Advocate* (January 29, 1914), 145.
[472] *Gospel Advocate* (November 5, 1914), 1166.
[473] J.R. Bradley, *Gospel Advocate* (Dec. 12, 1883), 787.

[474] Eris Bonner Benson, Personal interview with H. C. Warren and Henry B. Romine, Rogersville, Alabama (December 17, 1948,), 41–42.
[475] *Gospel Advocate* (December 15, 1892), 797.
[476] *Gospel Advocate* (September 7, 1893), 564.
[477] *Gospel Advocate* (October 26, 1893), 674.
[478] *Gospel Advocate* (November 9, 1893), 716.
[479] *Gospel Advocate* (June 26, 1906), 469.
[480] *Gospel Advocate* (July 8, 1909), 848.
[481] *Gospel Advocate* (July 22, 1909), 912.
[482] *Gospel Advocate* (May 16, 1912), 620.
[483] *Gospel Advocate* (September 5, 1912), 1005.
[484] *Gospel Advocate* (October 22, 1914), 1112.
[485] *Gospel Advocate* (November 12, 1914), 1194.
[486] John Campbell, of Killen, Alabama. December 17, 1948, Benson, "The Church of Christ in Lauderdale County, Alabama," 27.
[487] Larry Harper, *History of Antioch* (1969) and contribution by Tim McCafferty.
[488] *Gospel Advocate* (January 16. 1902), 36.
[489] *Gospel Advocate* (December 11, 1902), 789.
[490] Compiled by Mable Wright Parker, typed by Ethel Michael, (May 12, 1968).
[491] Larry Harper, *History of Antioch*.
[492] Larry Harper, *History of Antioch*.
[493] Larry Harper, *History of Antioch*.
[494] Wm. M. Behel, *Baptismal Records for 1905–1913*.
[495] Larry Harper, *History of Antioch*.
[496] Will Behel *Diary*, (unpublished, 1937), 12.
[497] *Gospel Advocate* (September 19, 1912), 1056.
[498] *Gospel Advocate* (September 26, 1912), 1078.
[499] *Gospel Advocate* (September 4, 1913), 852.
[500] *Gospel Advocate* (October 30, 1913), 1037.
[501] Larry Harper, *History of Antioch*.
[502] *Christian Standard* (October 9, 1875), 327

[503] *Gospel Advocate* (September 23, 1875), 911.
[504] William M. Behel, *Autobiography of William M. Behel* (Unpublished, 1937), 16.
[505] Benson, "The Church of Christ in Lauderdale County, Alabama," 33; Walter Bevis, of Florence, Alabama, to the author, (January 4, 1949).
[506] Wm. M. Behel, *Baptismal Records for 1903*.
[507] *Gospel Advocate* (August 15, 1912), 932.
[508] *Gospel Advocate* (November 12, 1914), 1194.
[509] *Gospel Advocate* (December 28, 1916), 1304.
[510] Like the one organized by Duckett at Piney Grove in 1893–94.
[511] *History of the Jacksonburg Church of Christ*, 4. Most of this history was condensed from notes written by Cultice Quillen who was assisted by Eula Abston. The notes were provided by Adine Butler.
[512] *History of the Jacksonburg Church of Christ*, 4.
[513] *Gospel Advocate* (August 22, 1907), 669.
[514] *Gospel Advocate* (October 17, 1907), 533.
[515] *Gospel Advocate* (June 4, 1908), 364.
[516] *Gospel Advocate* (September 10, 1908), 588.
[517] *Gospel Advocate* (October 15, 1914), 1086.
[518] *Gospel Advocate* (October 15, 1914), 1086.
[519] *History of the Jacksonburg Church of Christ*, 4.
[520] *Gospel Advocate* (September 30, 1915), 990.
[521] *Gospel Advocate* (December 28, 1916), 1304.
[522] *Gospel Advocate* (June 4, 1908), 364.
[523] Benson, "The Church of Christ in Lauderdale County, Alabama," 33; Walter Bevis, of Florence, Alabama, to the author, January 4, 1949).
[524] Personal interview with George McCorkle, in his home, 1979.
[525] Interview with Fred Bevis in 1974.
[526] Benson, "The Church of Christ in Lauderdale County, Alabama," 43; Walter Bevis, of Florence, Alabama, to the author,

January 4, 1949).

[527] See pages 331–332 in this document.

[528] *Gospel Advocate* (October 17, 1907), 669.

[529] William Behel's Baptismal Records for 1906.

[530] *Gospel Advocate* (July 18, 1907), 453.

[531] William Behel's Baptismal Records for 1907.

[532] *Gospel Advocate* (October 17, 1907), 669.

[533] *Gospel Advocate* (October 17, 1907), 669.

[534] Acts 14:23 (KJV).

[535] *Gospel Advocate* (September 10, 1908), 583.

[536] *Gospel Advocate* (June 4, 1908), 364.

[537] *Gospel Advocate* (October 7, 1909), 1280.

[538] *Gospel Advocate* (October 7, 1909), 1280.

[539] *Gospel Advocate* (November 13, 1879), 709.

[540] *Gospel Advocate* (November 6, 1879), 715.

[541] Benson, "The Church of Christ in Lauderdale County, Alabama," 37; V. J. Johns, of Florence, Alabama, to the author, March 31, 1949.

[542] William M. Behel, *Autobiography* (Unpublished, 1937), 10–12.

[543] William M. Behel Baptismal Records for 1905.

[544] *Deed Book 74*, Lauderdale County, Alabama, 17.

[545] *The Florence Herald* (December 15, 1905) 6.

[546] *The Florence Herald* (April 27, 1906), p. 7.

[547] William Behel's Baptismal Records for 1907; *Gospel Advocate* (October 17, 1907), 668.

[548] *Gospel Advocate* (June 4, 1908), 364.

[549] *Gospel Advocate* (October 7, 1909), 1280.

[550] *Gospel Advocate* (August 26, 1910), 976.

[551] William Behel's Baptismal Record Book for 1910.

[552] William Behel's Baptismal Record Book for 1910.

[553] William Behel's Baptismal Record Book for 1911.

[554] *Gospel Advocate* (October .30, 1913), 1037.

[555] William Behel's Baptismal Record Book for 1913.

[556] *Gospel Advocate* (August 27, 1914), 920.

[557] *Gospel Advocate* (December 27, 1906), 832.

[558] *Gospel Advocate* (November 21, 1907), 749.

[559] Benson, "The Church of Christ in Lauderdale County, Alabama," 39. H. C. Warren and Henry B. Romine, interview, December 17, 1948.

[560] *Gospel Advocate* (November 12, 1908), 725.

[561] *Gospel Advocate* (November 18, 1909), 1457.

[562] *Gospel Advocate* (August 4, 1910), 900.

[563] *Gospel Advocate* (August 18, 1910), 948.

[564] *Gospel Advocate* (August 17, 1911), 926.

[565] *Gospel Advocate* (September 5, 1912), 998.

[566] *Gospel Advocate* (September 4, 1913), 853.

[567] *Gospel Advocate* (August 20, 1914), 892.

[568] Benson, "The Church of Christ in Lauderdale County, Alabama," 39; Interview with Virgil Larimore on December 15, 1948.

[569] Benson, "The Church of Christ in Lauderdale County, Alabama," 39; Interview with Virgil Larimore on December 15, 1948.

[570] William Behel's Baptismal Records for 1900.

[571] Gospel Advocate (February 20, 1902), 127; William Behel's Baptismal Records for 1900.

[572] Benson, "The Church of Christ in Lauderdale County, Alabama," 39; Interview with Virgil Larimore on December 15, 1948.

[573] *Gospel Advocate* (February 28, 1907), 133.

[574] *Gospel Advocate* (October 17, 1907), 669.

[575] *Gospel Advocate* (June 4, 1908), 364.

[576] *Gospel Advocate* (September 10, 1908), 588.

[577] William Behel's Baptismal Records for 1908.

[578] William Behel's Baptismal Records for 1909.

[579] *Gospel Advocate* (October 7, 1909), 1280.

[580] William Behel's Baptismal Records for 1913.

[581] *Gospel Advocate* (October 30, 1913), 1037.

[582] *Gospel Advocate* (May 7, 1914), 500.

[583] *Gospel Advocate* (October 6, 1904), 640.//
[584] William Behel's Baptismal Record Book for 1906.//
[585] *Gospel Advocate* (August 22, 1907), 533.//
[586] William Behel's Baptismal Record Book for 1907.//
[587] *Gospel Advocate* (October 17, 1907), 669; William Behel's Baptismal Record Book for 1907.//
[588] *Gospel Advocate* (September 3, 1908), 572.//
[589] *Gospel Advocate* (September 30, 1909), 1232.//
[590] *Gospel Advocate* (August 25, 1910), 972.//
[591] *Gospel Advocate* (November 26, 1914), 1252.//
[592] Note from W. G. Harrison's daughter-in-law Nell Harrison, No date, sometime in the 1980s.//
[593] *Gospel Advocate* (February 20, 1890), 138.//
[594] Alabama, U.S., *Select Marriage Indexes*, 1816–1942.//
[595] *Romine Church Directory* (2005), 3.//
[596] Benson, "The Church of Christ in Lauderdale County, Alabama," 37; Interview, December 16, 1948, with Wallace Romine, Rogersville, Alabama.

Bibliography

Books

Benson, Eris Bonner. "The Church of Christ in Lauderdale County, Alabama." Thesis, Alabama Polytechnic Institute, 1949.

Cox, John D. *A Word Fitly Spoken*. Nashville, TN: Gospel Advocate Company, 1963.

Hall, B. F. *Autobiography*.

Holcomb, Hosea. *A History of the Rise and Progress of the Baptists in Alabama*. Philadelphia, PA: King and Laird, 1840.

Larimore, Mrs. T. B. *T. B. Larimore's Life, Letters, and Sermons*. Nashville, TN: Gospel Advocate Company, 1955.

McDonald, William Lindsey, *A Walk Through the Past*. Florence, Alabama, 1997.

Riley, B. F. *History of the Baptists of Alabama*. Birmingham, AL: Roberts and Sons, 1875.

Srygley, F. B. *Letters and Sermons of T. B. Larimore*. 3 vols. Nashville, TN: McQuiddy Printing, 1910.

Srygley, F. D. *Smiles and Tears: or Larimore and His Boys*. Nashville, TN: Gospel Advocate Company, 1989.

Periodicals

Apostolic Times
The Banner
The Baptist
Bible Advocate
Christian Magazine
Christian Messenger
Christian Reformer
Christian Register
Christian Review
Christian Standard
Firm Foundation
Florence Gazette
Florence Herald
Florence Times
Gospel Advocate
Gospel Guardian

Gospel Luminary
Millennial Harbinger
Nashville American
Octographic Review

Name Index

Askew, Aaron 55, 90, 110, 128
Askew, Murrell 41, 54–57, 63–64, 101, 109–121, 123–125, 128–131, 133–134, 136–137, 147, 150–151, 158–160, 162, 206, 225, 262
Behel, William 33, 44, 46, 91, 125, 136–137, 144, 157, 211, 213–215, 217–218, 221, 223–224, 226–227, 229–234, 241–245, 247, 265, 269–273
Bevis, T. F. 123
Bevis, T. O. 121–122, 124–125, 225
Bradley, J. R. 137–138, 151–153, 164–167, 206–207, 268
Brewer, G. C. 73–74
Campbell, Alexander. ix, xiv, xvi, 3, 6–7, 9–10, 17, 27, 50, 172, 208
Castleberry, John J. 91, 187–188
Chisholm, Esther viii, 5
Chisholm, John viii, 5, 15, 18, 35,–36, 173, 175

Clough, Simon 5, 9
Collins, L. D. 37–38
Collins, P. M. 38
Comer, William 111–112, 115–116, 120, 123, 129–131, 150–152, 155, 157, 262–264
Cox, John D. 166, 168, 265–266
D'Spain, Benjamin Lynn 5, 37, 49
D'Spain, Lynn 36, 38
D'Spain, Marshall D. 35, 37, 256
Despain, Marshall D. see D'Spain, Marshall D.
Dunn, J. H. 16, 18, 20–21, 23–25, 27–28, 58–59, 173, 255
Elam, E. A. 80, 176–177, 194
Ezell, J. Petty 209, 233, 244, 247–248
Fanning, Tolbert viii, 4, 6, 17–19, 21, 24, 26, 36–37, 39, 48–50, 52–53, 56, 59, 110, 129, 172–173, 175, 253
Freed, Avery Glenn 43

Fuqua, E. C.   44, 144, 166, 186, 192–193, 220–221, 223
Godwin, Brown   31, 65–66, 96, 123
Gresham, Andrew J.   21, 59–60, 92
Gresham, Philemon   20–21, 25
Gresham, William H.   22, 32, 67, 77, 82, 124–125, 139, 161, 189
Hackworth, James Matthew   18–19, 21, 24, 51–52, 56, 172–173
Hall, B. F.   viii, 4–7, 24, 36, 175, 253, 256
Harding, J. A.   239
Harris, J. T.   34, 44, 46, 106–108, 143–144, 157–158, 164, 166–168, 197, 199–201, 209–210, 213–215, 218–219, 236–238, 248
Harrison, W. G.   248–249, 273
Holt, C. E.   29, 33, 44–46, 121–122, 125, 141–144, 159, 191–202, 222, 224, 268
Holtsford, A. P.   57, 97, 140–141
Hooten, Percy H.   44, 190–191
Hoskins, Issac C.   82–83, 127, 197, 202–205, 221–223
Houston, Ross   18, 48, 50–52
Ijams. E. H.   18, 216, 254
Jones, J. P.   105, 207–209

Kendrick, Allen   viii, 36–38, 48
Kendrick, Carroll   39, 48–49
King, Thomas C.   238, 240
Klingman, George A.   188–190, 201, 203–205
Lanier, R. T.   111, 116, 130, 150–151, 154, 156–157, 237
Larimore, T. B.   xv, 18, 20, 28–30, 32, 59–67, 69–83, 85–86, 90–94, 98, 102, 109, 120, 122–124, 139, 150, 156–157, 160–161, 176 178–184, 186–187, 189–190, 199, 229–230, 241
Lefan, Matthew W.   140, 143, 211–213
Lipscomb, David   26, 59, 83, 93, 140, 182, 207–208, 212
Lipscomb, Granville   61–62, 96, 102
Long, W. S.   42–44
Lynn, Benjamin   36–37
Matthews, James E.   viii, 5–9, 11–12, 14–18, 24, 36–38, 50, 172, 175
Matthews, Mansell W.   8–9, 11, 36–38, 256
McQuiddy, J.C.   63, 80, 138, 192
Meeks, R. P.   71–72, 80, 181
Moore, Ephraim D.   4–5, 8, 11, 14, 24, 36–37, 50, 172
Morrow, Frank H.   209
Mulkey, John   36
O'Kelly, James   xiv, 3–4

Officer, Robert W. 63–64, 101, 103, 116–117, 135, 137, 147, 151, 160, 178, 262
Ott, J. C. 80, 161, 259
Pickens, J. M. 85, 259
Reynolds, G. A. 182–183, 189
Sanday, W. H. 104–105, 139–142, 208, 237, 251
Scott, Walter 17, 36
Sewell, E. G. 45, 191
Sewell, L. R. 124
Slayden, J. Paul 189
Speegle, O. P. 30
Srygley, F. D. xi, xv, 28, 30, 42, 59, 61–62, 72–73, 81, 85, 122, 177, 184–186, 256, 258–260, 263, 266
Stone, Barton W. xiv, 3–4, 12, 14–17, 36–38
Taylor, John 23–25, 27–28, 95
Thigpen, G. W. 113–114, 144
Thigpen, Gifford Carroll 136–139, 142–144, 165, 212–213
Trott, J. J. 21, 24
Trotter, Thomas B. 24
Underwood, John T. 30, 97, 104–105, 139, 157, 161, 167
Vandiver, John R. (N.) 39–41, 124
Wade, John D. 65, 96
Weatherford, Thomas L. 103, 105, 154, 156, 207, 250–251
Wesson, C. W. 21–22, 27

Wharton, W. H. 18, 91
Womack, S. W. 238–239
Wright, Percy D. 110, 141, 143, 170, 212, 261
Young, George P. 28–29, 92–93, 96, 216–217
Young, James 14–16, 18–20, 22, 24, 28, 49, 51, 53, 55–57, 91
Young, Thomas W. 59–60, 91–93, 95–96
Young, William B. 91–93, 96, 216–217

Also by C. Wayne Kilpatrick

An Early History of the Mars Hill Church of Christ: With a Collection of Memories by Members of the Congregation (2024)

J. R. Bradley: A Forgotten Larimore Boy (2019)

John Chisholm Church History Series

including

A Little Band of Disciples: The Beginnings of Churches of Christ in Madison County, Alabama

A Faithful Band of Workers: The Beginnings of Churches of Christ in Jackson County, Alabama

A Noble Band of Worshipers: The Beginnings of Churches of Christ Lauderdale County, Alabama

A Small Band of Brethren: The Beginnings of Churches of Christ in Limestone County, Alabama

HERITAGE CHRISTIAN UNIVERSITY PRESS

CYPRESS

To see the full catalog of Heritage Christian University Press and its imprint, Cypress Publications, visit www.hcupress.edu